Israeli Childhood Stories of the Sixties

Number 40

ISRAELI CHILDHOOD STORIES OF THE SIXTIES
Yizhar, Aloni, Shahar, Kahana-Carmon

by Gideon Telpaz

ISRAELI CHILDHOOD STORIES OF THE SIXTIES
Yizhar, Aloni, Shahar, Kahana-Carmon

by
Gideon Telpaz

Scholars Press
Chico, California

Israeli Childhood Stories of the Sixties:
Yizhar, Aloni, Shahar, Kahana-Carmon

by
Gideon Telpaz

Library of Congress Cataloging in Publication Data
Telpaz, Gideon.
   Israeli childhood stories of the sixties.

   (Brown Judaic studies ; no. 40)
   Bibliography: p.
   1. Children in literature. 2. Jewish children in literature.
3. Israeli fiction—History and criticism.
I. Title. II. Series.
PJ5030.C55T44 1983   892.4'3'0108355   82-24147
ISBN 0-89130-610-2

Printed in the United States of America

TABLE OF CONTENTS

ACKNOWLEDGMENTS

I am profoundly indebted to David Patterson, the president
of the Oxford Centre for Postgraduate Hebrew Studies, for his
encouragement and stimulating guidance, a source of inspiration
throughout; to Gloria Cigman for her immeasurable help; to J. B.
Bamborough, the principal of Linacre College, for his understanding and practical support. Many other scholars in Oxford were
generous with their time and knowledge. My special thanks are due
to N. S. Doniach, to Anthony Storr, and to Anne Lonsdale of the
Oriental Institute. I am also grateful to W. Hudson, M. Weaver,
A. Bron and other fellows and members of my college, Linacre
College, for a number of conducive ideas leisurely conceived in
the Common Room. Valuable assistance was given me by R. A. May
of the Bodleian Library, and G. Mandel, R. Judd, Hanna Safran and
the archivists of the Kressel Collection.

Work on this study was much facilitated by grants from B'nai
Brith, the Anglo-Jewish Association, the Israel Zangwill Memorial
Trust, the Arthur Davis Memorial Trust, the Humanitarian Trust,
and the Committee for Modern Middle Eastern Studies of Oxford
University.

I am particularly grateful to the Oxford Centre for Postgraduate Hebrew Studies for a bursary, and for enabling me to live
in Yarnton Manor, a most delightful and congenial setting, while
at work on this study.

PREFACE

The following procedures have been adopted in this study:

Titles of Hebrew books mentioned in the body of the text and the notes are given in transliteration and translation.

Titles of all Hebrew articles, as distinct from books, are given in the notes in translation only; the Hebrew titles of these articles are given in the Bibliography in transliteration.

Apart from excerpts from the *Jerusalem Post*, an Israeli daily published in English, all excerpts from Israeli newspapers and periodicals have been translated by the author.

All references to Hebrew sources are marked with (H) at the end of the relevant note.

The pagination of references to the stories discussed is given in the body of the text.

When proper names are mentioned, the transliteration follows the form in which these names are better known in English, or the form in which they appear in English in such sources as the *Encyclopaedia Judaica*.

The English translation of the title of a story, an article, or a book is in accordance with the published English translation of the source used, or the translation given in the Hebrew edition, except when the English translation supplied by the Israeli publisher was found to be inadequate.

Hebrew words used in the course of discussion are translated and, when necessary, explained the first time they occur.

INTRODUCTION

In the 1960s, childhood stories dealing with growing up in
Eretz Israel (Palestine) figured prominently in Israeli Hebrew
literature. These stories were written by authors who had been
born in the land, the *Sabras*, or who had been brought up there
from an early age. In Hebrew letters it was a period of a
changing of the guard: the first generation of *Sabra* writers was
making room for the next. This elder generation had come to be
known as the "Generation of 1948," the "Generation of the War of
Independence," or as "Dor ba-Aretz" ("Generation in the Land"),
after an anthology of the writings of sixteen poets and seventeen
fiction writers published to mark the anniversary of the first
decade of the State.[1] These writers are also sometimes known as
"Dor ha-Palmach" ("the Palmach[2] Generation"). Their early literary output demonstrated generationalism based on a belief that
the collective ranked higher than the individual. Historically,
it was an age of idealism. The young *Sabra* writer identified with
the values of the founding fathers, shared a belief in the same
cause and a deep commitment to it; his literature--a sort of
littérature engagée--was preoccupied with naturalistic depictions
of a *Sabra* stereotype consistent with the ideology of the collective. The incongruity began to be felt with the dramatic change
in the mental climate of Israeli society in the early 1950s.

The establishment of the State brought a release of the pre-
Independence tension and a political normalization, but the new
challenges generated a crisis of values. For one thing, the character of the population changed rapidly and drastically. In a few
years a population of 650,000--the Jewish population on the eve of
Independence--had to absorb twice its own number. The arrival of
immigrants from contrasting worlds caused a culture-shock which
was intensified by mounting social pressures. The sense of cohe-
sion was broken down. The gulf between the old Zionist ideology
and the new reality gave rise to a mood of disenchantment, especially among the excombatant *Sabras* who had to adjust to a normal
life. For many, the new reality was a bewildering anticlimax: the
promised land, for which they had fought and their friends had
sacrificed their lives, was not becoming what they had dreamed it
would be. Although by and large their generationalism never

1

assumed the role of a "lost generation," the malcontent excom-
batants clung nostalgically to the past, desperately trying to
adhere to values which post-Independence society had jettisoned
in its rush toward the utilitarian, the pragmatic and the material.

This ideological climate was hospitable to much of the literature written about the experience of the War of Independence in
the following years,[3] culminating in the outstanding fictional
expression of this experience in S. Yizhar's *Days of Ziklag* (1958).
Appearing ten years after the war, this anti-war novel gave vent to
suppressed emotions of nonconformity and disillusionment with the
hitherto sanctified ideals of the *Sabra*. An intervening span of a
decade seems to be a necessary incubation period before the emergence of a literature of revolt following a major war: ten years
elpased from the end of World War I before the appearance of Erich
Maria Remarque's *All Quiet on the Western Front*, and about the
same length of time elapsed after World War II before the emergence
of the "Beat Generation" in America and the "Angry Young Men" in
England.[4] In the *Sabra* literature, after exhausting the 1948 experience, the vivid reality of the past as an alternative to a
drab present found its expression in another major theme--the theme
of childhood.

The childhood story as a genre became popular in the late
fifties, and its popularity persisted well into the sixties. The
fifties saw the switch from the first-person plural, the collective voice of the first generation *Sabra* writers, to the first-
person singular, the voice of the individual, which from the outset marked the next generation. It is perhaps noteworthy that
this change was paralleled by a conspicuous shift in literary
orientation.[5] As Russian-orientated members of leftist parties
and kibbutzim, a considerable number of the 1948 writers sought
ideological inspiration in contemporary Russian literature that
expressed the World War II experience with which they could identify as fighters in Israel's War of Liberation. In those early
days, Russia was regarded as an ally. Disenchantment with the
Soviet Union began with the Prague show trial (November, 1952),
which was not only anti-Jewish but also explicitly anti-Israel.
This mood continued in the wake of the Russian onslaught against
Israel during the Moscow trials (January, 1953), which took place
during Stalin's last year, and which claimed to unveil "a con-
spiracy of doctors" described as agents of Zionist organization,
allegedly planning to liquidate Soviet political and military
leaders.

It is consistent with the political reorientation of Israeli
society that Israeli literature became Western-orientated. Writers
who began to publish in the 1950s and who had a substantial command
of English--the second language taught at school--were familiar
with contemporary English and American literature, and were particularly influenced by the current preoccupation with the estrangement of the individual. While in the early works of "Dor
ba-Aretz" the protagonist was by and large a figure in a collective, the protagonist who emerged now was an individual at odds
with society. Nonconformity replaced commitment; adherence to the
old values gave way to a growing sense of alienation and disorien-
tation. The myth of the heroic *Sabra* was cast aside while the
delinquent, the outsider and the dropout were brought to the fore.
No other genre enabled the writer to feel so much at ease in writing about these anti-heroes as that of the childhood story, for a
child could often serve as a more effective symbol of regression
and disaffection than an adult. "In a world given increasingly to
utilitarian values and the Machine," observes Coveney, "the child
could become the symbol of Imagination and Sensibility, a symbol
of Nature set against the forces abroad in society actively de-
naturing humanity."[6] As a metaphor, the child could help the artist "express his awareness of the conflict between human Innocence
and the cumulative pressures of social Experience."[7] As a theme,
he could allow the writer to express maladjustment, being "the
perfect image of insecurity and isolation, of fear and bewilder-
ment, of vulnerability and potential violation."[8]

In many instances, the Israeli childhood story of the 1960s--
in which the author reverts to his early years to explore his own
roots, take stock of his life and define himself--intimates a
malaise. The causes of this malaise are both ideological, as
indicated above, and psychological.

Discussing Mark Twain's recurrent urge to write about childhood, Van Wyck Brooks suggests that "when people in middle age
occupy themselves with their childhood it is because some central
instinct...has been blocked by internal or external obstacles."[9]
In their writing "their consciousness flows backward until it
reaches a period in their memory when life still seemed to them
open and fluid with possibilities."[10] Among the writers selected
for this study, this observation is particularly pertinent to
Yizhar who was forty-seven when his childhood stories were published in book form.

On occasion, the return to childhood in these stories concentrates on a specific situation depicting an initiatory failure that led into a psychological cul-de-sac. It may be arguable that, in writing about such points of past time, the author desires to achieve a cathartic reenactment: by recreating his childhood with retrospective insight he might free himself of it once and for all. It has been said that "in becoming conscious of the past one alters the present," and that "after self-examination a man is no longer the man he was before."[11] The writing of an autobiographical childhood story could help the author attain a change of perspective by dissociating himself from the state of innocence and incomprehension, and reaching a state of heightened self-awareness.

This study is limited to the reflection of childhood experience in Palestine and Israel in stories written in or around the 1960s by four native-born authors: S. Yizhar, Nissim Aloni, David Shahar and Amalia Kahana-Carmon. By reason of age, the four belong to the "Generation of 1948," and all of them took part in its major event, the War of Independence, to which Yizhar gave the most stirring literary expression. And yet, the writing of each of them is highly individualistic, and--with the exception of Yizhar's war stories--can hardly be regarded as representative of a group, or as displaying group consciousness.

A childhood story, for the purpose of this study, is one in which the narrator or protagonist is a child, or a boy or girl in early adolescence. The study is not concerned with children's stories, that is, stories meant for juvenile reading, but with stories about the experience of childhood written by adults for adult readers. Each writer is examined separately, but comparisons are drawn between the four. In each case an attempt is made to view the writer's childhood stories in the context of the body of his writing and, on occasion, to evaluate his writing with reference to the overall picture of Hebrew letters.

The mushrooming of the childhood story in the 1960s should be seen in the context of the proliferation of the short story in Hebrew literature at the time. A catalyst for this phenomenon was the large number of literary supplements and periodicals that were increasingly interested in publishing short stories by established as well as new writers who were experimenting with this genre. It was also possible at this time to publish long stories, sometimes the size of a novella, in periodicals with a large format. The most significant of these periodicals, for the purpose of this study, is *Keshet*, a literary quarterly, launched in Tel Aviv in

1958; from its very beginning it became the vanguard of the sixties. Its editor, Aharon Amir, defined its task in the manifesto
published in the first issue: "to serve as an aid to the growth of
original talents, an expression of nonconformity and experimentation."[12] Amir subscribed to the ideology of a small circle of
intellectuals, the "Canaanim," who believed that the native-born
youth had a major role to play in the revival of the ancient
Hebrew nation and its classic culture by dissociating himself from
the heritage of the Jewish diaspora, and creating an alliance with
other nations in the region such as the Druse and the Lebanese.[13]
Naturally, Amir was eager to encourage writing about growing up in
the Land, written by native-born authors. The very first issue of
Keshet carried a childhood story by Aloni, which set a trend to be
followed in subsequent issues with similar stories by other *Sabra*
writers.

The 1960s was a special period of growth in the history of
Israel. Although from its establishment the State was the abode
of a besieged society under a constant threat of war, the 1960s--
or more precisely the period between the Sinai War (1956) and the
Six-Day War (1967)--was the longest period of relative relaxation
it enjoyed, a period of continuous economic and political achievement. The State had emerged impressively victorious from her wars.
However, Israeli writers, like sensitive seismographs, were picking up undercurrents of suppressed anxieties and apprehensions beneath the prevailing mood of confidence, which they endeavored to
sublimate in childhood stories set in a period twenty or thirty
years earlier.

The stories allow us a first-hand glimpse into the inner
world of the young *Sabra*. In myths woven around him, he was re-
puted to be free of the defects that impaired the *shtetl* Jew,
"fearless to the point of recklessness, bold, extroverted and
little inclined towards, if not openly contemptuous of, intellectual pursuits."[14] It will emerge in this study that--except for
the portrait of the elder brother in Yizhar's work--the *Sabra*, as
revealed in these stories, was in reality far from the idealizing
myths.

Although in reverting to childhood some writers tend to look
back nostalgically, these were by no means days of bliss. The
Yishuv (the pre-State Jewish community) was engaged in a constant
struggle for survival and self-determination, and in several stories the personal trauma of the child on the verge of life runs
parallel to traumatic events of the community, reflecting them and

being intensified by them. The interaction becomes the background
for the child's attempts to define his self-image, to grasp the
extent of his new capacities, and state his position in the conflict between himself, as an individual, and the collective.

    In analyzing these stories a number of psychological aspects
are adduced in support of the critical interpretations put forward.
It is suggested, for instance, that a reluctance to grow up and
leave behind the carefree world of the child--the "Peter Pan syndrome"--plays a significant role in some of these stories.
Another aspect, which combines the psychological and the ideological, relates to the theme of the *Akedah* (sacrifice of Isaac). In
their new interpretation of this fundamental Jewish archetype,
drawing on generational thinking, Israeli writers, within the
first decade of the State, began to give voice to a protagonist
belonging to the generation of the sons, who is not identified
with the traditional figure of Isaac, but is instead protesting,
bitter, and disillusioned. Bringing to the fore such a defiant
approach mirrors a culmination of the crisis of values in post-
1948 Israeli society, and attests to the ambivalence of the sons
toward the founding fathers, whom they partly envied for their
experience and partly blamed for the outcome.[15] On another level,
the *Akedah* as a major symbol of initiation was highly pertinent to
the biography of the "Generation of 1948" and its preoccupation
with death. Death became a fact of life for the generation that
had lived through the Arab riots of 1929, 1936-39, the wars of
1939-45, 1948, 1956, and the recurrent border incidents which had
resulted in military retaliatory incursions during the fifties and
the sixties.

    In examining the art of these short stories, which often come
close to autobiography, the historical authenticity of the artistic reconstruction is immaterial. No one can step twice into the
same river, as Heraclitus observed. "Autobiography is not simple
repetition of the past as it was, for recollection brings us not
the past itself but only the presence in spirit of a world forever
gone."[16] The question should not be whether a story is faithful
to a certain historical reality, but rather how the author treats
the reality that he perceives.

    The literature examined here belongs to a period that drew to
an end with the Six-Day War. The time that has elapsed since then
allows for some historical perspective in its evaluation. The
critical analysis undertaken in this study utilizes a wide selection of contemporary responses to the works scrutinized, to

demonstrate their immediate impact and their reception by critics
who, belonging to various schools, mirrored different moods and
opinions within Israeli society. The selection includes reviews
and essays published in literary supplements which appeared in the
weekend issues of Israeli dailies such as *Haaretz, Davar,
Lamerḥav*,[17] *Al Hamishmar, Hatzofeh, Jerusalem Post, Maariv, Yediot
Aḥronot*; literary monthlies such as *Moznaim*; bimonthlies such as
Ammot; quarterlies such as *Keshet, Mibbifnim, Siman K'ria*; annuals
such as *Meassef*. At the same time selected theories of literary
criticism as expressed by American and European scholars are in-
corporated into the discussion whenever their views offer significant insights.

Ultimately, although this study is aimed at exploring one
genre of literature, written by one generation in one particular
decade, it is hoped that it may assist the reader in coming closer
to understanding the nature of Israeli literature as a whole, ex-
tending beyond that which is seeking to express the experience of
a *Sabra* in search of his roots and identity. For the childhood
story is at the core of this literature.

CHAPTER I

GOODBYE TO ARCADIA: S. YIZHAR

S. Yizhar (originally Yizhar Smilansky) was born in 1916 in
the *moshavah* Reḥovot, one of the first modern agricultural settlements in Palestine, into a family of pioneers and writers. One
of his uncles was Moshe Smilansky (1874-1953),[1] a farmer and a
popular storyteller, who wrote about the life of Jews and Arabs
in the pre-State era. Another uncle was the writer Meir Smilansky
(pseudonym M. Secco) (1876-1946).[2] Yizhar's father, Ze'ev Smilansky (1873-1944),[3] who had immigrated to Palestine in 1891, was one
of the founders of *Hapoel Hatzair*.[4] Growing up in a *moshavah* made
a strong impact on Yizhar, and became a recurrent theme in his
fiction, particularly in his childhood stories. He was trained
to be a teacher and taught in Yavne'el, at the Ben Shemen Youth
Village and at the Reḥovot High School. After participating in
the War of Independence he became a member of the Knesset, serving
six terms from its inauguration in 1948 until 1967, when he gave
up his seat and returned to the field of education.

Of the "Dor ba-Aretz" writers, Yizhar was the first to be
published, the first to sound loud and clear the voice of the
Sabra in literature. The appearance of his first story, "Ephraim
Hozer la-Aspeset" ("Ephraim Goes Back to Alfalfa"),[5] has subsequently come to mark the date the native-born generation burst
into the scene of Hebrew literature.[6] His writing provided a
vital link between the emerging Israeli literature and the introspective, soul-searching Hebrew literature at the beginning of the
century, especially with two of its major writers, U. N. Gnessin
(1879-1913) and Y. H. Brenner (1881-1921). Like Gnessin, Yizhar
made an extensive use of the interior monologue, and "the technique of detailed description of sensory impressions as a continu-
ance and an expression of the character's internal experience";[7]
like Brenner, his stories are "about a personal and public moral
issue, which forces the individual to a decision of broad existential implications."[8] These features, noticeable already in
"Ephraim Goes Back to Alfalfa," are consistently present throughout Yizhar's writing.

"Ephraim Goes Back to Alfalfa" deals with the conflict between the wishes of the individual and those of the collective.

9

After three years in the alfalfa field of the kibbutz, the unful-
filled Ephraim asks to change to the orange grove; but when given
the option he chooses to stay in the alfalfa field. The story's
strength lies in its inner plot, in depicting the struggle which
takes place within the protagonist, the agonies of hesitation and
indecision, and in the landscape descriptions which were distinctly innovative in Hebrew literature. It was followed by the
stories "Mish'olim ba-Sadot" ("Paths in the Fields"),[9] "Laylah
Beli Yeriot" ("A Night Without Shooting"),[10] and "Massa El Gedot
ha-Erev" ("A Journey to the Banks of Evening").[11] Yizhar's first
book, *Be-Fa'atei Negev* (*On the Edge of the Negev*),[12] depicts a
well-drilling in the Negev and demonstrates a remarkable ability--
rare in Hebrew letters at the time--to give minute technical descriptions. It was followed by "Ha-Horshah ba-Givah" ("The Grove on
the Hill").[13] Written before the War of Independence, these stories generally reflect an optimistic and idealistic mood, in keeping with the spirit of the *Yishuv* in the pre-State years. The war
shattered that mood and introduced unexpected, troubling doubts
about the morality and ideology of the war-time Israeli.

The early war stories "Sippur Hirbet Hizah" ("The Story of
Hirbet Hizah") and "Ha-Shavui" ("The Prisoner"), published in a
book named after the former story,[14] dealt openly, for the first
time in Hebrew literature, with the shock the sensitive Israeli
soldier experienced at the brutality of war and the destruction it
brought to the pastoral world of the Arab village. The moral dilemma the protagonist faced threatened his integrity: he could not
accept military authority, yet could not muster enough courage to
defy it. His sense of justice was affronted by what he saw done
to Arab villagers. He felt an urge to protest but found himself
unable to do so for fear of what his comrades might think of him,
or because of other inhibiting factors. *Shayyarah Shel Hatzot*
(*Midnight Convoy*),[15] another story that took its setting from the
the War of Independence, is, again, an attempt to say that war,
including the War of Independence, is an obstacle to a better
life.[16]

These three war stories turned out to be merely exercises for
Yizhar's mammoth book on the War of Independence, *Yemei Ziklag*
(*Days of Ziklag*),[17] that provoked much controversy.[18] The seven
days of battle, the time span of the novel, provided Yizhar with
ample opportunity to examine the ideological crisis of his generation. More than in any other work, he became in *Ziklag* the mouthpiece of this generation and of its ambivalent sentiments toward
its pioneer fathers.

It took Yizhar most of the 1950s to write *Ziklag* and it ex-
hausted him. He later published only one more work of fiction,
Sippurei Mishor (*Tales of the Plain*),[19] its major theme being
visions of childhood.[20] As the purpose of this study is to examine childhood stories written or published in the 1960s, of all
the previously mentioned stories, only those included in the last
book will be discussed. The rest will be referred to only where
it is felt that they shed light on the stories under discussion.

Tales of the Plain: A Brief Summary and General Comments

   Tales of the Plain[21] consists of four stories: "Aremat ha-
Deshen" ("The Dunghill"); "Ha-Nimlat" ("The Runaway");[22] "Habakuk"
("Habakuk");[23] and "Sippur she-Lo Hithil" ("A Story That Did Not
Begin").[24] The first three are considerably shorter than the last,
which occupies more than half of the book: over one hundred pages.
   Each story contains two active layers of time--the present
and the past. The present provides a point of departure from which
the disillusioned adult narrator goes back to the "idyllic" days
of childhood, during which the episodes he is narrating take place.
Although the exact time when these episodes occurred is never disclosed, a reader familiar with life in Palestine and with Yizhar's
biography can hazard a guess that the first two stories relate to
the late 1920s when the author was in his early teens. The background of the third story is apparently the 1930s when the author
was studying at the Jerusalem Teacher's Seminary. The problem of
the chronological background of the last story is more intricate
for reasons which will soon be pointed out. In each story, when
depicting an episode that happened in childhood or adolescence,
the narrator does so through the viewpoint of a boy or an adolescent, while commenting on it from the perspective of an adult.
But both viewpoints, the boy's and the adult's, blend harmoniously
and the reader cannot always tell them apart.
   In "The Dunghill" (hereafter: "Dunghill"), a story about the
buying of dung from the Bedouin to fertilize citrus groves, the
protagonists are the narrator's elder brother and his Arab middle-
man. They team up as a pair of confidence-tricksters who swindle
the Bedouin in a comic, theatrical ritual, cultivated almost to
perfection. While admiring the "show" of his brother and his Arab
helper, the fascinated boy-narrator feels sympathy for the poor
Bedouin, but is in no position to inferfere. When he finally expresses his faltering protest, his patronizing brother dismisses
him with a cynical remark and unscrupulously goes about his business.

"The Runaway" (hereafter: "Runaway") depicts a horse that breaks loose and runs away to freedom after its owner unhitches it during a break in the work of levelling the ground in the narrator's yard. Through the eyes of the sensitive, fanciful boy, we are given an enthusiastic and graphic account of the horse running through the open countryside, and of the rural landscape with its flora and fauna. The horse galloping to its heart's content becomes the symbol of the narrator's great yearning for freedom. But Aryeh, its owner, is filled with distress. The narrator's clumsy attempt to console him turns out to be cold comfort. When he asks Aryeh whether he is positive that the horse ever wished to belong to him, implying that the horse's escape to freedom is justifiable, the horse-owner tells him off. When the horse is captured and brought back, it is of course to the joy of Aryeh and the great distress of the boy-narrator.

The business of "Ḥabakuk" is actually adolescence rather than childhood. It will be brought up here only to illuminate the themes, ambience and narrative of the other stories. Ḥabakuk, a violinist and astrologer, introduced to the narrator by the latter's mother, becomes the spiritual mentor of the narrator and his friends. They frequent Ḥabakuk's Jerusalem basement apartment, where he acquaints them with Beethoven and Mozart. Although his playing leaves much to be desired, for the admiring youths it is an experience of exaltation. Habakuk meets his death in the War of Independence, hit by a shell, when he volunteers with other civilians to help in building the fortification of a kibbutz.

If the aforementioned stories offer very little plot, the last story in *Tales of the Plain* (hereafter: *Tales*) offers even less. For the most part it is a chaotic amalgamation of rhetoric--chiefly expressing protest, disquiet, rage and despair with the quality of urban life emerging in Israel--and nostalgic description of nature into which the narrator takes the reader as a means of escape. Yizhar calls it "A Story That Did Not Begin" (hereafter: "A Story"); had it begun properly it would have been about the untimely death of the narrator's brother in a motorcycle accident. The tragic event provides the only element of plot, but it remains in the background for much of the story, as the narrator, unable to cope with the trauma of his grief, cannot muster the strength to bring it to the foreground in explicit narrative. When he finally manages to do so, it is with the help of a device borrowed from the theater: an evocative dramatization of the moment the accident happened. A hint of another potential--but undeveloped--plot is given in a brief evocation of a singular experience embedded in

the narrator's memories of his childhood, when his elder brother
took him to a festivity in an Arab village. This memory triggers a
nostalgic flow of reminiscences of Arab villages before they were
conquered and blotted out in 1948.

A comparison of these four stories, which were written for
the adult reader, with *Shishah Sippurei Kayitz* (*Six Summer Stories*),[25] his book of children's stories, may help us understand
some of the significant changes that have occurred in Yizhar's
writing since 1950 both artistically and ideologically.

The first thing that strikes the reader of *Six Summer Stories*
is their simplicity, ease, economy, and their graceful, restrained
humor; each one of them is a narrative with a linear plot. These
attributes are almost entirely absent from *Tales*, which seems to
have been written by a completely different author. The narrator
of the 1950 children's stories displays the lucid, scrutinizing
eye of an adult who has a clear, objective grasp of his subject
matter; the narrator of the 1963 childhood stories clearly lacks
such lucidity and is characterized instead by a growing sense of
perplexity.[26] There were indeed vital ideological and psychological changes that Yizhar had undergone during the passage of time,
and that were of fundamental significance to his writing. In 1950,
although the two disturbing war stories ("Ḥirbet Ḥizah" and "The
Prisoner") were already in print, Yizhar was still fully committed
to the pre-State ideals. *Ziklag*, the book of disenchantment, had
not yet been written. During the long years of his labor on this
magnum opus, as Yizhar became doubtful about the Israeli quality
of life, he lost his "simplicity" as well as his confidence in
conventional literary technique. *Tales*, written after *Ziklag*,
marks the culmination of these ideological-artistic changes.

It has been suggested that beneath the light, jocular cover
of the 1950 children's stories evidence can be detected of the
problems which haunted Yizhar all through his writing career, and
which surfaced so harshly in *Tales*.[27] Accordingly, *Six Summer
Stories* too implies a lack of confidence in society and its values.
The plot exposes an Yizharian character in his development from
the stage of illusion to the stage of disillusionment. The boy-
protagonist, particularly in the story "A Dip in the Pool,"[28] is a
variation of the insecure, introvert protagonist, who appears in
all Yizhar's stories, and his story already incorporates a number
of major themes in his later childhood stories. First, the theme
of the boy who refuses to grow up and is unable to accept responsibility or a structure of rules and conventions. Second, the

escape to nature which provides the shelter in which this sensitive, frightened Peter Pan is free to be himself. Third, the alter
ego of the weak protagonist, the strong, virile, natural leader
whom the ambivalent protagonist admires but can never imitate suc-
cessfully. In "A Dip in the Pool," it is Yoel, the protagonist's
friend. In *Tales* it is the protagonist's elder brother.

It is remarkable that after *Ziklag* Yizhar chose to withdraw
from the literary scene with a collection of stories containing
visions of childhood. Perhaps this move was predictable for, after exhausting his war experiences, childhood became a natural escape. Turning to the present meant a definite (personal or public)
commitment, and a clearcut orientation of a mature man. In the
absence of such orientation, only childhood, which does not bear
with it any obligation, could serve as a scheme of life.[29] More
often than not, Yizhar's inability to say goodbye to his childhood
did not meet with his critics' approval. His rhetoric has been
labelled as that of an adolescent.[30] He was accused of being overly
attached to one age group--youth,[31] and that his heroes "(or rather
his only hero, who keeps changing names and situations) find it
difficult and even refuse to cut themselves off from the egocen-
tricity of childhood...this is the mental age of his heroes."[32]
Ephraim, his first protagonist, is said to be the prototype of all
his maladjusted heroes. If maturity implies coming to terms with
the necessary cycle of life, Ephraim--who is given to childhood
illusions--deliberately refuses to mature, preferring to remain
the eternal adolescent.[33]

But such a response to Yizhar seems to overlook his need to
hold on to childhood visions less as expression of rebellion than
as an invigorating vehicle to cope with a stifling reality. In
actual fact, these visions serve as a source of liberation, a
guiding light in an existence that for the disillusioned idealist
in him seems bereft of a raison d'être. In this respect, these
childhood stories should not be taken as merely a regressive expression of escape from an intolerable reality, but as an expression of Yizhar's romantic desire to transcend it. This is the
romantic urge which causes one of his reviewers to proclaim, "The
greatness of Yizhar's romanticism lies precisely in its failure;
its heroes are always yearning for an ideal reality even though
it stands no chance of being achieved."[34] And another reviewer,
picking up this thread and rejecting the common notion that regards
Yizhar as looking back to childhood, argues: Yizhar is actually
turning towards "the possible, the open" that has not yet come to

be and that forever stands at the threshold, because he cannot be
satisfied with a fait accompli.[35] In at least one place in "A
Story," Yizhar seems to provide good ground for such an argument.

> But I do not wish at all to brag about or praise the
> Yesterday....If you think, perhaps, that I too like many
> people...walk with my eyes in the back of my head looking
> back with yearning and nostalgia, like Lot's wife whose
> heart cries for what already was, neat and orderly as it
> was, and not for what has not yet come to be--you could
> not be more mistaken. (124)

And yet it would be erroneous to take this particular statement of
Yizhar at face value, for "A Story" is indeed filled with "yearning and nostalgia." A nostalgic escape to nature from the confine-
ment of the urban scene, and a nostalgic escape to the past (to
childhood) from the disheartening reality of the present pervade
Tales, giving rise to an interpretation of them as essentially
pastoral. This view is explored in the ensuing discussion.

About Pastoral

     In his book *The Uses of Nostalgia*,[36] Laurence Lerner formu-
lates a view about pastoral literature which, despite his focus on
European culture, appears to bear upon the critical analysis and
evaluation of Yizhar. Writing on pastoral, Lerner proposes, is
entering a region of the mind that has several names. "In terms
of time it is the Golden Age. In terms of space it is Eden or
Arcadia. Its goddess is Astraea, its worship is nostalgia. Its
chronicle is pastoral."[37] To establish the theory that nostalgia
is the basic emotion of pastoral, Lerner goes back to Virgil's
first Eclogue, a dialogue between two shepherds, Tityrus and
Meliboeus, about their home. Meliboeus, exiled to Africa, does
not know if or when he will return. The Eclogue is drenched in
nostalgia, for Meliboeus sees the beauty of home through the eyes
of loss. Lerner maintains that "the nostalgia that impregnates
the *Eclogues* never left pastoral; and eventually it came to the
surface, as the evident shaping spirit of poems."[38] In the nine-
teenth century, when the pastoral convention was no longer used,
poems continued to deal openly with the emotion to which that convention corresponded. Baudelaire, in his fascination with tropi-
cal landscapes to which he longed to escape from the mud and gas-
light of Paris, is one example;[39] in fiction, Proust is another.[40]
The title *A la recherche du temps perdu* announces an ambiguous
nostalgia: one looks for the past in two ways, with memory, and--
in some mysterious manner--with one's whole self. The point of

Proust's novel, which becomes clear in the last volume, is that
these two manners can be combined, provided that the remembering
process is done by the "involuntary memory" and not by the "volun-
tary memory" which, being at the mercy of defense mechanisms, is
likely to produce conventional and insignificant images. Proust
uses his *mémoire involontaire* to reconstruct accounts of his childhood, thus, the famous *petite madeleine* that reminds him of his
aunt drinking her herb tea takes him back to the account of childhood in *Du Côté de chez Swann*.[41] What mattered to Proust was the
joining of a sensation from the past with one from the present,
and the fact that at the moment of recalling the past one was actually there. Proust's recognition of the importance of nostalgia
emphasizes that longing is what makes art possible. Deprivation
leads to creation. When one is not part of the life one longs for,
"the longing retains its intensity, and can even offer the joy of
attainment," by enabling imagination to have "the illusion of
dealing with what is real and not just what is longed for."[42]
Hanna Segal, after Freud, even goes so far as to maintain that
"all creation is really a re-creation of a once loved and once
whole, but now lost and ruined object, a ruined internal world and
self....The wish to create is rooted in the depressive position
and the capacity to create depends on successful working through
it."[43] Art, then, resembles mourning for it is the experience and
the acceptance of loss. Only when loss has been acknowledged and
mourning experienced can re-creation take place.

     Milton's *Paradise Lost* may serve as a perfect illustration.
There is little doubt which way Milton saw Eden: it is growing
luxuriantly, uncontrolled, bursting with abundance and fertility.
But it is doomed and tinged with sadness. Adam is going to fall.
Both he and Eve must be banished. The destruction of the garden
is inevitable. Milton's lines are permeated with the melancholia
of this loss. The message is clear: one cannot live in Eden forever; one must leave it behind and emerge into the real world.[44]
The loss, traumatic as it may be, is not undesirable. Eden is
analogous to childhood. The loss of childhood is in retrospect
excruciatingly sad, but in the final analysis favorable. For the
outcome of leaving childhood behind is growing up, accepting the
need to obey the cycle of life.

     Often pastoral and nostalgia are associated in childhood
stories with another motif which for convenience will be named here
the Peter Pan syndrome. A modern classic that exemplifies this is
J. D. Salinger's *The Catcher in the Rye*.

To be sure, *The Catcher in the Rye*[45] is not exactly a childhood story but that of the adolescent Holden Caulfield, who at the
outset of his narrative observes retrospectively, "I was sixteen
then, and I am seventeen now. And yet I act sometimes like I was
only about twelve."[46] So, although biologically he is no longer
a child, psychologically--by his own admission--he considers himself as such. This narrator recounts in an authentic teenage
idiom his flight from the hypocrisies of the adult world, his
search for innocence and truth, and his final collapse on a psy-
chiatrist's couch. His story, "a 'sick' version of Huckleberry
Finn,"[47] is classified by Lerner as a pastoral satire.[48] A close
look at Holden Caulfield's narrative may offer support to such a
supposition. Holden cannot adjust to his society, and is not sure
that he wants to. He looks at Pencey, the prep school in Pennsyl-
vania from which he eventually "got kicked out," at the boys and
teachers and parents, and finds them all phoney. He comes to the
same conclusion about almost everybody he meets on his way to New
York and in New York. His sharp, observing eye, which distin-
guishes between the phoney and the authentic, is the eye of a
satirist, but he has a soft spot for the weak and the underdog.
He loves his little sister tenderly and is full of pain and grief
at the memory of his dead brother Allie.

One of his chief paradoxes is that he is and is not part of
the world he hates, being both its victim and its judge. Frustrated and disgusted with his reality, Holden, the romanticist-
idealist who is unable to find his salvation in the urban environment, dreams about escape to nature, to the pastoral cabin camps
in Massachusetts and Vermont or out West. But he does not wish to
withdraw totally. He would like to have a mission.

> I keep picturing all these little kids playing some game
> in this big field of rye and all. Thousands of little
> kids, and nobody's around, nobody big, I mean--except me.
> And I'm standing on the edge of some crazy cliff. What
> I have to do, I have to catch everybody if they start to
> go over the cliff--I mean if they're running and they
> don't look where they're going I have to come out from
> somewhere and *catch* them. That's all I'd do all day.
> I'd just be the catcher in the rye and all.[49]

This vision of an open field and a carefree life is the extreme of idyllic idleness: all Holden wants to do is to keep the
children in Arcadia; that is to say, protect the innocent children
and stop them from entering the dangerous zone of maturity. The
rye field is analogous to childhood; the carefree children who play
there are threatened because childhood is temporary. What he wants

is to stop the flow of time to allow them to remain children forever. Like Peter Pan, Holden finds it painful to grow up because
he resents what he is meant to grow up into. If he comes to the
rye field as a protector, he will have an excuse to re-enter this
field, the only older person around. Childhood is clearly equated
here with the idea of the idyllic. But unlike the passages in
which he speaks of going to Vermont or "out West," in this passage
Holden finally realizes that what he wishes to be can be perceived
only in a dream.

When comparing Yizhar with Salinger, one is immediately aware
of a basic difference between the two. While the pastoral element
is common to both, Yizhar lacks Salinger's capacity to create the
distance from his subject matter necessary to render narrative
satirical. Moreover, satire is incompatible with his temperament.
Even so, enough of the elements mentioned here can be found in
Tales to suggest some sort of affinity. The malcontent narrator
in Yizhar's stories who is constantly offended by the coarseness
of his environment, and who is unable to hold his own in a tough
world but able to see through it is, in this respect, similar to
the narrator in Salinger's book. Another similarity is in the
rejection of maturity and the negation of the present. From the
latter stems Yizhar's ideology of escape, which takes two forms:
escape to the world of childhood, and escape to the open country,
the idyllic.

The theme of the malcontent in the role of the catcher in the
rye, as Salinger perceives it, can be found especially in "A Story,"
in which the narrator keeps urging his listener (towards whom he
adopts a protectively paternal tone)[50] not to join the established
order, and whom he advises to escape to a place which is still uncontaminated, where he can still retain his childhood innocence.
All the stories in *Tales*, particularly the last one, are characterized by an over-use of intrusion and digression, a narrative
technique of which Holden is fond, finding it more intriguing than
that of the linear narrative.[51]

These elements are considered at length in the following discussion of *Tales*. The first aspect to be examined is one high-
lighted in Salinger's book--the rejection of the present, which in
both Salinger and Yizhar can be interpreted as a form of rebellion
against the world of maturity.

Rejection of the Present

In his refusal to join the ranks of adults and the race for
success, and in his wish to remain forever with the young children
in the rye field, Holden Caulfield is manifesting a quixotic attempt to make time stand still or, to borrow Lerner's phrase,
"refusing history."[52] This Peter Pan syndrome can result in regression and withdrawal as a form of escape from reality, or in an
open revolt against it. Indeed, the themes of revolt and escape
run through *Tales* like a common thread. In this respect *Tales* is
an Israeli counterpart of contemporary trends that surfaced in
American and English literature in the 1950s which, in M. C. Bradbrook's observation, glamorized "the Dionysian image of Delin-
quency."[53] In America it began with the "Beat Generation," and in
England with the "Angry Young Men." Yizhar's rage, as expressed
in "A Story," calls to mind his English counterparts--Amis (*Lucky
Jim*, 1954), Osborne (*Look Back in Anger*, 1956), Braine (*Room at
the Top*, 1957). His rejection of the cult of success, his
preaching against conformity, and his incitement to search for
alternative lifestyles, to drop out and take to the road, were
not dissimilar to the credos of the "Beat" writers who substi-
tuted for success and conformity "a cult of unsuccess."[54]
Inspired by Jack Kerouac (1922-1969) the major figure among the
"Beat" writers, and his book *On the Road* (1957), many began
restlessly hitchhiking across America in a mixture of rebellion
against Establishment, conformity, authority in general; an
escape which had no particular goal beside the romantic concept of
total freedom, and the avoidance of commitment. Those beatniks of
the fifties paved the way for the hippies, the young rebels of the
sixties, whose escape to the hallucinogenic drugs was one form of
rejecting the mores of established society and a boisterous freedom from social constraint.[55]

The literary image of the delinquent, the maladjusted and the
outsider, can be reflected, according to Bradbrook, in two ways.
The first one is "the Dionysian or Ecstatic version" which recog-
nizes no Delinquents; the second is "the Estranged," which implicitly places, but does not positively judge, the Delinquent, and
which prefers to use the style of irony and a tone of alienation.[56]
By this definition, while Osborne and the "Beat" writers are
"Dionysian," Salinger is among the "Estranged." By the same token,
Yizhar is a "Dionysian." Throughout "A Story" he lashes out in a
diatribe against reality, inciting his listener (reader) to rebel
against it--a conspicuous paradox, since the revolt is supposed to

be against a reality in which Yizhar was himself a major "Establishment" figure: a prominent member of the ruling party in the Knesset.

Yizhar repeatedly declares that his environment is irrevocably contaminated in a way that has ruined his beloved country for good. No wonder he "refuses history"; history has failed him; it has made possible the disintegration of the idealistic values on which he grew up, the world which had shaped him. What were these values? In a speech[57] given a year before publishing *Tales*, he allows us to have a glimpse of them. These were the values of the *rishonim*, the early pioneers, the founding fathers, who heroically elevated themselves to meet the challenge of the harsh reality of the land. Nonconformists, they nevertheless had a strong sense of commitment and mission. In this speech Yizhar rhapsodizes about his father and uncles who, as young pioneers, settled in Ḥadera (1890), at the time a desolate and malaria-ridden swampland. Not knowing that the swamps were the source of malaria, they opened their hut windows to the breeze. Seventy years later Yizhar exclaims in his speech, "Ah, how I wish I could have now a bit of the breeze[58] that blew in into one old, distant hut that stood there on the sand hill."

Without such a spirit he is a malcontent ("I am a man who lost his world. I had it once but it is gone" ["A Story," 198]), one who is unable to find anything of positive value in the present. He is disgusted with the vulgarity, ugliness, greediness of society, the destruction of pastoral. One of the major symbols of his childhood and of pastoral was the orange groves[59] and now they too were "dried up and sold to the land-speculators" ("A Story," 113). The state has become the "land of petty pedlars, paradise of the castrated, the abode of peanut crackers" (113). The old sycamore and the magnificent eucalyptus yielded their place to the "grey, drab concrete *shikkunim*,[60] the product of a castrated, frustrated, ulcer-ridden architect" (113).

Yizhar's diatribe stems from his reaction to the radical changes in Israeli society and landscape in the wake of the materialism and pragmatism of the 1950s and 1960s, which replaced the idealism of the pre-State years. The 1950s and 1960s were the years of mass immigration, and of the construction boom which originated from the need to settle multitudes of immigrants. With sentimental and aesthetic factors in many cases ranking low in the scale of priorities, landscape was damaged beyond repair. In a claustrophobic tone Yizhar cries out:

> Ugly *shikkunim* will breed ugly men, ugly men will breed
> ugly women, ugly women will breed ugly children and
> ugly children will breed an ugly world. And an ugly
> world will breed nothing but will be blocked up and
> choked up and that will be that. (114)

His only advice to his listener is to cut himself off completely from such a reality and to drop out: "Do not associate
yourself with anything, do not buy a house, nor a plot, nor even
a table" (105). This dissent is aimed at enabling one to break
loose: "Run, run. That's all that's left. Run like a roe-buck.
Run breathless and blindfolded, as though escaping from smoke, or
from the stench of a carcass" (104). He talks to his listener
with a sense of impending disaster, urging him not to conform but
to escape: "Flee, run for your life...and don't look back lest you
perish" (103).[61]

In their rejection of society and its false materialistic re-
wards, and in their preaching to escape to a yet uncontaminated
Arcadia, these sermons resemble Holden Caulfield's fantasies of
escape to Vermont where he can live in "a cabin" (for him it was
what the "hut" of the *rishonim*, in contrast to the *shikkunim*, was
for Yizhar), or to the rye field where he can "keep the children
in Arcadia." The Yizharian narrator assumes the responsiblity of
Holden in the rye field when he addresses the listener as a child
in need of protection, calling him: "my son," "my darling son,"
"my beloved son." Like Holden, he does not attempt to be engaged
in an active campaign to fight for his principles, but prefers to
escape, either because he believes the situation is hopeless, or
because he is not cut out to be a fighter. In the context of real
life, this particular aspect is even more conspicuous in Yizhar's
case than in Salinger's. Yizhar, after all, had the opportunity
to put up a fight for his ideas as a member of the Knesset for
many years. He chose to refrain from this option. For most of
his political career he was unwilling, or unable, to become an
iconoclast in his public life, contrary to the defiant mood of
"A Story." Ultimately, however, his writing preaches escape, not
a fight.

Escape for him means not having to come to terms with the
present, not toeing the line, avoiding stagnation and, above all,
retaining the Peter Pan within him. *Tales* advocates two modes of
escape: escape to the past (to the days of childhood), and escape
to nature; the two sides of the same pastoral coin.

Escape to Childhood, or the Idea of Freedom

Throughout *Tales*, Yizhar constantly depicts the *now* in sharp
contrast with the *then*, the present serving as a device by which
the perspective of the past is accurately defined. The opening
sentence of "Runaway" is: "Things haven't always been as they are
now." "Dunghill" begins with the comparison between the technique
of buying dung in the 1960s, when the story is narrated, and buying it in the days when the story took place--the 1930s. "Ḥabakuk"
starts with the narrator informing us how sad his story is going to
be and why he had put off telling it so many times in the past.
The past is overshadowing "A Story" from its first sentence: "And
you know there are roads that one can't go through any more,"
bringing to mind the contrast between how roads used to be in the
then and how they are in the *now*.

How does the narrator invoke the memories of the *then*, which
in these stories refers almost always to his childhood? In contrast to Proust, Yizhar's memories are mostly voluntary--that is,
when he sets out a priori to tell a story. But when he does not
attempt to reconstruct a definite episode, he allows himself to be
carried away by his *mémoire involontaire*. Where the taste of the
petite madeleine triggers Proust's flow of associations, it is
smell that starts Yizhar on his "stream of consciousness" monologue
about the sad fields of his childhood. The sharp, bitter smell of
camomile ("A Story," 136) and smell of scented grass (164) or the
smell of the dusty road (204). All his smell-stimulated memories
are pastoral; they are associated with his escape to the plain,
which is nothing but the escape from the present to the past, to
the years of childhood.

To judge from *Tales*, the finest attribute of childhood, in
Yizhar's view, is the concept of freedom. He thus goes along with
Coveney's theory about the "cult of the child" in literature, which
maintains "that the child indeed becomes a means of escape from the
pressures of adult adjustment, a means of regression towards the
irresponsibility of youth, childhood, infancy, and ultimately nes-
cience itself."[62] Underlying these stories is a lament of a man
of forty-seven (Yizhar's age at the publication of this book) who
can no longer be part of "that most envied thing of all, the state
of eternal youthfulness, the Country of the Ever-Young,"[63] and yet
is unable to accept that "Paradise...must be left behind."[64] His
futile attempts to return to it are really the *leitmotiv* of these
stories.

Freedom is first and foremost the freedom of mobility which,
as mentioned above, played a major role in the philosophy of the
"Beat" writers. Mobility means ability to run away from (confine-
ment and stagnation--the horse in "Runaway"), and to run towards
(excitement, adventures, and a carefree and uninhibited life--the
brother on his motorcycle in "A Story"). Yizhar relishes watching
the horse and the motorcycle--the instruments of mobility and
liberty. Their descriptions are seasoned with overtones of excitement, admiration and fascination.

The Jungian belief that wild horses often symbolize "the uncontrollable, instinctive drives that can erupt from the uncon-
scious--and that many people try to repress,"[65] may well be applicable to Yizhar's equine descriptions in "Runaway." Wild horses
embody for him beauty, strength, purity and the freedom of roaming
the wilderness--qualities which he cannot find in the "castrated"
reality around him. As Bruno Bettelheim points out, "Children
have a natural affinity to animals and often feel closer to them
than to adults, wishing to share what seems like an animal's easy
life of instinctual freedom and enjoyment."[66] The escape of the
runaway horse thus expresses Yizhar's longing to escape from the
present, so explicitly expressed in "A Story."[67] The descriptions
of the horse breaking loose and running away ("Runaway," 45f.) are
given in time sequences, as though recorded by a camera in slow
motion, with great care not to miss any gesture. The movement is
from the tamed to the wild, from the *here* to the *there*, from the
now to the *then*, as seen through the eyes of a fascinated boy-
narrator, savoring each little detail. As this narrator becomes
increasingly identified with the runaway, his ecstatic feelings of
total freedom intensify and on a semi-conscious level his Peter
Pan traits emerge. These traits express themselves in the wish to
be always on the road (the beatnik's concept, after Kerouac's book)
and never to arrive--for arrival means completing the course,
reaching maturity, and giving up mobility (freedom).

> Ah, always to be afire and never extinguished. Always to
> want and never to be satisfied. Always to set out and
> never to arrive. To be alive and not sluggish. Free and
> not bound....To be swept along in this flowing movement,
> this running, to be carried aloft, to beat upward and
> fly--beyond all fences and all enclosures and all allot-
> ments, and all duties and obligations, out into the wide
> open. Ah, yes. ("Runaway," 112f.)

Running (motion) then, is, by his own admission, escaping duties,
obligations. It has no other purpose but to be itself; it is the
truest form of self-fulfillment.

You don't have to get anywhere, reach any place; all you
do is just gallop....No restraint and nobody to stop you.
No accounts to render and no regrets. You just live your
running to the full. You become everything you have ever
wanted to be deep down inside you. Out there, whatever
has been quivering inside you, whatever you have ever
longed to be, to attain, comes into being in that won-
drous running.[68] ("Runaway," 106)

The brother's motorcycle in "A Story," just like the runaway
horse, is a wild and powerful thing that loves to live its running
to the utmost; the narrator regards it as an extension of his elder
brother. However, the difference here is in the relations between
the motorcycle and its owner, the brother. The motorcycle, always
well behaved, like a tamed horse ("A Story," 140), resembles more
the horse Bubkah[69] than the runaway horse. Bubkah is meek, fond
of its owner, whom it would never leave voluntarily. When stolen
it is happy to return to its owner--exactly the reverse of the
runaway. Communication between Ḥanoch and Bubkah is excellent
just as it is between the brother and his motorcycle: it is enough
for the brother to look at his motorcycle for it to come to life
(139).

Unlike the runaway horse, the motorcycle is directly linked
with death. The way the brother rides it, experiencing an ex-
hilarating sensation of freedom, is actually courting death. The
fatal ending is inevitable in Yizhar's stories: the runaway horse
is captured, the motorcyclist is killed in an accident, and Ḥabakuk is struck down by a shell. There are no happy endings.[70]

Among the critics who have commented on Yizhar's idea of escape to freedom, Kurzweil's reaction is certainly the most sarcas-
tic and vitriolic.

The lyricism of adolescence does not forsake Yizhar even
when he is approaching his fifties, and the eternal "Ah"
and "Oh" do not convince and do not add an epic weight to
the story...."Ah, that horse! Ah, that horse of mine!
Ah, that horse!," this is the final sentence of the story.
And the free, desert horse, ran, ran, galloped, galloped,
towards the desert, and suddenly, "Ah, that horse! Ah,
that horse of mine! Ah, that horse!"--he changed direction
and ran, ran...until he reached the building of the
Knesset.[71]

While refraining from scoffing at Yizhar for his many years
in the Knesset, another critic, Schweid, nevertheless cannot repress an ironic tone when referring to the runaway horse.

He ran and ran and ran (one must admit: to measure by the
patience of a modern reader, he ran a bit too much, but
what can one do? Apparently that's how it was, nothing
that the author could do...) until he is finally captured

> to the great relief of the reader and the great sorrow of
> the reminiscing child....Truth to tell, had the running
> of the horse been much shortened and the theory about run-
> ning in the fields replaced by description only, and had
> the style been less sentimental and clumsy, the story
> could have been convincing. The wish to compress too
> much acted against Yizhar. He had pretensions to raise
> a situation to the level of a *Weltanschauung* but only
> managed to create an expression of bothersome sentimen-
> talism.[72]

In the same context, Miron, who sees in the escape of the
runaway horse an instance of Yizhar's inner resistance to a world
of duties and order--traceable throughout Yizhar's writings, beginning with "Ephraim Goes Back to Alfalfa"--maintains that Yizhar's
idea of freedom suffers from an "intellectual feebleness" and is
unduly adolescent; a fact which Yizhar tries to cover up by "sensuous colorfulness and the gentle emotional fabric of the inner
monologue."[73]

The theme of total freedom is related in Yizhar's childhood
stories to the pastoral theme of escape to nature and to the theme
of nostalgia for the pre-State Arab, with the runaway horse serving
as the linking element. The formula is as follows.[74] The horse
(the embodiment of freedom) escapes towards the open country and
the Arab village (both are representatives of pastoral and of nostalgia for the lost world of childhood), and from there on towards
the desert, the homeland of the noble Arab horses (and the reverse
of the "land of petty pedlars and paradise of the castrated"). On
a symbolic level this escape, an act of defiance, can be seen as
reflecting Yizhar's disillusionment with society, and his desire
to retreat from the constrictions of reality to an inner time, in
which "life still seemed...open and fluid with possibilities."[75]

Escape to Nature

Yizhar's best remembered speech in the Knesset (he made very
few during the many years he served as a member) was the one in
which he introduced a bill for the preservation of wild flowers.[76]
It was charged with the love of wild flowers, love of nature, which
is displayed in abundance in his childhood stories, particularly
in their landscape descriptions. Miron, who considers Yizhar "the
greatest poet of landscape in Israeli literature,"[77] finds the
source of Yizhar's reverence for nature in the writer's belief
that it is both more pure and more complete than man.[78] It stands
to reason that this romantic antithesis of nature and society derives from the author's quest for compensation in nature for his
own inadequacy.[79]

An outdoor man in his narrative orientation, the natural
arena of Yizhar's stories is the open countryside, the landscape
of fields, wild patches, sands and desert reaches of the south.
Whenever he introduces a vision of a domestic world in his stories
it serves only as a setting for an exit to the wilderness, or for
a return to it.[80] When Yizhar begins to narrate the glory of nature, Barzel observes, "he releases his descriptive power and reveals the treasures of his language...his sentences voice the
whispers of fields which give off intoxicating scents, paint multi-
colored sights, sweep into the open landscapes."[81] And Miron sees
Yizhar's linguistic treatment of the outdoors as "the greatest
artistic achievement, both of Yizhar himself and of Hebrew fiction
in his generation."[82] While this assumption seems to be accepted
by all, opinions differ as to the technique employed. Yizhar is
said to have learned much from the landscape descriptions of
Gogol, Turgenev and Tolstoy. But while the Russian masters believed that landscape by itself has no justification in their work,
unless it penetrates the consciousness of man--therefore its descriptions never became independent and were always limited--Yizhar
often allows landscapes to burst into the plot and take its place,
diverting the reader from the main story.[83] Disagreeing, Miron
maintains that Yizhar does not take "descriptive interest in landscape and object as such," even though he obviously enjoys his
ability to create verbally "a detailed and sensuously living reconstruction of the physical, scenic reality."[84] In Yizhar's
stories, Miron holds, this scenic reality is never regarded as
merely an object of artistic description but "it serves simultaneously as the background of an intense human drama and as a
participant in that drama, an active factor demanding its place as
an equal, alongside, and in opposition to, the human factor."[85]
Precisely the opposite view is expressed by S. Zemach, who claims
that Yizhar is not interested in people, individual or collective,
and that landscape descriptions are the most fundamental element
in his writing, for which he enlists all his power.[86] Disputing
this premise, Shaked argues that the function of nature in Yizhar's
stories is to cut man off from his loneliness and integrate him in
the sweeping flow which is bigger than himself.[87]

The diversity of opinion about Yizhar's approach to nature
stems from the ambivalence that characterizes the way nature is
depicted throughout his writings. On the one hand, some of his
stories may confirm the opinion that the principal relations between man and landscape in them are of enmity and mutual distrust,

with man attempting to conquer the wilderness by means of cultivation and refinement, and with the landscape showing fierce resistance. This enmity is particularly displayed in *Ziklag*, where the
characters, as D. Patterson points out, "are dominated by the in-
hospitable wilderness in which they find themselves, and with
which they can establish no emotional rapport."[88] On the other
hand, throughout *Tales* Yizhar displays his recognition of nature
"as an exalted, spiritual value, a superior moral standard, capable of annulling all opposing standards."[89] When viewed from
this aspect, landscape may become a symbol of total liberation.

But does the narrator really feel exaltation in nature?
"There is always sadness over the open country," he tells us
("A Story," 136), his mood consistent with Lerner's view that
"Eden is tinged with sadness"[90] due to its impending doom. Perhaps because he is so aware of it, the narrator does not miss an
opportunity to give us excessive inventories of wild life and wild
flora (135-36, 184-88), as though writing an obituary to something
dear to him which has perished. His compulsive habit of naming
birds, insects, beasts, flowers, grasses, brings to mind the biblical verse: "And Adam gave names to all cattle and the fowl of
the air and to every beast of the field."[91] Since this is his
Eden, he feels like Adam. Is it just a result of his sense of
loss ("When you name a thing you really lose it"[92]), or is it a
wish to create an exotic effect ("Sometimes the exotic is achieved
by simple naming of objects"[93])? To the possibility of a positive
answer to both suggestions, another suggestion may be added, and
that is that Yizhar does it also to impress the reader that he is
a man who knows what he is talking about when he takes us on a grand
tour of his Arcadia, so that we may trust him as an expert guide.

The landscape visibly evokes his sentimentality. His eyes
linger lovingly on each rural sight, and in this respect he is not
unlike Meliboeus, Virgil's about-to-be-exiled shepherd, who sees
the beauty of his home through the eyes of loss,[94] or from Eve in
Paradise Lost, in her lament on the loss of Eden.[95] Coveney
clearly links this nostalgic feeling with childhood: "Regret for
childhood takes on the same obsessive emotional quality as the
exile's nostalgia for 'home.'"[96]

Like Milton's Eden, Yizhar's rural landscape, when not yet
ruined or spoiled by civilization, grows luxuriantly, and everything in its flora and fauna is on friendly terms from "the good
old days" of childhood. Once the narrator manages to escape there,
he stops being the malcontent. Sometimes, however, the sensation

he experiences while being tuned to the sounds that keep coming at
him from the open countryside borders on the mystical; there is in
these landscape descriptions an inherent striving for the unknown,
for a transcendental reality. When in the open country, he waits
to hear God speaking to him, or he cries out to his dead brother.
It is noteworthy that, with the exception of Miron, none of the
critics seems to pay attention to these metaphysical strivings in
Tales. [97] When discussing Yizhar's landscape, they relate only to
the physical landscape. This landscape was indeed the point of
departure in *Tales*, but, as the stories unfold, nature and landscape become a vehicle for transcendence from the here and now. A
mere undercurrent in the first three stories, it emerges and accelerates towards the end of "A Story," as the narrator is finally
able to face the death of his brother. Reaching this stage, he
finds himself in a totally different "plain." All his remarkable
skills in describing the physical plain fail him when he tries to
apply them to this esoteric plain, and the virtuoso lapses into
obscurantism. The vague perception of this awesome sphere serves
as a moment of illumination ("A Story," 195-97). Yet it frightens
the narrator more than it exhilarates him, because he realizes
that it goes beyond his cognizance. Despite his superior command
of language, when it comes to grasping such an experience he finds
words inadequate.

The Arab Question

    In a post-Yom Kippur War symposium organized by the literary
quarterly *Keshet*, Yizhar stated:

        Ever since the arrival of the *Biluim* [98] discussions
        about the "Arab question" have not ceased. This motif
        is repeated in endless variations and each time the
        variation becomes more difficult and more total and
        all inclusive.[99]

    As far as his own stories are concerned, the "Arab question"
is probably his most controversial theme, particularly in his war
stories. In his childhood stories, however, it is strongly linked
with the escape to nature.

    The war stories, which voiced the protest of the Jewish hu-
manist against the injustice done to the Arab villagers by his
comrades, threw many of his readers off balance. What baffled and
vexed them was not so much the shock that the morally sensitive
protagonist registered in view of the brutality displayed by his
comrades, but rather his refraining from taking any course of

action to stop it. For those who speculated that this protagonist actually represented the persona of the author, this inertia cast serious doubts on his moral integrity.

Critics from the left wing accused him of inconclusive humanism,[100] and warned him against the risks of not demonstrating courage and moral and intellectual consistency.[101] Critics from the right wing accused him of playing a double game: "Yizhar's war against sadism is only lip service....He is a partner to his hero's emptiness";[102] and: "Yizhar's hero realizes well the ambiguity of his moral stand. He is aware that he is evading the issue and that it means moral failure."[103] He was taken to task for displaying literary courage to cover up political cowardice.

> Twice at least the narrator of "Ḥirbet Ḥizah" mentions
> the prophet Jeremiah, as a symbol of crying out against
> oppression. But the man from Anathoth was put in jail,
> as we know, and was not among the King's advisors. Not
> so Yizhar. For many years he sat in the Knesset....We
> never heard him raising his voice about the oppressed and
> persecuted Arabs. In such a cry of conscience, even if
> voiced despite a possible ban by his party, he would not
> have risked going to jail. At the most he would have
> risked his seat in the Knesset....One thing must be
> clear: using prophetic pathos without risking anything
> does not convince. On the contrary, it jars the ear
> and depresses.[104]

As a rule, Yizhar avoided answering his literary critics in public. However, in "A Story," he did it indirectly in the long monologue of which this story consists:

> Am I the address for questions?...Is this what people
> miss--the answers that I can give?...I do not have even
> one good, satisfying answer....And when I am pushed to
> the wall I am only squashed....Do I have one solid thing
> on which I could stand safely and suggest beneficial
> alternatives? All I have in my hands is the conviction
> that it should not be done this way. (126)

Miron, who often demonstrates more insight and openmindedness with regard to Yizhar than other critics, offers this explanation of Yizhar's ambivalence:

> Yizhar is a definite romanticist who nevertheless became
> the poet of a pioneer-group enterprise, which demands a
> conquest of the self and the individual will, and utterly
> nullifies them whenever they clash with the collective
> will of the society....The moral solution of this con-
> flict is, as has been noted, unfixed, and generally un-
> clear as well, and this fact has definite bearing upon
> the method of artistic exposition of reality, which is
> uniform and regular in most of Yizhar's stories.[105]

As far as the aforecited critics are concerned, Yizhar's treatment of the Arab question stems from moral and humanistic

attitudes. In sharp contrast, U. Shoham offers a completely different theory.[106] It should be stated at the outset that his
thesis is generally more in keeping with the theory that relates
to Yizhar as a writer of pastoral.

Shoham's point of departure is that it is mistaken to expect
to find behind Yizhar's "prophetic" outbursts a moralistic attitude. Rather than denouncing horrors inflicted on Arabs by Jews,
Yizhar aims to use the Arab as a literary device in his lament on
the loss of pastoral. There are in *Tales* two basic, contradictory
and simultaneous situations: one is a departure to (or a yearning
for) a world that has not yet come to be; the other--nostalgia for
a world that has been. The narrator's fluctuating position between the future and the past is his position between the *open*
(the distance that has not yet been travelled) and the *closed*(the
object of his nostalgia). The *open* is symbolized in the plain
(the Negev, the desert), while the *closed* is symbolized in the
orange grove (that grew in the narrator's *moshavah* in his childhood). The narrator's simultaneous attraction to these two poles
confuses them in a paradoxical manner, so that sometimes the departure looks like arrival, the future looks like past, and past
like future. The Arab, in this context, is branching off from the
world of the orange grove, while at the same time belonging to the
wilderness (the Negev), thus serving as a link between the *closed*
and the *open*. The Bedouin that come from the Negev to the orange
grove to sell dung, their merchandise, in "Dunghill," exemplify
this theory. There is a camaraderie and partnership between the
Jew (the narrator's brother) and Suliman the Arab (the brother's
intermediary in his dealings with the Bedouin). This camaraderie
turns into a brotherhood bond in "A Story," in the dramatic episode of the accident in which the brother and "his Arab" were
killed. A minute before the accident the brother is reported to
have thought: "[I am riding] this motorcycle of mine to be on time
for the landsale[107] and my Aḥmed is with me, the same old Aḥmed
who is always with me" (176). Shoham interprets this as expressing
Yizhar's belief in the possibility of perfect harmony between Jews
and Arabs. But the ride (the idyll of the Golden Age) does not
last long: the accident (the war) happened in a most senseless way,
Jews and Arabs alike died together. In other words, with the War
of Independence the legend of the Golden Age exploded: Eden was
lost. The new reality brought the end of pastoral, the end of
harmony between Jews and Arabs. A reading of Yizhar's war stories
in this light explains why the protagonist was so infirm when, on

the face of it, as a humanist, he should have taken measures to
help the Arab in his predicament and not just stand aside in a
silent protest. The reason: the impulse behind the urge to write
such stories is not moral but pastoral. In "Dunghill," the moral
rage should have been directed at the elder brother. Nevertheless,
despite a timid protest, the story is far from rebuking him. Quite
the contrary, he is portrayed with much admiration. The author's
point of departure seems to be that both the brother (the cheat),
and the Bedouin (the cheated), belong to the vision of the orange
grove, and if there is injustice, it is "all in the family."

To sum up Shoham's theory: the conflict in Yizhar's stories
is not a moral conflict but a constant tension between the *open*
and the *closed*, with the fictional Arab acting as the most authentic image of the *closed* within the *open*. And since the tension
between these two poles (or his constant simultaneous gravitation
to both of them) always left the Yizharian protagonist paralyzed,
one can see why this protagonist experiences the same inaction
whenever he has to relate to injustice done to Arabs.

Although Shoham's theory seems attractive, it would appear to
be short-sighted to eliminate altogether from Yizhar's characters
moral considerations concerning Arabs, for the sake of emphasizing
the author's pastoral inclinations. Pastoral does not cancel
morality; as Empson points out: "The realistic sort of pastoral...
also gives a natural expression for a sense of social injustice."[108]

That moral impetus was conducive to the writing of a story
that dealt acutely with the Arab--contrary to Shoham's supposition--
is disclosed in one of Yizhar's rare attempts to defend his stories
publicly. Shortly before a controversial screening of a television
adaptation of "Ḥirbet Ḥizah," the following statement of his appeared in an Israeli daily.[109]

> Most of what is told in "Ḥirbet Ḥizah" are facts of which
> I was an eyewitness....I was not the only witness....Of
> course, like in any other literary composition there is
> much fiction in its arrangement and characters, but the
> basic facts remain. When I wrote the story I did not
> write it as a Jew or an Arab, and not as a conflict be-
> tween Jews and Arabs. I was mainly concerned with the
> human situation. I wrote it as a man who was hurt by
> what he saw, and who came to bear witness before people
> how things really were.

The sense or bearing witness is felt throughout his descriptions of rustic life and landscape; the tone is that of pastoral
elegies. The disappearance of the primitive Arab village, which
had added an exotic dimension to the world of his childhood, also

meant the vanishing of innocence, simplicity and that exotic charm
from the land. Underlying the detailed, idyllic portrayal of pastoral Arab villages (in the chapter "The Silence of the Villages,"
"A Story," 145-62), is the same nostalgia that accompanies the
descriptions of wild life and flora of his childhood landscapes.
Eden is doomed; writing about it is erecting a monument to it.

      True to his romantic impetus, Yizhar's inclination in these
childhood stories is to portray the Arab as some sort of a "Noble
Savage," the simple child of nature. At the same time, the Arab's
submissiveness, as symbolized by the camel ("A Story," 160f.), is
consistent with Lerner's observation that "there is an intimate
link...between the theme of rural content and a meek submissiveness
to authority."[110] This feature, easily discernible in the Bedouin
who come to the orange grove to sell dung, increases the narrator's
distress when he witnesses his brother's deeds. However, his
timid, ambivalent protest, when he questions his brother about his
act can be seen as suggesting a moral standpoint which seeks abso-
lute justice,[111] just as it can be seen as a futile wish to question for the sake of questioning, without really intending to re-
form his brother or to bring about a clear-cut moral decision.[112]
While each of these theories may be an oversimplification--as is
often the case with a complex author such as Yizhar, who is full
of contradictions--these two conflicting opinions may be equally
right when considered together, both reflecting various aspects of
his polymorphous interior life.

      In *Tales*, unlike in his war stories, Yizhar refrains from de-
picting the destruction of the Arab village as resulting from the
ruthlessness of its conquerors. Nevertheless, his lament in "A
Story" on the Arab village that perished is imbued not just with
elegiac overtones, but with obvious implications of a collective
guilt, reinforced by the fact that he himself was among the conquerors of this village (152).

The Concept of Death

      The fact that these stories were written by a man who has
difficulty in acknowledging the death of his childhood has much to
do with the way death is grasped in them.

      To begin with, writing these stories can be seen as a form of
bringing about a symbolic death; that is, if one accepts the assumption that such autobiographical writing is a cathartic experience that enables the author to say goodbye to childhood, and
brings him to the realization that "Paradise must be left behind."

In this respect, the act of writing these stories contains an element of symbolic initiation, in the Jungian sense;[113] and since
initiation is a noble cause--an act of liberation as well as of
commitment--and since death is related to initiation, it follows
that, in this context, if death has to take place it ought to be
associated with a noble cause. Indeed, in Yizhar's war stories
death is inseparable from liberation; that, after all, was "The
War of Liberation."[114] It could be suggested, then, that if there
is a "justifiable reason" for death, *that* war provided it. But if
indeed this is so, what is one to make of the death of the fool-
hardy brother in the motorcycle accident? Like most road accidents
caused by miscalculation, it was unjustifiable; it did not serve
any noble cause. If anything, it was a consequence of a daredevil
wish to court danger. Yizhar's attempt to introduce a nuance of
nobility into his dramatization of the accident does not work.
One recalls teacher Antolini's remark to Holden Caulfield as he
quotes from Wilhelm Stekel: "The mark of the immature man is that
he wants to die nobly for a cause, while the mark of the mature
man is that he wants to live humbly for one."[115]

   The romantic malcontent, the narrator of "A Story," repeatedly
expresses his readiness to die for a noble cause if God asks for
the sacrifice. He is waiting for God to give him a sign (197),
ready to answer God with *hinneni* "הנני" ("Behold, here I am") and
to hear God instructing him *kumm lekh lekha* "קום לך לר" ("Arise,
go") (197). By using these biblical phrases, Yizhar links the
motif of death in his story with major motifs which are originally
associated with them. The phrase *hinneni* echoes the sacrifice of
Isaac, the *Akedah*. When God tempted Abraham He called Abraham's
name, and Abraham replied: *hinneni* (Gen 22:1). This phrase is
associated also with the reply of young Samuel, when he heard God
call his name (1 Sam 3:4). *Hinneni* connotes both readiness for
mission and for sacrifice which in Yizhar's mentality marks the
heroism of the *rishonim* whom he wished to emulate. The phrase
lekh lekha is again associated with Abraham who was told by God:
lekh lekha me-artzekha ("Get thee out of thy country, and thy kin-
dred, and from thy father's house, unto a land that I will shew
thee," Gen 12:1). Once again the motif of mission (connoting the
rishonim, the founding fathers), is given in an analogy to Abraham,
the archetypal founding father, but this time with an interesting
nuance which stems from Yizhar's duality: Yizhar adds to the *lekh
lekha* which is connected with Abraham, the word *kumm* ("arise"), and
thus he associates the motif of Abraham with the motif of Jonah,

the motif of escape. When told by God: *kumm lekh el Nineveh*
("Arise, go to Nineveh," Jonah 1:2), Jonah tried instead to escape.
Here, then, in a nutshell, Yizhar discloses his troubled dichotomy:
the wish to have a mission, a commitment, even if it involves self-
sacrifice on the one hand, the wish to escape on the other.

As for the actual fear of death, it takes the narrator of "A
Story" an ocean of words and a few direct curses--when he personi-
fies death in the dramatization of the accident scene[116]--to overcome it and find solace in the belief that death is not the end,
that nothing is lost, and that "the living carries his dead" (204).
Becoming philosophical helps him to recover from the death of his
brother and thus end his adolescent, romantic rebellion against
time. It enables him to conquer his futile attempt not to let go
of the latent child in his self, and to take a decisive step towards facing maturity. We leave him alone at the end of the story,
after the storm of his verbosity subsides, with the impression that
this man stoically resigns himself to whatever maturity holds for
him. The irony is that death, such as his brother's, which was
caused by a reluctance to lead a life of compromise, now teaches
the narrator himself to accept this sort of life.

The Brother Motif

To judge from *Tales*, the footloose and fancy-free elder
brother, the embodiment of the ideal of youth, is the paragon of
Yizhar's childhood. He is first seen in "Dunghill" riding a
donkey, he is last seen in "A Story" riding a motorcycle to his
death. His death is what "A Story" was meant to be about. But
the trauma caused by it was so overwhelming that it prevented the
author from recounting it in a conventional narrative, and made
him attempt to circumvent it with long "sermons."[117] Consequently,
the brother motif too becomes linked with the recurrent theme of
escape. The narrator's grief for the loss of his brother is similar to Holden Caulfield's grief for his dead brother, Allie.[118]
Holden admires Allie who, in his eyes, possessed qualities that
Holden is looking for and cannot find in his peers or, for that
matter, in the adults with whom he has contact. Without Allie he
is forlorn in an impoverished, worthless world. The absence of
Allie and his like allows the "phonies" to gain power, spread all
over, and ruin the world. The narrator of "A Story" shares much
the same feeling. The dead brother was the epitome of all that
was positive and authentic in a *Sabra* who was the true heir to the

rishonim. His untimely exit left the stage in the hands of his
unworthy compatriots.

Both in "Dunghill" and in "A Story," the elder brother is
portrayed as feeling at home with the Arabs, familiar with their
language, folklore, manners, customs, and commands their respect.
He associates more with them than with Jews; his own Jewish friends
"complete in Arabic what they can't say in Hebrew" ("A Story," 143).
One of the narrator's most thrilling memories of his childhood is
about the night his brother and his brother's friends took him to
see an Arab festivity (142-44).

In contrast to the "petty pedlars" and the "land speculators"
who uprooted the orange groves to build instead the ugly *shikkunim,*
the brother is described at the end of "Dunghill" as standing on
top of the dung hill which he has just bought from the Arabs, pro-
claiming joyfully: "The orange grove will be fertilized and we'll
have a fantastic yield" (37). And when he purchases land in "A
Story," it is for the Jewish National Fund, to be used for the
establishment of new Jewish settlements, not for speculation.

The brother incorporates outstanding virile and potent elements. His motorcycle is a sexual symbol, an extension of his
machismo, and while riding it is a show of bravado, his contact
with it is not without erotic allusions. It is enough for the
brother to gaze at the motorcycle for "a quiver of attentive
stretching to run through it" ("A Story," 139). Describing the
ride on the motorcycle, the narrator uses a biblical circumlocu-
tion for sexual intercourse: "Horse and rider became one flesh"
(140; cf., Gen 2:24).

It should be noted, though, that in contrast to most of the
other childhood stories discussed in this study, Yizhar's are
conspicuously lacking in eroticism. His is a masculine world,
devoid of girls (Naomi, who briefly appears in "Ḥabakuk" which is
not really a childhood story, is not mentioned in any erotic
context). The link here is not between love (Eros) and death
(Thanatos), but between freedom and death. Freedom is associated
with speed, the uninhibited mobility, for which the brother will
pay with his life. In a way, the death of the brother is the outcome of a rebellion against the limitation of life, matter, speed,
time, the rules of nature as embodied in the train with which the
brother collides.[119] Death is inevitable because in the final
analysis death is the ultimate expression of the freedom of life.
Therefore, a sense of fatalism marks the re-enactment of the accident scene, as the narrator involves himself in an attempt to

interfere and stop the inevitable, begging his brother and the
engine driver to slow down, asking the Arab passenger to stop his
brother, beseeching the Angel of Death to spare his brother, all
of course to no avail.

The Brother motif energizes Yizhar's narrative power in
"Dunghill" and in "A Story." In the latter only when the narrator
describes his brother or an episode associated with him is there
a story; otherwise, "A Story" is nothing but loosely connected
sermons, nature descriptions, and some metaphysical contemplation,
all of which are held together by the memory, or the sense of
loss, of the brother.

The narrator's taking us to the open country, his brother's
natural habitat, is a desperate attempt to communicate with the
dead. He is hoping to hear his brother's voice, his advice, his
guidance. His cry to the dead brother at the end of "A Story" is
not unlike his cry to Ḥabakuk at the end of "Ḥabakuk," for both
played the role of a mentor: the brother--the earthly mentor;
Ḥabakuk, the musician and astrologer--the spiritual. On both occasions the narrator is left without response. The mentors are
gone; he is destined to find his way without guidance or protection. To judge from these stories, he had very little success in
doing so.

The Father Image

In sharp contrast to the elaborate literary treatment of the
elder brother, the narrator's father lacks definition and is never
brought into focus throughout *Tales*. This may seem odd--particu-
larly in the light of Yizhar's effusions when referring to his
father and uncles in the *rishonim* speech--and could lead one to
believe that the father's role in the narrator's childhood was
insignificant. One is bound to ask: is the father ignored in
these stories because he is of no importance, or because the narrator has difficulty in relating to him? The following is an attempt to formulate answers to these questions, drawing on the
ideological background of the Father motif in the *Sabra* literature.

The father appears briefly and marginally on the setting of
"Runaway," for the first time when he asks his neighbor Aryeh to
plow the yard (84) and for the second time, and equally negligibly,
as he leaves to go to work (88). As for the mother--she is seen
also briefly, in "Ḥabakuk" (70), when accompanying her son, the
narrator, to Jerusalem, where she introduces him to Ḥabakuk. Both
parents are mentioned together only once in the whole book, again

tersely, in "A Story" (143). We are told that because they had to
take a trip somewhere, the narrator, a young boy at the time, was
left with his elder brother. The fact that the brother took him
that night to the Arab festivity is not mere coincidence; it provides a possible clue to the parents' almost total absence from
these childhood stories: they cannot act as his initiators into
the Arab world as does the elder brother. They are never touched
on in an Arab context. For the narrator, only the brother, the
true son of the land, could become a model and a guide to the
world of pastoral, in which the Arab figured prominently. These
roles could not be filled by the immigrant parents. As his
rishonim speech reveals, Yizhar, who admired these pioneers, would
almost certainly endorse the observation that the record of these
founding fathers "was probably unparalleled in modern history,"
and that they "had not only revolutionized their society but also
to a large extent created it."[120] Ignoring these parent figures
in stories in which he tries to take stock of his roots could only
mean that as far as he--the acclaimed "first *Sabra* writer"--is
concerned his personal history does not begin with them but rather
with his elder brother.

The theme of the revered and resented fathers haunted the
first-generation *Sabras*, who were troubled by the idea that historically they had to measure up to the standard of their fathers
in every aspect of their lives, while not being allowed to disturb
the fathers' goals. The sons' ambivalence is bluntly expressed by
the poet Ḥaim Gouri, another leading figure of the first-generation
Sabra writers (b. 1923), in the aforementioned post-Yom Kippur War
Keshet symposium: "There is in us a bitter revolt against these
generations [of the diaspora]. There is in us clearly a wish
both to kill the father and to seek him."[121] Such a repressed
parricidal impulse played a major role in the writings of Yizhar,
which became, as Miron put it, "the most faithful literary expression of a generation...caught in a tension between its great,
historic destiny and its basic experience of life, which is identical to the parallel tension between the group's sense of its
destiny and the personal life experience of the hero."[122]

The image this generation had of itself had undergone tremen-
dous changes in the post-Independence era. In the pre-State days,
and during the War of Independence, the *Sabra* youth was identified
with the image "Silver Tray," after a famous poem by the poet
Nathan Alterman (1910-1970), that took its name from a saying
attributed to Dr. Chaim Weizmann and which appeared as a motto to

the poem: "A State is not given to a nation on a silver tray."[123]
The poem symbolized the *Sabra*'s willingness to sacrifice his life
as the "Silver Tray" on which history hands the Jewish nation its
State.

An heroic symbol, the "Silver Tray" could be viewed as tantamount to the old biblical symbol of the *Akedah* that, in Jewish
thought, came to represent the supreme instance of self-sacrifice
in obedience to God's will. However, in the wake of the ideological shift in the Israeli society, and especially as it became increasingly obvious that the 1948 war was not to be the final one,
the "Silver Tray" was cast aside to be replaced by a disenchanted
re-interpretation of the *Akedah* theme. In this new context, the
son did not identify with the saintly Isaac as depicted in the
biblical text, but rather with a possible alter ego who might not
have been entirely free of parricidal leanings, in view of his
father's filicidal inclinations.[124] Gouri gives a hint of it in
his poem *Yerushah* ("Heritage"),[125] which ends with the following
lines:

> Isaac, as we're told, wasn't taken up for sacrifice
> He lived a long time,
> Seeing things prosper, till his eyesight dimmed.
> But that hour he made a heritage for his descendants.
> Each one born with a knife in his heart.[126]

If *this* Isaac could have spoken his mind when taken to be
sacrificed, his words might not have sounded unlike the defiant
utterances of the young *Sabra* soldiers whom Yizhar portrayed in
Ziklag, who refusing to accept the *Akedah* concept of self-sacrifice
resented their fathers for going along with this concept (i.e., the
war) and not manoeuvring them out of it.

It should be pointed out that this remarkable change in approach to the *Akedah*--a principal cause of the malaise of the generation of the sons in the immediate post-Independence era--is not
new. It can be traced to certain legends from centuries ago that
dealt with this subject. One such legend that dwells on Abraham's
eagerness to sacrifice his son, and which Spiegel cites,[127] tries
to explain the biblical verse in which the angel says to Abraham:
"Lay not thy hand upon the lad" (Gen 22:12):

> Why did the angel refer to *hand* and not to knife? (For
> from the eyes) of the ministering angels tears dropped
> onto the knife, and it dissolved completely and evaporated.
> Said Abraham: Perhaps (this has happened because the lad)
> is not fit to be a sacrificial gift. May I strangle him,
> may I burn him, shall I cut him up in pieces before Thee?
> Said He to him: "Lay not thy hand!" Said Abraham to Him:

In that event, I have come here in vain. Let me bruise
him, let me extract some blood from him, let me remove
from him one drop of blood! Said He to him: "Don't you
do anything (*meuma*) to him," don't you bruise (*muma*) him.

The emergence in *Ziklag* of a new approach to the *Akedah* paved
the way for the development of this theme in Israeli literature
and drama. In Israeli drama, ever since the end of the 1960s (a
decade after *Ziklag*), a reversal of roles takes place. Isaac becomes not only the accuser, but also the *oked* (one who offers
sacrifice), while Abraham becomes the *ne'ekad* (the sacrifice).[128]
In the theater this trend began to manifest itself with the controversial satirical revue *Malkat ha-Ambatyah* (*Queen of the Bathtub*), written by a representative of the second *Sabra* generation
(if Yizhar represents the first), Ḥanoch Levin[129] (b. 1943), in
the aftermath of the 1967 war. This period saw also the appearance
of two published symposiums of young members of the kibbutz movement, in which the "Isaacs" expressed their defiant voice: *Siaḥ
Lohamim* (*Seventh Day*),[130] and *Shanah le-Aḥar ha-Milḥamah* (*A Year
After the War*).[131] In the latter, one of the participants said:
"We are a generation of doubters and sceptics. We are left only
with contradictions and ruined faith. What remains for us to believe in?...I want to know and understand where I am going and
what I am fighting for. I am not willing to be an eternal Isaac
climbing onto the altar without asking why or understanding...."[132]

The preceding discussion may explain the marginal role of the
father in *Tales*. It is not beyond the bounds of possibility to
regard the exclusion of the father as resulting from a wish on
Yizhar's part to avoid having to deal in his childhood stories
with the controversial theme of the *Akedah*.[133] At the same time,
on a metaphysical level, one can detect in "A Story" a dramatic
transformation in Yizhar since *Ziklag*, with regard to his relations
to another father, the "Cosmic Father," to borrow Kurzweil's
phrase. In *Ziklag*, Yizhar exclaims: "The God of the *Akedot* is the
father of evil."[134] Outraged by this blaspheming, Kurzweil, an
orthodox Jew, lashes out: "Yizhar needs the Cosmic Father for a
negative purpose, to blame Him for making reality what it is."[135]
As Kurzweil sees it, the rebellion against the *Akedah*, which is a
rebellion against death, is aimed against the Father.[136] In this
respect it appears that Yizhar has come a long way in the brief
interval between *Ziklag* and *Tales*, for Yizhar's last story suggests
a full acceptance of the "Cosmic Father." Near the end of "A
Story," the narrator cries out: "Talk to me, talk, talk, leave a
sign, Father, Father--" (197), meaning the "Cosmic Father." And

he offers himself as a sacrifice, an act which has now assumed for
him the ultimate purpose of his life. Moreover, by using biblical
phrases associated with Abraham, as noted above, he indicates an
identification with Abraham. He wishes to be put to the test like
Abraham. This surprising realization marks the end of the cycle:
Isaac (who Yizhar has been until now) has become an *Abraham*.
Furthermore, he now wants to sacrifice the "Isaac" that remains
within him. Psychologically speaking, he has reached maturity, a
task which required undergoing a complete change of perspective.
Becoming the father may mean the end of rebellion against the
fathers, and, in his case, perhaps the end of the need to write
altogether. For as one who was until now the voice of the sons in
literature, he could no longer go on writing once realizing that
he could no more write as a son, but as a father, an ineluctable
biological fact. To become the voice of the fathers in literature
was simply against his grain.

Yizhar's world is a man's world. In all of his stories there
is not a single clearly-defined heroine; he does not even attempt
to create such a character.[137] It has been argued that "a painter
of man only," he is unable to read a woman's mind,[138] or that
whenever women appear in his stories they are in a state of "calculated sobriety and beyond any struggle."[139] These opinions give
some indication why most critics do not find it worth their while
to evaluate Yizhar's female characters, including the mother. Yet,
it does not seem proper to end a discussion of the literary treatment of the father image without mentioning the mother image.
Writing about "Ḥabakuk," Barzel[140] maintains that the mother plays
a significant role in this story. The fact that she introduces
Ḥabakuk to the boy indicates that the author does not really advo-
cate rebellion (as could be assumed from "A Story") but continuity.
The mother, who represents the world of tradition, brings her son
to Jerusalem where she will leave him to continue his education
with her advice and with an ally who takes over her role, Ḥabakuk.
She thus bears witness to the fact that Yizhar is basically a tra-
ditionalist and a conformist rather than an iconoclast.

Barzel's theory attests to the futility of any attempt to
capture the essence of Yizhar's writing with one epithet. Yizhar's
relationship, as a *Sabra*, to his father (and in this context the
father represents all antecedents of past generations of the diaspora, regardless of the fact that Yizhar's father himself rebelled
against these same generations by going to Palestine), bears the
mark of the ambiguity which Gouri phrases in the *Keshet* symposium.

This ambiguity is an intrinsic element in the *Sabra*'s search for
identity. In no way could Yizhar have escaped it, his work being--
to borrow again from Miron--"the most faithful literary expression
of his generation."

A Last Look at *Tales*

   As a writer whose forte lies in dealing with his protagonists'
inner struggle rather than with their actions, Yizhar cares very
little for the element of plot in *Tales*. If such an element is
still evident in the first three stories, the last one displays an
unmistakable wish to discard it altogether. All four stories are
written in the first-person, the narrator being a character in the
story. As such, he can observe or experience almost all that is
finally pertinent to the story. One of his most conspicuous flaws
is an inability to refrain from interpreting his tale over and over
again by way of intrusions, as though distrustful of the implicit,
or as though trying to challenge the supposition that "an episode
shown is more effective than the same episode told."[141] The obvious results are a prolixity which is foreign to the short story,
and a certain lassitude that overtakes the reader. It seems extremely unlikely that an experienced writer such as Yizhar was
unaware that "the structure of the short story is too delicate,
too tenuous, for a load of verbal pomposity."[142] If he nevertheless went ahead and wrote these stories the way he did, it was
either as a result of a wish to be innovative or, which seems more
likely, as a result of a waning mastery of the genre.
   It is symptomatic that he chose "A Story That Did Not Begin"
to reveal his thoughts about narrative art, for, as its name suggests, this is a story whose narrator has no power to unfold.
Throughout it, Yizhar makes a fetish of inhibitions. The symptom
of inhibitions that block the narrator whenever he is about to
start his story, and disrupt its flow by intrusions and digressions whenever it gets underway, is manifested distinctly in the
first three stories, but it becomes the prevailing factor in the
last one. In all four, Yizhar uses the device of an anonymous
listener who has little patience for digressions, and who constantly attempts to steer the narrator back to his tale, while the latter cannot help procrastinating and indulging in lengthy asides.
The narrator's restlessness and his urge to break away from conventional ways of living become linked with his breaking away from
conventions of the literary form. The conventional framework of

the story, like that of life, impedes him and he must escape
(another escape) it, to retain his potency.

His description of artistic potency resembles that of sexual
potency. The act of writing is depicted by metaphors which seem
to endorse Hanna Segal's assumption that "there is clearly a genital aspect of artistic creation which is of paramount importance.
Creating a work of art is a psychic equivalent of procreation."[143]
Reflecting on his ineptitude, Yizhar admits: "If only I knew how
to come..." ("A Story," 135). And later in the same paragraph:
"Here I am, filled with all that I have and with what is hidden in
me...which hasn't yet come...which is repressed...." And he follows that with a long description of a liberating outburst of
energy that is seemingly referring to the act of writing, except
that the metaphors he chooses allude as well to the male genitals
and the sexual act.

This outburst calls to mind the liberating outburst of the
runaway horse, and the liberating, wild ride on the brother's
motorcycle. Both the horse and the motorcycle, as noted, are
sexual symbols and both are linked with the idea of total freedom.
Hence, the act of writing is analogous to total freedom, and the
story itself--to the male genitals. As if to remove doubts from a
sceptical reader, Yizhar goes on to compare the story with an even
more recognizable sexual metaphor, an eel. The reluctant story,
which refuses to begin, is like "an eel that slips away from the
hands of the catchers," who are too eager to find "the right word"
("A Story," 199f.). Coming upon the ultimate, "redeeming" word,
which escapes Yizhar throughout the story, is tantamount, in a
sexual context, to orgasm.

The promised story's refusal "to come" leaves us with "A
Story That Did Not Begin," a massive non-story, an overelaborated
display of linguistic dexterity, versatility, tautology, and flamboyant rhetoric marked by uneven syntax; a torrential verbal chaos,
incoherent, uncontrolled. At one point, after several one-word
and two-word sentences followed by an extraordinary sentence of
462 words (198-200), the author confesses to his inability to find
the one true word, concedes his narrative failure, and lapses into
silence. His silence is one in which statements such as Herbert
Gold's gain in cogency: "The storyteller must have a story to tell
not merely some sweet prose to take out for a walk."[144]

Yizhar's verbal intoxication is typical of the first generation of Israeli writers whose mother tongue was Hebrew.[145] These
writers, especially in the 1940s and 1950s--when modern Hebrew was

still very much engrossed in self-discovery and dynamic growth--in
their eagerness to demonstrate technical mastery while searching
for their own voice, often indulged in flaunting rare words, lifted
from various old linguistic layers, artificially synthesized into
a literary, modern-day, but not yet wholly standardized, language.
The result was excessive loquacity, overlabored and affected Hebrew.
Instead of being artless, writers turned artful. This did not seem
to disturb the critics at the time. In an attempt to justify such
anomalies, ideological reasons were employed. Expressing the view
of many of his colleagues, the critic Zussman, complimenting Yizhar
on his sumptuous language, remarks: "That which is not acquired
through the language will never become an earthy property of a nation."[146] Such theories helped the writer feel like a pioneer
(which was in keeping with the spirit of the age): the conquest of
language is complementary to the conquest of the land and a prerequisite for the forming of a new nation. Ideologically fitting,
when it comes to literature such theories invariably misfire.
Confusing the end with the means when executing a short story often miscarries. Although Yizhar's eye for color, texture, earth
and sky, in these stories is superb, in the acid test of the art
of the short story *Tales* turned out to be a setback. Of all the
critics who discussed *Tales* only Miron appears to respect Yizhar
for his courage to write in a manner that ran the risk of "artistic suicide."[147] He conceives of Yizhar as trying to rebel against
the boundaries of literature and language, and break out of the
narrative into something beyond it. While this may be so, paradoxically though, in "A Story," as a result of his quest for the
single, precise, "redeeming" word, Yizhar got entangled in an endless, imprecise tirade, losing his way and becoming, in the process,
the Roget's Thesaurus of the Hebrew language. This could hardly
have been his intention when he tried to begin his last story, the
story which symbolically enough has never begun.

CHAPTER II

THE HIDDEN MYTH: NISSIM ALONI

Nissim Aloni, born in Tel Aviv in 1926, is set apart from the other writers whose stories of childhood are explored here by the fact that while the ethnic origin of the others is Ashkenazi he comes from a Sephardi home and environment, and by the fact that he alone chose eventually to pursue his artistic impulse through drama rather than narrative fiction.

The four childhood stories[1] included in his book *Ha-Yanshuf* (*The Owl*),[2] the subject of the study, were written between his first play, *Akhzar mi-Kol ha-Melekh*[3] (*The King is the Cruellest*), staged by the *Habimah* theater in Tel Aviv, 1953, and his second, *Bigdei ha-Melekh ha-Ḥadashim* (*The King's* [Emperor's] *New Clothes*), staged by the same theater in 1961. Aloni's decision to give up writing short stories for playwriting was expressed by, among other things, the establishment of his own theater, *Teatron Ha-Onot* ("The Theater of the Seasons"), in Tel Aviv in 1963.

His first play was an innovation in the Israeli theatrical scene.[4] It broke with the contemporary documentary drama, drawn from the background of the 1948 war, and established him as the most intriguing playwright in Israel. Its biblical theme--the conflict between the kings Reḥoboam and Jeroboam--an allegory of the contemporary political scene,[5] indicated Aloni's tendency to look for reference in history and mythology. Aloni introduced a fresh, brilliantly vivacious synthesis of biblical and modern Hebrew, which revealed his extraordinary linguistic concern. In the eight years that passed between this play and his second, he underwent an ideological and artistic metamorphosis that transformed his theatrical style. During this period he spent five years in Jerusalem studying history and French literature at the Hebrew University, and became aware, in his own words, of "the divergence of things, their complexity,"[6] his intimation that cynicism and disillusion had now replaced his initial innocence. In 1956 he left Israel for Paris where he came under the influence of the Theater of the Absurd. Abandoning realism for surrealism, his plays seem henceforth to lack interest in reflecting or dealing with current affairs. Instead, their subject matter, characters, and theatrical components construct an imagined and highly original

45

universe which seems to have very little in common with actuality.
Baffled critics registered their reservations, doubted his artistic integrity. He was charged with covering up by glitter and
fireworks a shallowness of content; with preferring flamboyance to
subtlety; with the use of boisterous verbal and theatrical virtu-
osity to avoid a straightforward, committed expression.[7]

In almost all his plays Aloni demonstrates a longing for a
"kingship" as a legend which compensates for a dull reality. Acknowledging his predilection for writing plays about kings, beg-
gars, clowns and prostitutes, he asks: "What else is there to
write about?"[8] These characters, although not as major dramatis
personae, made their appearance in his childhood stories as well.
The fact that the stories preceded the plays in which such characters are fully developed, indicates their experimental role. Examined from the standpoint of the plays, the stories could be regarded as an attempt to escape from a threatening reality by regression to the world of childhood; at the same time these childhood stories, technically speaking, served as a convenient literary
vehicle for shaping the early portrait of a character who in the
plays sets out to struggle with major existential issues.[9] The
plays and the stories alike are the work of a writer who oscillates
between an inability to struggle directly and without disguise with
the Israeli reality, and a reluctance to take up that struggle.

The stories are told in the first-person through a narrator
nicknamed Edirne. The perspective of each story is bifocal: the
reality of the Sephardi *shekhunah* (neighborhood) with World War II
as background, and the perception of this reality by an extremely
sensitive, highly imaginative and naïve boy on the threshold of
life. The geographical, sociological, psychological and cultural
milieu of the narrator correspond to Aloni's own childhood world
in the working class Sephardi *shekhunah* in the south of Tel Aviv.
Although the historical background also fits, there is a slight
chronological discrepancy: Aloni was fifteen when the battles of
Tobruk and Mersa Matruh (1941-1942), which are mentioned in the
stories, took place. In the stories the narrator is no older than
twelve.[10] The personal trauma of this boy in his transition from
childhood to adolescence is intensified by juxtaposition with the
public trauma of the *Yishuv* when the war drew close to home; the
boy's anguish, contrasted with his ignorance of the meaning of the
historic events and their possible consequences, interacts with
the community's apprehensions.

In analyzing these stories in the context of the connection
between psyche and environment--psychological insight and social
grasp--a suggested point of departure is the assumption that beneath the ostensibly innocent narratives lies a subterranean network of active archetypes and symbolic associations drawn from
Jewish legends and Greek myths. Identifying the mythic elements
and decoding them involves an interpretation based on clues scattered throughout the stories, as well as interviews with Aloni
over the years, and it will be divided into two sections: a discussion of the realistic level and a discussion of the mythic
level of these childhood stories.

The Arrangement and Content of the Stories

     The arrangement of the four stories in *The Owl* does not re-
flect the order in which they were originally published. Chrono-
logically the order was: "Hayal Turki me-Edirne" ("A Turkish
Soldier from Edirne"),[11] "Ha-Yanshuf" ("The Owl"),[12] "Liheyot
Ofeh" ("To be a Baker"),[13] "Shmeel" ("Shmeel").[14] In the book the
order is as follows: "A Turkish Soldier from Edirne," "The Owl,"
"Shmeel" and "To be a Baker." The rearranged order suggests a
pattern of inner development, a sort of *Bildungsroman* in minea-
ture.[15] Each story focuses on an unusual event which ends as a
sad revelation; as a unit the four express the intense sensibility
of childhood at the moment of onset of self-awareness. The vivid
and immediate quality of the stories derives from the young narrator's revelation of himself; the author intrudes nowhere and his
adult self seems to be totally absent from the narrative. The
narrator is too young and inexperienced to understand or comment
on the psychological, historical, sociological or anthropological
aspects of his tale, and his innocence accounts for the absence of
the ironic, the ideological, or the didactic in his tone. Since
the stories observe the dramatic unities, one might regard them--in
keeping with Aloni's dramaturgic leanings--as four acts of a play,
each one illuminating the narrator from a different aspect,[16] in
addition to demonstrating the slow process of dissociation from
the fantastic as a precondition of his coming of age.[17]
     The first story, "A Turkish Soldier from Edirne,"[18] intro-
duces as an exposition the narrator's world. We meet characters,
locality, ambience, chronological background and symbols to be met
again in the subsequent stories. It is an aggressive world, non-
intellectual, superstitious and colorful. The narrator's friend,

Salomon, the leader of the *shekhunah* "gang" of boys, brags about a
thousand-year-old owl that lives in his attic. Another friend,
Shmeel, boasts of his father, a soldier in the British army on the
Western desert. The narrator himself tells a tall story about an
heroic Turkish soldier whose head was cut off when he was attack-
ing his Bulgarian enemies. The severed head flew through the air
while its mouth continued to shout a Turkish battle cry and the
headless body continued to charge. The boy had heard this grotesque story from a down-and-out shoeblack whom he fantasized to
be the Turkish soldier. The *shekhunah* serves as a theatrical setting, while in the background the war is raging. The story cli-
maxes with the narrator "reviving" the shoeblack who he thinks is
dying, though in actual fact he is only suffering from an epilep-
tic fit.

The fantasy at the center of the second story, "The Owl"
(hereafter: "Owl"), was briefly alluded to in the opening story:
the mysterious thousand-year-old owl. The narrator believes in
its existence as firmly as he believes that the shoeblack is the
heroic Turk. His tale begins with a description of a girl who
lives at the outskirts of the narrator's *shekhunah*, and ends with
him taking her to Salomon's home to show her the owl. When they
arrive there, Salomon beats the narrator and humiliates him in
front of the girl, denying the myth of the owl. From then on the
narrator is ostracized by all the boys of the *shekhunah*.

"Shmeel," the third story, takes place immediately afterwards.
The narrator's isolation and exasperation betray a growing awareness of the difference between himself and his peers. The fantastic
element in this story is Shmeel's intention to blow up the world,
which a Chinese knifegrinder once told him he could do by holding
a mirror up to the sun. Why does Shmeel intend to blow up the
world? As is his habit in these stories, Aloni refrains from ex-
planations. There are several oblique suggestions of Shmeel's
mother's presumed infidelity, while Shmeel's father is at the
front, but since the narrator's credibility is doubtful, the reader
is never satisfied that the boy's suspicion is not fabricated by a
feverish imagination. Shmeel does not blow up the world, Salomon's
"gang" makes peace with the narrator, and the story ends with a
description of Shmeel's father being brought home in an ambulance,
his legs covered with blankets. Shmeel walks alongside the
stretcher holding his father's hand, but upon seeing the narrator
he drops his father's hand, pushes the narrator away, throws stones
at him and curses him.

The last story, "To be a Baker" (hereafter: "Baker"), depicts
the narrator's most urgent attempt to achieve independence, and in
this respect its initiatory aspects stand out sharply in comparison with the previous stories. As the long summer vacation comes
round, the narrator's parents suggest to him that he should go to
stay with his uncle in the *moshavah*. He refuses and insists instead on going to work in the Sasson bakery. For the boy the job
means assuming responsibility, joining the ranks of the adults,
boosting his self-esteem. But his joy is overshadowed by the pres-
presence of Sultana, the mother of the bakery owner, a blind old
woman who both frightens and fascinates the boy. Avramino, an old
man who runs a drinks stand near the bakery, warns him against her,
but the boy ignores the warning. The fantastic tales that he hears
from one of the bakers about Sultana's past excite and stimulate
his fancy, and he comes under her spell. When she first asks him
to steal bagels from their clients' trays for her he is shocked,
but miserably obeys. Soon he does it for her every Friday "even
happily," until he is caught by Izakino, the baker. In a confrontation, Sultana denies sending him to steal for her, and the boy
does not contradict her. Shortly after the narrator is thrown out
of the bakery, Izakino dies. At the end of the story when his
father once again suggests going to his uncle, the boy agrees.

In all four stories the boy moves uncomfortably between childhood and adolescence and looks for ways to overcome the resulting
tension, and in each case the stories seem to convey the feeling
that the initiation fails.[19] By the end of each story the narrator is in retreat to an earlier stage of incomprehension. His
attempts to reach maturity prove to be premature.

The Tangy Flavor of the Levant

Aloni's fascination with eccentric characters and ambience is
closely related to his concept of the Levant as he came to know it
in his childhood, growing up in a Sephardi, Ladino-speaking *shekhunah*. Unlike most of the Ashkenazim, the Sephardim in Palestine--
during the time of the British Mandate and the preceding Turkish
rule--originated in Mediterranean countries where they were in
touch with the culture of the Levant, and acquainted with its particular approach to life, its customs, mentality, morality and
folklore. Moreover, they integrated much of it into their own way
of life.[20] And yet, it appears from Aloni's own disclosure[21] that
the realization of his spiritual kinship with the Levant dawned on
him only during the years between his first and second plays, the

period of gestation and birth of his childhood stories. At that
time he discovered and admired two writers famous for capturing
the spirit of the Levant: the English Lawrence Durrell (*The Alex-
andria Quartet*, 1958-1960), and the Greek poet Constantine Kavafis,
an Alexandrian by birth and spiritual inclination. During that
period, as Aloni discloses,[22] he conceived the idea of writing a
play about a naked king and a child, which was later to become the
theme of *The King's New Clothes*. If we substitute for "King" the
word "adult," we have the essence of the four stories collected in
The Owl.

Unlike those of Yizhar, Aloni's childhood stories are not for
the most part a result of nostalgic or elegiac attachment to the
golden days of childhood. They do not begin with a point of departure in the present--as do Yizhar's--from which the narrator
sets out an evocative voyage into his past; in Aloni there is no
distance in time between narrative and narrator. An eloquent observation made about Bruno Schultz[23] is equally applicable to
Aloni: "He does not conjure up memories--he fulfills his yearning;
he writes no obituaries to the past--he recreates it; his is not a
distant view of childhood--it is an immersion in it."[24] In this
respect Aloni's childhood stories may be regarded as period pieces,
each one representing an attempt to encapsulate a phase of the
narrator's childhood with a flash of insight, and recreate it
artistically.

For Aloni, writing these stories at this particular stage
was quite inevitable; he had to pause, take stock of his life,
define his roots and his true subjects. Asked in an interview
what happened in the years between his first and second plays, he
avoided direct answer and, typically, replied with a riddle:
"Doesn't it seem to you some sort of incest (*gilluy arayot*)?
Suddenly everything was exposed."[25] The cryptic reference to
incest in this context is not a Freudian slip; as will emerge
from this study, incest fires the imagination of his young narrator. "Suddenly everything was exposed" may be telling us that in
the period when these stories were written he experienced a sudden
insight into his past, his destiny, an illumination which eventually enabled him to move to the next stage of his artistic development: playwriting.

Coming to terms with a sense of belonging to the Levant also
meant discarding any residue of inferiority which might have im-
peded him as a Sephardi in a society dominated by Ashkenazi
values. He could now proudly explore the charm and nobility in

the crude Sephardi environment; he could now become the Chagall of
the pre-State Sephardi *shekhunah*.

The Masculine Bravado

The juvenile narrator of Aloni's childhood stories shares
with the narrator of Yizhar's *Tales* an attraction for the concept
of machismo; but the two differ dramatically in respect to the
Peter Pan syndrome. The Yizharian narrator is reluctant to lose
the child's carefree existence, Aloni's (especially in "Baker")
cannot wait to become adult. Being a child is an exasperating
handicap. He is weak, beaten, ostracized by his friends, belittled
by his parents, and (except for the last story) has no say at home
or in the *shekhunah*. Far from being happy, his childhood is full
of apocalyptic fears, incomprehensions, frustrations. Like a
Dickens child, Aloni's is moving "in a world of terror, fantasy,
melodrama and death";[26] becoming a man is escaping it. A product
of his society and its concepts of manhood, and in accordance with
the spirit of the time (World War II), he cherishes an ideal of
virility in the soldier. Fierce, arrogant, daredevil, the soldier
is the embodiment of heroism.[27] The derelict shoeblack ("Soldier")
cannot be anything but an heroic fighter. The same standard applies to Shmeel's soldier-father, to the girl's brother ("Owl")
who joins the army, and to the soldiers the narrator meets in the
street or watches in the café. Even Shmeel, when planning to blow
up the world, is portrayed like a soldier ("Shmeel," 190, 198,
200); presumably the capacity to perform such an act satisfied the
prerequisites of a soldier. The brave soldier is an antithesis to
the narrator with his fears (of his friends, his parents, his
school teachers, Sultana, his "sins," the Germans). The nickname
Edirne suggests a wishful identification with the heroic Turkish
soldier.[28]

Soldiers are generally associated in Aloni's stories with the
erotic. They are seen "walking about wearing fierce shoes, throw-
ing quick glances as they talked...and very beautiful girls, shak-
ing their hair, looked over their shoulders, their mouths twisted.
The line of their panties showed through their skirts" ("Shmeel,"
164f.). Or, they "sat around marble tables [in the café] and drank
yellow beer and the radio played tunes. Blackhaired girls with
blue eyelids sat with them, their backs always straight and their
eyes, glass" (166). The boy-narrator, who is at a stage in which,
as Coveney describes it, "sexuality enters feverishly into his
growing awareness,"[29] keeps peeping into the café, driven by his

erotic curiosity. In his comprehension, sex is the major business
of a soldier apart from killing the enemy. The worst that might
befall a soldier is returning from the battlefield with his geni-
talia impaired, as was the case with Shmeel's father. Naturally,
the boy's account contains no glimpse into the true world of a
soldier, his fears, anxieties, sorrows, disillusionment, as this
would contradict the glamorized perception of his paradigm.

The Titilation of the Neophyte

    Among the Israeli writers who contributed to the genre of
childhood stories, Aloni stands out in his emphasis on the erotic.
If George Steiner is correct in assuming that "the absence of the
erotic produces varieties of sentimentality,"[30] eroticism, as it
is manifested in Aloni, can make it possible for the author to
escape the traps of sentimentality to which, by his own admission,
he is temperamentally vulnerable.[31] In accordance with the awakening sexuality of the young narrator, the erotic, in the form of
explicit descriptions, implicit references, and symbolic content,
is a device extensively used in these stories, which could be regarded, to use Steiner's phrase, as "graphically Freudian."[32]

    The tall, lonely monastery, a prominent fixture in the back-
drop of the *shekhunah*, whose steeple is often described looking
toward Jaffa (a city connected in Aloni's imagination with prostitutes[33]), is one of several phallic symbols; another is the hose
which Sapporta the shoemaker is pulling from his shop "like a
stubborn snake" ("Shmeel," 184).[34] To this category also belongs
the locomotive of the train which is swallowed in the Jaffa tunnel,
and which is again mentioned in the context of the relationship
between Shmeel's parents (196, 198). Similarly, sharp weapons
such as a penknife, often mentioned in "Shmeel" (168, 170, 171,
176), and a bayonet, stand, in the Freudian view, for the male
genital.[35] The latter is actually made explicit: "Mulla stuck
himself near me like a bayonet and pointed with his hand to his
penis" (174).

    Although as a rule Aloni refrains from interlarding his
stories with obscenities, he does not shy away from introducing
taboo words to illuminate the narrator's awakening sexuality.
Thus, when the narrator tells how one of his classmates found a
condom he confesses: "when he said this word my heart jumped"
("Owl," 38). The impact of this word on him is considerable, provoking his sexual imagination. This happens also when Salomon

tells him that the Swiss cottages in the pictures in Sauliko's
café are a brothel ("Owl," 23); or when he imagines the fat prostitutes bending in their rooms (40); or when he watches the girls
climbing over the fench of the railway tracks, to get a glimpse of
their underwear (38).[36]   A woman's hair is often associated with
wantonness. The fact that teacher Margalit comes to school with
her hair hanging loose is presented in the same breath as the ru-
mor that the police raided a brothel and the finding of the condom.
Quotations cited earlier illustrate that Aloni's eyes are drawn to
a girl's hair when describing girls with soldiers. But the erotic
meaning of a woman's hair is particularly associated with the woman
who arouses the narrator's sexuality--Shmeel's mother, standing on
her balcony in a red dressing gown with her hair dishevelled
("Shmeel," 172). Her ruffled hair is touched by her hand, then
tickles his cheek (176) when she asks him to look for Shmeel. The
full erotic impact of this hair-tantalizing, however repressed
during daytime, emerges in the boy's nighttime dream and reaches
a climax.

> Shmeel's mother had fallen on top of me, her hair
> dishevelled and her arms trembling. I covered my ears
> with my hands but her voice whispered in the darkness
> with her hand, "call him, boy, go call him, boy, boy,
> go call him, call him, boy, boy, boy." Soundlessly
> she slammed the balcony shutter door. Tedious noon was
> in the shaded room and [her] flesh, white, trembling,
> murmured weakly on the bed. Her hand drooped to the
> floor and a sea of yellow hair rose to choke me.

The dream ends with:

> Then we were in the half-dry cistern near the palm-tree
> lot, defecating, and the noon breeze was sliding off
> the palm fronds, fluttering on our bare thighs and she
> turned into a white mountain smooth as marble and flowed
> to me like a river of warm milk, all over the cistern,
> and I fell. (184f.)[37]

This dream seems to be the furthest Aloni allows himself to
venture into pornography. Psychologically revealing, it is not
sexually very daring, considering the complicated energies of
erotic sensibility and sexual symbolism released in these stories.
Aloni is extremely careful not to exceed the limits he sets for
himself with regard to the distance between sexual awareness and
idiom, for the boy-narrator, being sexually inexperienced, is deprived of verbal freedom. Accordingly, the author's wish to maintain the narrator's plausibility, more than his reluctance to
challenge the taboos of respectable speech, accounts for the narrative's verbal reticence in sexual matters. At the same time,

Aloni's reticence could be rooted also in his wish to preserve erotic mystery, the presence of which dominated the world of his narrator just as much as the mystery of war and death.

This mystery is the essence of "Baker." An examination of the mythic elements of this intriguing story will follow in the section dealing with the mythic aspects of Aloni's stories. In the context of Eros, it is illuminating to look into the erotic implications of its principal metaphor, the bakery.

The ambiguous meaning of the story's opening words elucidates its main theme: "When the *ḥofesh ha-gadol* (חופש הגדול) came round...." The simplest meaning of *ḥofesh ha-gadol* here is the long summer vacation from school. But *ḥofesh* means also freedom, liberty--a stage which the boy-narrator is yearning to reach, and which he associates with adults. When the long summer vacation came round, he declared he wanted to work in a bakery. For him to be a baker means joining the world of adults, being liberated from prohibitions and inhibitions imposed on him as a child.

The symbolic meaning of the oven as a womb is embodied in the saying: "She has a bun in the oven." The association of an oven with sex has been pointed out by Freud.[38] Lévi-Strauss talks about the custom of various Californian tribes of putting women who had just given birth and pubescent girls into ovens, hollowed out in the ground.[39] He also mentions an early nineteenth-century French custom, in the St. Omer district, according to which, when an unmarried woman's younger sister was married first, the elder sister would be "lifted up and laid on the top of the oven, so that she might be warmed up, as the saying was, since her situation seemed to indicate she had remained insensitive to love."[40]

The descriptions of the encounter baker-oven in "Baker" are often suggestive of sexual intercourse, with the oven being always hot and the baker pushing the shovel in. Sasson is described standing near the oven, holding with both hands a shovel full of unbaked loaves.

> He lay in wait for the flames.[41] Suddenly he pushed the shovel in, and immediately, as if he had stuck a spoon into an angry lion's mouth he pulled it out again, and it was empty. (308)

The analogy oven-womb-lion's mouth suggests that love is a dangerous undertaking. Furthermore, since the story often links anger with Sultana, Sasson's mother, the analogy also introduces Oedipal overtones in the description of Sasson pushing himself into the oven as well, swimming in the "waves of the fire," to see

how his bread is being baked. On an allegorical level, Sultana is
the spirit of the oven, which is one of the reasons why the narrator, in his eagerness to be a baker, gravitates towards her.[42]

When Izakino invites the boy to work in the bakery he promises
him: "Come, we'll make a real, proud baker out of you" (*Tarmil*,
109).[43] The boy's ambition is to be like Sasson, to push his
shovel into the fire. But all he is allowed to do is paste the
bakery's labels on the loaves. His frustration finds its expression in an erotically suggestive way.

> Sometimes, as my fingers passed over a shiny unbaked
> loaf, I could hardly keep myself from sticking my finger
> in.[44] I said to myself, Izakino promised to make a
> baker out of me. He won't forget. (312)

Izakino, the mentor, offers guidance not only into the world
of manhood, but--as this story appears to suggest symbolically in
the passages in which Izakino talks to the boy about the art of
creating bread--also into the world of creativity. In this respect, Izakino is comparable with Ḥabakuk of Yizhar's story
"Ḥabakuk." When viewed in this context, it could be inferred that
the description of the boy-narrator's failure to become a baker is
a projection of an acute double fear on the part of the author
himself: the fear of failing as a man and as an artist.

As was the case with Adam, the fall of the neophyte, the sin
that caused him to be expelled from his paradise (the bakery),
originated in his succumbing to a femme fatale. Such a woman appears also in "Shmeel" (Shmeel's mother), and to some extent in
"Owl" (the girl). In the latter, the girl unwittingly inspires
the boy to take her to see the owl, an act that causes him to fall
out with his friends and which, in his notion, could have proved
fatal to him, as he truly believed that whoever sees the owl brings
death upon himself.[45]

A Touch of the Macabre

The war ominously looming on the horizon serves here as both
a psychological and a chronological framework. By interpolating
the Western desert, in general ("Soldier," 8, 10, 12, 21; "Owl,"
52; "Shmeel," 164, 168, 206, 212) and names of particular places
on this front associated with fierce battles such as Mersa Matruh
("Soldier," 8; "Owl," 32), or Tobruk ("Owl," 48, 49, 52), the
reader can date the narratives in 1941-1942, the period of battles
between the British army and Rommel's Afrika Korps, when the latter were advancing swiftly into Egypt; but no later than November

1942, the time of the decisive British victory in El Alamein.
Other places connected with the war in other parts of the world
are also mentioned: London ("Soldier," 24), Voronezh ("Shmeel,"
214), Sevastopol (206). News of the war is continuously reaching
the narrator's home through radio bulletins. Thus he learns that
the Germans are on the offensive ("Owl," 36), or that Tobruk has
fallen (48). Discussing the news, his father is always optimistic,
believing that the end is near and that the allies are beating the
Germans "good and proper" ("Shmeel," 164), while his mother fears
that the war will never end. Every night the *shekhunah* is blacked
out. Blankets cover the windows of the bakery ("Baker," 303, 315,
317), blackout curtains hang across the café windows ("Soldier,"
18), dark blue paint obscures the streetlights (8, 14, 18; "Shmeel,"
164), buses roll with dimmed headlights ("Soldier," 19, 22, 23),
and air-raid wardens patrol the streets to keep the blackout complete (8, 18).

The community's apprehensions surface in the narrator's dream
when, echoing his mother, he exclaims: "The war will not end, the
war will not end" ("Shmeel," 186). But more often war and death
are romanticized in these stories as, for example, in the shoeblack's macabre fable about the sad king of Edirne. The valleys
around Edirne were full of roses that were irrigated by rivers
flowing down from the mountains ("Soldier," 12f.). Each night the
neighing of thousands of war-horses drowned in the rivers made the
famous singers of Edirne stop singing in the cafés. Once, to
celebrate a victory over the Greeks, the king made a great feast.
The big square of Edirne was filled with corpses of Greek soldiers
and all the great singers came to perform before the king. On
that night the drowned horses did not neigh, so sweet were the
voices of the singers. The king cried: "God of mercy, if there
were no wars there would be no sweet voices." Subsequently they
opened barrels of wine and drank all night at the king's expense.
The romantic mind of the boy sees nothing wrong with the association of the horrors of war with roses, sweet singing and wine.
Death itself is not horrendous once conquered, and it can be conquered, as Shoeblack informs the boy-narrator: if the mourners
rise and hold the dying man with both hands, and if he holds on to
them, he will be brought back to life ("Soldier," 22). The boy-
narrator, never one to distinguish facts from fantasy, does not
doubt this piece of information just as he does not doubt Shoeblack's tale of a man in Edirne who died eight times. All he
thinks about is to remember to tell the secret to Shmeel in case

Shmeel's father dies in the Western desert; Shmeel ought to know
that his father can die another seven times ("Soldier," 21).

Although the argument that Death rules the narrator's world[46]
cannot be ascertained beyond doubt, it is probably correct to assume that fears of death prompt the narrator to identify it with
various objects, people, or other creatures. Because the sign of
the skull and crossbones is hung on every lamppost as a warning
against climbing it, and because the streetlights are dimmed with
dark blue paint, the narrator associates the symbol of death, the
skull, with the blue color, and comes up with the following image:
"On moonlit nights Death would climb down from the top of the
lamppost and sit with us, a little old man, blue, bald" ("Soldier,"
8). Another personification of Death is the tousand-year-old owl,
whose powers differ from story to story. In "Soldier" its curse
brings blindness (7), in "Owl" it causes death (55). Thus, the
boy's taking the girl to see the owl could be regarded as a manifestation of a death-haunted eroticism; as a lover in search of
death, his love is a dangerous undertaking. His fascination with
Sultana, similar to his fascination with Shoeblack, is also
grounded in a deathwish, for death is often mentioned or implied
when Sultana is mentioned, from the moment she is introduced to us
as "an embalmed owl" ("Baker," 306). Death is in the wrinkles of
her face, and "her blind eyes could look upon the face of the
secret death, which stretched like pale cobwebs across the reaches
of this beautiful summer" (306).[47]

From association with the demonic Sultana and Shoeblack (he
frequents the local café where the Devil sits and drinks arak from
a "flask made out of bat skin" ["Soldier," 7]), some demonic elements inevitably rub off on the boy himself. In one instance he
fantasizes slaying Goldberg--presumably the lover of Shmeel's
mother and therefore a rival--in a symbolic act of witchcraft at
the breakfast table.

> I took the sharpened pencil and with its point lifted
> the skin off the milk. As I put it on the plate I said
> to myself, here is Mr. Goldberg's skin. I made two
> holes in it and I pushed into them two splinters remain-
> ing from the night. His face was torn and his eyes
> blurred. I said to him, You'll never wear glasses
> again, and I poured coffee on his face. ("Shmeel," 172)

This episode follows another night of erotic dreams about
Shmeel's mother in which, somewhat reminiscent of *Hamlet*, Shmeel's
father makes a ghostlike appearance, "his head with a soldier's
hat touching the roof" (170). The narrative implies that Shmeel's

father is furious with the dreamer because he senses the boy's
lust for his wife: "when he saw me his face was drained, his hands
were on his hips, and his boots stomped on my sandals" (170).

This subtle Oedipal passage, followed by the "breakfast-
table witchcraft," links violence and guilt with sexual arousal
and heightens our awareness of the elements of sin and retribution.

Sin and Retribution

By his own admission, Aloni refrains from preaching, teaching,
or passing judgment;[48] in this respect he is the opposite of Yizhar
in *Tales*. All he wants is to tell an entertaining and interesting
story. But here he faces the dilemma which Northrop Frye has formulated: "If literature is didactic, it tends to injure its own
integrity; if it ceases wholly to be didactic, it tends to injure
its own seriousness."[49] Sensitive to the consequences of such a
dilemma, Aloni manages to skirt them by skilfully keeping the adult
author out of his childhood stories. He thus minimizes the risks
of exposing his own credo in matters of morality, while subtly and
in a noncommittal manner revealing it under the disguise of the
naïve and inarticulate narrator.

His stories may be regarded as "confessional autobiography,"
as defined by Coveney in his discussion of *Huckleberry Finn*.[50] He
feels an urge to elucidate not only his roots but his moral development in his formative years, attempting to reconcile himself
with his childhood.[51] And yet these "memoirs" are clearly not an
apologia. He seems to derive pleasure from exposing his "sins,"
as though such an act enables him to grasp better the simple truth
of his life. But this is the ambiguous truth that Booth suggested,
reflecting that "there is a pleasure from learning the simple
truth, and there is a pleasure from learning that the truth is not
simple."[52]

The stories mirror the boy-narrator's attempt to define one
of the vitamins of personality: his self-concept.[53] In the process of moving toward self-identity it is important for him to
understand the boundaries of his new capacities. His adjustment
depends on harmony between the self that reflects reality and the
self he would like to be. Like Huckleberry Finn, he constantly
defines his virtue "in terms of sin and wickedness."[54]

A product of his environment, his concepts of sin--often
heightened by juvenile innocence--are strongly influenced by the
behavioral code of his peers and the adults of the *shekhunah*. He
mentions sinning against himself, his parents, his friends. His

only religious sin is eating on Yom Kippur, twice mentioned: when
he contemplates the defiant act of breaking the fast of this holy
day,[55] and when his friends actually force an apple into his mouth
("Owl," 35). He has no share in other religious sins mentioned.
These include violations of the Sabbath, by Mr. Green, the English
teacher, who bathes in the sea (37), and by others who play foot-
ball, or ride cars, bicycles and motorcycles (45ff.). Apart from
his mother's advice that he should recite "Hear O Israel!" before
going to bed ("Shmeel," 172), there is no reference to prayers,
synagogues, or religious practice. The fact that the presence of
the Devil (*Satan*) in the *shekhunah* is more tangible than that of
God is recorded in the second sentence of the first story which
reports the Devil as an habitué of the local café. Apart from its
contribution to the ambience, this very "fact," when presented at
the outset, prepares the reader to anticipate the boy's persistent
gravitation to the "Thou shalt nots." His relationship with Sultana clearly demonstrates the pattern: he is afraid of her but at
the same time fascinated by her, and allows himself to be drawn
towards her, making his fall inevitable.

An inherent self-destructiveness is one possible reason for
his behavior;[56] another is his curiosity about the mystery hidden
in the "forbidden fruit." Secrets, both of the thanatotic and the
erotic nature, have power over him. In this context, Aloni's
phrase *gilluy arayot*, in the *Keshet* interview, carries extra
weight, as it literally consists of the word *gilluy*, unveiling,
uncovering (as well as discovering), and *arayot*, which implies the
genitals (of a relative belonging to the opposite sex) that are
supposed to remain covered and concealed, a secret.

The attempt to unveil challenging secrets thrills the boy.
After being caught peeping into the café and watching a soldier
push his hand under a girl's blouse, he flees in the darkness of
the street "my eyes aflame with a quivering and slick secret and
my whole body throbbing" ("Shmeel," 166). On this occasion he
escapes unscathed, but he is not so lucky when Salomon and the
"gang" catch him trying to come too close to the secret of the owl.

Aware of breaking the rules, he is distressed by a sense of
wrong-doing. He acknowledges his "sins." These include: fantasizing for self-aggrandisement, lying to his parents, lusting after
his best friend's mother, peeping at the girls' panties near the
railway, and worst of all, stealing and breaking Izakino's trust
in him. In addition to his shame, and his constant fear of impending punishment, he is exasperated by a nagging awareness that he

does not deceive anybody, that even the drunken Shoeblack can see
through him: "He slowly raised his head and looked at me a long
while, his grin twisted, his eyes blinking, as though he exposed
my vices in the darkness" ("Soldier," 16). Likewise the school
librarian, Salomon's "gang," his parents, the girl's brother
("Owl," 44). He even imagines guards standing along the railway,
pointing their fingers at him (38). And he confesses: "I am a
sinner. They know. They are right" (44). Scrupulous by nature,
he knows he deserves to be punished. Izakino, catching him stealing, tells him: "God will punish you" ("Baker," 319), and when
Izakino dies shortly afterwards, the boy takes it to be the
punishment.

At Home, or The Dichotomy of Distress

     The boy's life revolves around two centers: indoors--his home,
and outdoors--the *shekhunah*. From the scant information about his
school, one gets the impression that rather than a place to acquire
knowledge and satisfy intellectual needs, it is a place where the
boy's erotic awareness is stimulated. The house in front of the
school is rumored to be a brothel ("Owl," 38); the teachers Margalit and Green are mentioned in ways which suggest dubious conduct
(37). Pedagogically, the school is inadequate: the Bible teacher
makes fun of the narrator and intimidates him when he asks a question in class (35).
     The values of his home and its pattern of human relationships
are the prime factors in the development of the narrator. The ambivalent depiction of this home, which emerges from Aloni's stories, could be traced to the dichotomy between the actual author--
the adult Aloni--and the boy-narrator. The understanding and
compassion of the mature adult are fused in the creative process
with the disconcerting memories of the uncomprehending and immature protagonist.
     The patriarchal Sephardi home is not child-orientated. In
the family constellation the boy feels thwarted. The discipline
he is subjected to is uncompromising; the father lays down the
rules, expects to be obeyed, and punishes if he is not. This sets
the tone of the intra-family dynamics. A study dealing with parental coerciveness and child autonomy has concluded that parental
coerciveness, which could be related to lack of parental trust,
"arouses hostility and the need to be self-assertive in boys. Although engendered by coerciveness, hostility leads to a high degree
of autonomy."[57] As brothers or sisters are not mentioned, the

family nucleus consists of him and his parents. The parents' behavior, grounded on authoritarian concepts of upbringing, is the
cause of the credibility gap. The boy does not permit himself
emotional responsiveness. On the few occasions when he tries to
confide in his parents and reveal his innermost fears he gets the
wrong response. They display a harmful insensitivity to his distress; they are sure he is up to mischief. In the absence of ade-
quate home guidance he searches outside and finds the antithesis
of his parents in Shoeblack and Sultana. Shoeblack actually serves
as a mentor[58] who helps to usher the boy into the world of adults
when he offers him a drink ("Soldier," 11), and a cigarette (20).
While the boy is fascinated by Shoeblack, he is intimidated by his
ordinary father whom, ironically, he twice sees as a threatening
wizard[59] ("Owl," 34; "Baker," 305).

Only the last story registers a noticeable change in the
parents' attitude, which corresponds to the intensified process of
the boy's individuation, as expressed in his insistence on going
to work in the bakery. This is the first time they show respect
for him. After he has stolen for Sultana, his father senses his
distress. Not knowing the real reason, and not inquiring, the
father comforts him and demonstrates his paternal love by gently
caressing the boy in a scene of father-son intimacy (314f.). A
similar situation takes place between mother and son at the end of
"Baker." After he tells her about Izakino's death, her reaction
is summed up in a moving, laconic sentence: "She wiped her hand
slowly on her apron and then sat down at the table, next to me"
(320). Their nonverbal communication touches the boy: his mother
treats him as an adult. Trust is built between them. He can now
confide in her and tell her: "It is my fault." This is the
moment they come to terms with each other on a new basis, the moment in which something important concerning the boy's initiation
takes place. Izakino's death comes to represent the symbolic
death of the narrator's childish innocence--a necessary factor in
a successful initiatory process. Accepting responsibility implies
comprehension, seeing reality as it is and, most significantly,
dissociation from childhood fantasies.

The apron of the narrator's mother is her trademark: when not
cooking, she is darning socks or seeing that the boy does his
homework. (She is not an intellectual, we know nothing about her
reading habits, and as for the father--he reads only the newspapers.) There is nothing sensuous or erotic about her. In sharp
contrast, Shmeel's mother is never described wearing an apron, but

a red dressing gown; her nails are painted red too--red being
associated in Aloni's stories with Eros.[60] Unawares, the narrator
projects onto Shmeel's mother his repressed Oedipal feelings. She
is erotically provocative, standing on the balcony[61] with her hair
hanging loose over her red dressing gown. By contrast, the narrator's mother is never mentioned on a balcony (just as her hair is
never mentioned as hanging loose but rather as "pinned up," [168]).
Her lifestyle revolves around the kitchen, the warm and cosy living
room where she can play her role as the affectionate leader of the
family, the specialist in childrearing, while the father can play
his traditional role of protector and provider. The coalition of
mutual support between the parents lends unity and direction to
the development of the family, but the boy is sometimes inclined
to interpret this coalition as being aimed against him: "I was
afraid of them. We were alone in the room and the rain closed in
on us. They stood like two big people and hated me" ("Owl," 35).
In such a mood, like Huckleberry Finn and Holden Caulfield, the
narrator begins to entertain thoughts of escape; like them he is a
potential runaway. Huckleberry Finn wishes to escape from his
abusing father and from the widow who wants to adopt him and
"civilize" him. His sailing down the river and hiding in the
woods is enacting "the revolt of 'natural and healthy instinct'
against its suppression by a 'moral' society."[62] And Holden Caulfield, in search of his Arcadia, dreams of going to the woods of
Massachusetts and Vermont or out West. But in the case of Aloni's
narrator, who has no dreams of Arcadia or the idyllic, the
fantasies of escape are tinted with overtones of self-mockery:
"I will go to main street. I will go to the lonely monastery[63] on
the green hill outside the city. I will go to the groves in the
Hatikva Quarter" ("Shmeel," 176). The "pastoral" parody of these
fantasies is obvious: there were no groves in the Hatikva Quarter;
it was just a Tel Aviv slum.[64]

The *Shekhunah*, or The Thrill and the Wounded Dignity

Answering a question in the *Keshet* interview, Aloni says:
"How do I look at the world? From the *shekhunah*."[65] And earlier
in the same interview he reveals a significant aspect of his ars
poetica: "I always believe that somehow what I write, actually
what everyone writes, is designed for some height and width."[66]
Indeed, it appears as though he recreates his Sephardi *shekhunah*
for a stage. Characters larger than life (Sultana, Shoeblack),
along with mysterious figures (the Chinese knifegrinder) and

imaginary wizards, legendary kings, real-life prostitutes, soldiers
and dwellers of the *shekhunah*, adults or youngsters, interact as
dramatis personae in a plot knitted together by a narrator who
sometimes sees himself as a clown, a Harlequin ("Soldier," 18;
"Owl," 47; "Shmeel," 166), moving about in a haunting setting.

The *shekhunah* is seen with the boy and largely through his
eyes, and in his imagination reality acquires legendary dimensions.
The folkloristic mood introduced at the opening lines of the first
story (with the description of the Devil as an habitué of the local
café and the ancient owl in Salomon's attic) keeps developing as
the stories unfold, to spice up the atmosphere. The fertile imagination of the child which allows him to see summer "sprawled over
the whole grey neighborhood, like a golden giant made of cotton-
wool" ("Baker," 305), and "golden summer children taller than the
houses and naked" (306) tossing their heads out of the palm trees,
enables him also, in accord with home and street influences, to
believe in the supernatural, in magic, devils and demons.

The *shed* (demon or devil), as a hostile chthonic entity out
to ruin people, has an active role in the lore of the *shekhunah*.
As a figure of speech or as an image, it is mentioned seven times
throughout the stories ("Soldier," 23; "Baker," 304,[67] 308, 311,
315, 319). This numinous number, a meaningful one for the superstitious, is mentioned twice in connection with the *shed*. The
narrator's mother tells him that only because of him the *shed* sent
them "seven lean years which never seemed to end" ("Baker," 304).
On another occasion she informs him that reciting the incantation
of "Hear O Israel!" seven times before going to bed wards off the
shedim ("Shmeel," 172). Mention of the *shed* serves as an omen.
When the mother premonitorily says: "The devil hasn't forgotten"
("Baker," 304), she is proven right as the story unfolds. The
shed is mentioned several times in connection with Sultana,[68] and
once in an entirely different connotation: "In the dim lights of
the bus, the driver's head gleamed like a *shed*" ("Soldier," 23).

For luck and against the evil eye the Sasson bakery has a
hand made of silver paper with one finger cut off, a horseshoe
covered with gold paper, and heads of garlic hung on both sides of
the horseshoe ("Baker," 308). For the same reason, the narrator's
mother feeds him a lump of sugar ("Shmeel," 206). No wonder that
in such an ambience primitive beliefs in the mysterious powers of
the owl or in the magical powers of a mirror flourish.[69] As
pointed out, the narrator himself practices "the occult" to hurt
Goldberg; and in another instance he does it by cracking watermelon

seeds to annihilate Sultana's image and destroy the effect of her
words ("Baker," 314). Superstition is common in these stories
possibly because they are told by a narrator fascinated by the
irrational and supernatural. However, it would be erroneous to
conclude on the basis of his account that superstition is just as
active in the mentality of all other dwellers of the *shekhunah*.

His childhood stories being tales of a *shekhunah*, Aloni's
human panorama is larger in scope than that of Yizhar, with a far
greater sense of group vitality. While avoiding commentary on the
Jewish community,[70] he nonetheless stresses the conflict between
the individual and the collective--in his case the peer-group.
In "Owl" and "Shmeel" it is a conflict between the boy Edirne and
Salomon's "gang"; but in an earlier story, "Kayitz Aharon" ("The
Last Summer"),[71] which deals with the same *shekhunah*, the same
"gang" of boys, and which Aloni did not deem fit for inclusion in
The Owl, a peculiar switch occurs. This story is about Salomon,
not about Edirne, the narrator of *The Owl* stories; Edirne is missing here. The narrating voice is the first-person plural of the
collective, the peer-group, that calls itself *The Shekhunah*; indeed, it is a *shekhunah* story par excellence. \The conflict is
between the group and its leader. The group wishes to be free of
Salomon's leadership, but is reluctant to make a move because he
is still loved and admired and nobody knows what would happen
without him. The most intriguing switch is in the portrayal of
Salomon, who is not the guttersnipe of the later stories but a
"decent" boy on his way out of the slum and moving up in society.
Neglecting his *shekhunah* chums, he joins a youth movement where he
associates with boys and girls from the affluent Ashkenazi neighborhood of the north of Tel Aviv, dances with girls, wears the
uniform of the youth movement, lets himself be indoctrinated by
its kibbutz-orientated ideology and even contemplates going to
high school--all of which makes him a traitor in the eyes of the
boys from the *shekhunah*. To top it all, it becomes known that his
mother plans to move the family out of the *shekhunah* to a more
respectable address. But he is still the leader and the boys do
not defy him even when he begins to organize gymnastics for them.
Only after he had left in the summer to join the youth movement's
"work camp" in a kibbutz did the boys accept the advice of a
rival leader to send Salomon a letter of dismissal. "The Last
Summer," with its faltering style, remains no more than an experiment in which Aloni sought to find the right voice and point of
view for his subsequent *shekhunah* tales. The social tension of

the Tel Aviv society is not yet internalized here, and the myth of
the *shekhunah* is not yet sufficiently developed to emerge in the
shape of the fantastic, the demonic, and the erotic which color
the later stories. Awareness of all these flaws was apparently
Aloni's reason for excluding this story from *The Owl*.

If Erich Fromm is right in assuming that "Man's main task in
life is to give birth to himself, to become what he potentially
is,"[72] the major problem of the boy-narrator in *The Owl* is his in-
capacity to establish harmony between this "task" and his wish to
be accepted by his peers. Salomon, the decision-maker, sets the
pattern when he beats the narrator and ostracizes him. The puni-
tive impact of silence is powerfully conveyed when the narrator is
ignored by his friends; he has to summon all his resources to
withstand its devastating effects. Bruised, frightened, and tormented by self-pity when he thinks about the good times his
friends, with their delinquent energy, are having, he nevertheless
endeavors to maintain his dignity. His relationship with his
friends is, for that matter, reminiscent of Joseph and his
brothers; they cannot accept his imagination and must reject him
as well. He would never choose to become an outsider, but they
leave him no choice. The only solace left for him is to take re-
course to a world in which he excels--the fantasy world.

The Fantasy World

A child's retreat into his fantasy world is a defense mechanism that makes frustration bearable. It has been argued that the
consolation of daydreaming prevents violent acts.[73] There is a
fusion, an interpenetration of the fantastic and the realistic
elements in these stories, with the fantasy world playing a major
role. On the one hand, it is expressed in the richness of fantasies, fantastic deeds, beliefs and daydreams of a make-believe
world; on the other hand, in the wealth of the imagery employed.

The hypothesis that the fantasy of a boy in the 1940s is
analogous with that of the whole of the pre-State Jewish society
on the threshold of its political and psychological self-realization[74] may seem far-fetched, in view of the fact that Aloni refrains from dealing openly with ideological aspects and restricts
his narrative to the *shekhunah* as seen through the eyes of a boy
ignorant about ideological or political matters. Many of the
boy's fantasies are intimate, largely erotic, and even if one
tries to view them as an allegory it would hardly seem plausible
to regard them as a reflection of contemporary political or

psychological facets of the community. Nevertheless, the hypothesis is valid in the context of one particular aspect of the boy's
fantasies: the thanatotic. The boy's fantasies reflect apocalyptic anxieties and premonitions that can be seen as foreshadowing
the preoccupation of "Dor ba-Aretz" with death, and particularly
with the new approach to the old theme of the *Akedah*, which surfaced in Israeli literature and was brought to the fore in the
late 1950s with Yizhar's controversial *Ziklag*.

The boy-narrator's fantasies flow from daydreaming or reverie
or from intuition. There is hardly a passage in these stories in
which his imagination is not at work, if not as a component of the
situation then in his choice of imagery, often with no dividing
line between fact and fancy. Almost everything absorbed by his
sensory perception stimulates him in a way which is often unre-
lated to external realities. His imagination is "magical" in the
sense formulated by Sartre: "It is an incantation destined to
produce the object of one's thought, the thing one desires, in
such a way that one can take possession of it."[75]

Of Aloni's senses, the sharpest is that of sight, which defines the nuance and detail of many of the images and descriptive
passages. His heightened acoustic sense is manifested in dialogue
which consists of terse, colloquial sentences, arranged in the
staccato manner which was later to become characteristic of his
plays.

The stories exhibit a brilliant coloration, in keeping with
the vivid role of the pictorial in them. There are eleven colors
in Aloni's palette. The following list is arranged according to
the number of times (in brackets) each color appears in the four
stories: white (44), red (34), black (26), yellow (24), grey (20),
green (17), blue (14), brown (8), orange (7), silver (4), pink (2).
The fact that white and red are the dominant colors may not be
accidental as they symbolize the two aspects locked in conflict
throughout these stories: the spiritual and the sexual.[76]

The more one looks into Aloni's reconstruction of his childhood world, the more one senses behind or within it the vibrating
presence of concealed knowledge. The stories set the reader asking questions such as: What does the owl symbolize? What is behind
the apocalyptic act of blowing up the world by holding a mirror up
to the sun? Who does the peculiar Sultana stand for? Sooner or
later the reader comes to feel that there is a secret pattern
underlying these stories, a secret code.

What this code might be, and what additional meanings these
stories might convey once decoded on another level, is considered
in the next section which explores the hidden mythical elements
submerged in Aloni's childhood stories.

Aloni's Hidden Myth: A Prologue

It appears that to decipher the secret code one has to turn
for clues to the world of myth. Aloni himself steers us in this
direction, admitting his fascination with myth and his dependency
on it: "When I get stuck I recruit all my friends from Greek mythology and try to take something from them. I cry to them: Help!"[77]
He was familiar with Greek mythology from a very early age;
when he was thirteen he wrote a play called *Oedipus*.[78] His themes
are interwoven and knitted together with mythic motifs. He does
not try to conceal it: "I feel myself constantly living with a
legend and with a very ancient tale,"[79] echoing Francis Fergusson's
observation: "Drama, the lyric and fiction live symbiotically with
myths, nourished by them, and nourishing their flickering lives."[80]
On another occasion, Aloni discloses: "The ancient myths are broken
but they exist. Many things that I see are reflected in me, as
though in a mirror, on the mythological plane."[81] He admits that
in all his writings he looks for references, in the Bible, Greek
mythology, history, or other previous sources.[82] When writing a
play about Herod, he took the story of Herod and Mariamne, mixed
it with Greek legends and concocted a modern story.[83] In the case
of *The King is the Cruellest* the source was the Bible; in *The
King's New Clothes*--Andersen's tale; in *The Revolution and the
Chicken*--Mark Twain; in *The American Princess*--the Greek myth of
Persephone. Aloni's justification for using this ploy is his belief that mythic elements enrich the scope of the narrative and
its meaning.[84] Since his childhood stories demonstrate an extensive use of mythical material, incorporating mythico-ritualistic
elements, it is necessary to consider them from this aspect in an
attempt to find answers to questions which otherwise leave the
reader baffled.
Jung's definition of myth as "the natural and indispensable
intermediate stage between unconscious and conscious cognition"[85]
is one attempt to simplify an intricate term. Francis Fergusson
argues that it is almost impossible to use this term without
apologetic quotation marks: "Ill-defined for centuries, it is now
used in many senses and for many purposes: to mean nonsense or
willful obscurantism in some contexts, the deepest wisdom of man

in others."[86] Much the same feeling is echoed in Block's statement: "There is no doubt that Myth is one of the most muddled and
abused concepts in our critical vocabulary."[87] This concept has
been defined "as a lie, a popular delusion, as mystical fantasy,
as primitive science, as a record of historical fact, a symbol of
philosophical truth, a reflection of unconscious motivations, indeed, any unconscious assumption."[88] Kirk's contention is that
there is "no Platonic form of a myth against which all actual
instances can be measured," as myths "differ enormously in their
morphology and their social function."[89] The problematical state
of dealing with myth is acknowledged by Lévi-Strauss in *The Raw
and the Cooked*, his book about myth. At its outset he states:

> Apart from the fact that the science of myths is still
> in its infancy, so that its practitioners must consider
> themselves fortunate to obtain even a few tentative,
> preliminary results, we can already be certain that the
> ultimate state will never be attained, since were it
> theoretically possible, the fact still remains that
> there does not exist, nor ever will exist, any community
> or group of communities whose mythology and ethnography
> (and without the latter the study of myths is ineffectual)
> can be known in their entirety. The ambition to achieve
> such knowledge is meaningless, since we are dealing with
> a shifting reality, perpetually exposed to the attacks
> of a past that destroys it and of a future that changes
> it.[90]

A methodological shortcoming which Lévi-Strauss points out
lies in the fact that "since it has no interest in definite begin-
nings or endings, mythological thought never develops any theme to
completion: there is always something left unfinished."[91] Wellek,
who thinks little of applying myth in criticism, warns against
irrational mysticism that "reduces all poetry to a conveyor of a
few myths: rebirth and purification. After decoding each work of
art in these terms, one is left with a feeling of futility and
monotony."[92] On the other hand, Bidney who believes that through
the image myth fuses the real and the ideal, claims that "myth,
like great art and dramatic literature, may have profound symbolic
or allegorical value," and that is "not because myth necessarily
and intrinsically has such latent, esoteric wisdom, but because
the plot or theme suggest to us universal patterns of motivation
and conduct."[93] And C. S. Lewis, speaking of the importance of
the study of myth, explains that the peculiar attraction of this
study "springs in part from the same impulse which makes men
allegorize the myth. It is one more effort to seize, to conceptualize, the important something which myth seems to suggest."[94]

As for using myth as an approach to a work of literature, there are, according to Blotner, two possible assertions: (1) the author "knowingly used myth as a basis for his creation"; (2) "all unaware, he used it as it welled up out of the subconscious layers of his psyche where it resided as forgotten material, as an archetypal pattern or a fragment of the collective or racial unconscious."[95] In view of Aloni's own testimony that he consciously draws from mythical material, it would seem natural to assume that he belongs to the first category. But how credible is his testimony? The ensuing discussion of his use of myths shows that a conscious employment of certain mythical elements leads him in a mysterious way to other mythical elements he was not aware of at the outset. Admitting a process in which his mind oscillates between the conscious and the unconscious, he says: "I am going to write and mysterious wheels start to work. Then I sit down and write and suddenly I realize that the most important thing has emerged without my even being aware of it."[96]

The mythological thought appears to indicate that Blotner's aforementioned classification is somewhat simplistic. Lévi-Strauss, pointing out that "divergence of sequences and themes is a fundamental characteristic of mythological thought, which manifests itself as an irradiation,"[97] believes that "themes can be split up ad infinitum. Just when you think you have disentangled and separated them, you realize that they are knitting together again in response to the operation of unexpected affinities."[98] In the case of Aloni's childhood stories, it seems that all the mythical motifs which are embedded in them are interconnected, if not entangled. Touching one automatically activates another, and intuitively his mythopoeic impulse starts to work.

An initial impression that these childhood stories are just a personal myth of the *shekhunah*, drawn from the experience and imagination of a neophyte with a distinctive poetic resonance, runs into trouble in view of textual allusions that draw attention to their relation to a much larger scope, as biblical and mythical motifs become noticeable. Bearing in mind that "myths explain the structural principles behind familiar literary facts,"[99] one can use these allusions as clues in an attempt to decode another, obscure layer of meaning which was at the heart of the creative process. However, while following these clues it should be remembered that poetic structure transforms the mythic material, disciplining and subjecting it to logical and psychological motives that eventually alienate it from its origins.

By sticking to his chosen convention--stories narrated by a
naïve raconteur--Aloni does not facilitate this task for his reader. Faulty comprehension on the part of the narrator, which accounts for a certain obscurity in his report, could also be used
as a ploy by the author to camouflage mythic elements. But apparently Aloni does not wish to disguise his intention altogether.
From various clues that can be put together, it emerges that at
the center of these stories--which relate the induction of a neo-
phyte--lies the myth of the *Akedah*, with which most themes, motifs,
archetypes, and symbols in these stories[100] are basically inter-
related. Submerged in the first three stories, this myth, "so
central to the nervous system of Judaism and Christianity,"[101]
surfaces in the last one with the appearance of characters named
after the three principal participants in the biblical drama of
the sacrifice of Isaac: Abraham (Avramino), Isaac (Izakino), and
Sarah (Sultana--a possible synonym for the Hebrew Sarah). Because of the biblical allusions these characters--two of whom are
marginal in the story--attain intense symbolic value. Since Aloni
is often more interested in the mythic figure rather than in the
traditional story, he has allowed himself to diverge from the biblical source and transform radically the biblical archetypes, most
notably in the case of Sarah-Sultana.

The *Akedah*, Metaphor and Grotesque

The *Akedah* has previously been discussed in the context of
Yizhar's *Tales*, and Gouri's poem "Heritage." Belonging to the
"generation of Isaac," the generation of the sons, just as Yizhar
and Gouri do, Aloni's obsession with death could perhaps be regarded as related to his reaction, as a potential victim (an
Isaac), to the *Akedah* theme. As one who participated in the 1948
war, Aloni shared the idealistic commitment of his contemporaries.
But when the war was over, his ideology had undergone a dramatic
change. In his *Keshet* interview, he brings up his disillusion and
the indignation he and his contemporaries felt. Recalling his
mood in 1951, he speaks about

> ...bitterness against the government. Presumably because
> the land was conquered. Because suddenly it became
> small....Suddenly they made the country small for us.
> They conquered. It became their land, and everybody was
> singing in Jerusalem "alles is dreck!" (Yiddish: "It's
> all shit!") Yes, this was the famous song. Why?
> Because all the tough fighters suddenly realized that
> it was all over...shall we say, Jesus is dead, Paul takes
> over....I was 22-23. I ask myself: what did I feel at

the time? I don't recall exactly. There was bitterness--
this I remember. And the word "non-conformism" was in.[102]

This "non-conformism" on the part of the soldiers was aimed
mostly against the fathers who had sent them to war. The Isaacs
were challenging the authority and the rights of the fathers to do
so.[103] If, among other things, the concept of fathers stands for
the world of the antecedents, or the world of tradition, such an
expression of defiance should be taken for rejecting tradition.
When the boy-narrator exclaims: "On Yom Kippur, God willing, we
will light up the streets" ("Shmeel," 214), or: "I said to myself,
on Yom Kippur, God willing, we will eat dates" (212), the intentional ironic use of the traditional phrase "God willing" in the
context of purposefully committing sinful acts on the holiest day
of the Jewish calendar, the day of Atonement, indicates a direct
contempt for Yom Kippur and an indirect defiance of the *Akedah*,
for Yom Kippur, according to some traditions,[104] was the day on
which the *Akedah* took place, the day in which the penitential
prayer called *Akedah* is recited.[105]

Scattered throughout Aloni's childhood stories are the three
main features of the biblical tale of the *Akedah*: the knife, the
wood, the fire, mentioned in Gen 22:6, "And Abraham took the wood
of the burnt offering, and laid it upon Isaac his son; and he took
the fire in his hand, and a knife; and they went both of them
together."

The knife, referred to several times in "Shmeel,"[106] is introduced with a meaningful connotation in "Baker," a story subtly
suggestive of the *Akedah*. After the boy-narrator announces his
wish to work in the bakery and he awaits his father's response,
the following thought crosses his mind: "I was afraid that he
would utter a verdict like a knife from his mouth" (*Tarmil*, 104).[107]
In the Akedaic-Oedipal context of the father-son relationship, the
knife as a metaphor assumes a heightened significance, the acute-
ness of which borders on the grotesque, when the story presents
the father as a man handy with a knife when dealing with a watermelon (122). "The distant projection from the present event or
deed to the ancient myth is of course grotesque," says Aloni in an
interview.[108] Indeed, the allusions to the myth of the *Akedah*, as
it is transformed in Aloni's tales, often acquire a grotesque
twist. Giving the knife to Isaac (Izakino) ("Baker," 312), is
another example.

The wood of the burnt offering may well be implied in the
simile that describes Shmeel sitting on the roof "like a scorched

tree" ("Shmeel," 188), and Sultana, at the entrance to the bakery
like "an old tree trunk, scorched by the fire, but not consumed"
("Baker," 307). In this respect, it is perhaps possible to regard
Sylvan--the baker, whose name, conspicuously neither Hebrew nor
Jewish, represents a being, a deity or spirit of woods--as another
allusion to the element of wood.

  As for the fire--it is brought up numerous times in connection with the bakery, with reference to the flames in the oven.
In the earlier examination of the element of Eros in Aloni's childhood stories, the oven was discussed from the viewpoint of the
erotic. But the motif of the burning oven, or the fiery furnace,
associated with Abraham and Daniel,[109] is also loaded with initiatory and transformatory implications. Lévi-Strauss noted that
"the raw/cooked axis is characteristic of culture...since cooking
brings about the cultural transformation of the raw."[110] Fire is
a transmuting element, a device of purification, it changes whatever is put in it. And as in the case of Abraham (who in the
legends was not affected by the fire, just as his son Isaac in the
initiatory story of the sacrifice that did not happen) and Daniel,
fire challenges the courage of man. Facing fire represents in
this case a test of masculine courage, a quality Aloni's narrator
clearly desires. Fire also carries a Promethean connotation of
something divine and forbidden--a secret which endows one with
godlike powers--and the boy-narrator's fascination with forbidden
secrets has been indicated.

  One instance of the grotesque Aloni mentioned in his
interview is manifested in the description of Abraham (Avramino).
The man whose biblical namesake is the glorious patriarch is reduced to an old ex-boxer, now a street vendor of soft drinks
("Baker," 306). Except for warning the narrator against Sultana,
and providing some biblical allusions, his role in the story is
peripheral. Abraham's monotheism is alluded to in Avramino's
words: "Aren't we all children of one very strange God?" (306).
His Akedaic allusion, when he refers to Izakino, is obvious: "He's
a good man, that soft bastard. A saint. How the good Lord lets
him remain among us, I'll never know" (307). And when he sarcas-
tically calls Sultana "my beauty!" (307), he may well be alluding
to Sarah's famous beauty.[111] In another context, the love of the
biblical Sarah for Isaac is suggested in the narrator's remark,
when observing a change that came over the furious Sultana: "Izakino's name has calmed her down. When he comes, she will get down
on her knees before him" (309).

One of the baffling elements in "Baker" is Izakino's death--
a striking contrast to the original *Akedah* story in which Isaac
survives. As will be shown in a moment, various midrashic versions
that differ from the biblical version of the *Akedah*, give rise to
a hypothesis that Aloni's use of this element may not have been as
random as it would otherwise seem.

In his introduction to *The Last Trial*, Goldin offers "the
possibility that the biblical account itself may be but the selected, the adopted version of a much more ancient narrative which
once upon a time circulated orally and which possibly included
elements now no longer in the written record."[112] In Gen 22:19,
immediately after the story of the *Akedah*, it is said: "So Abraham
returned unto his young men, and they rose up and went together to
Beer-Sheba; and Abraham dwelt at Beer-Sheba." The fact that Isaac
was not mentioned here intrigued the sages as to his whereabouts.
Abraham ibn Ezra in his commentary on Gen 22:19 records an opinion
that Abraham actually killed Isaac, who was later resurrected from
the dead. One midrash has it that God brought Isaac into the
Garden of Eden where he stayed three years.[113] Another midrash,
quoted by Isaac ben Asher ha-Levi, limited Isaac's sojourn in
Paradise to two years and explained that Isaac was secreted there
"to be healed from the incision made in his by his father when he
began to offer him up as a sacrifice."[114] Supporting this midrash,
R. Eleazar ben Pedat maintains that "although Isaac did not die,
Scripture regards him *as though* he had died and his ashes lay piled
on the altar."[115] No wonder Rebecca was so startled when she first
saw Isaac (Gen 24:64), given that she was seeing a man descended
from Paradise, who "walked the way the dead walk, head down and
feet up."[116] In another midrash "Isaac was in the grip of fear as
he lay bound on top of the altar, and his soul flew out of him,
and the Holy One, blessed be He, restored it to him by means of
the dewdrops for Resurrection of the Dead."[117] In yet another
midrash, when Isaac was bound on the altar and "reduced to ashes
and his sacrificial dust was cast on to Mount Moriah," God immediately revived him with the aforementioned dew.[118] The tradition
that Isaac was slain or burnt was especially strong at the time of
the Crusades when many thousands of Jews killed themselves to
sanctify the Name of God.[119] Isaac's death was explained in these
midrashim as "stored-up merit and for the atonement" of all the
generations to come.[120] In "Baker," as Avramino observes, there
is an air of sainthood about Izakino. In the narrator's perception, Izakino's death is associated with the idea of

atonement: he dies because of the narrator's sin. In this sense
it is a sacrificial death, with Izakino being the scapegoat.[121]
The description of Izakino as "white" from the flour (*Tarmil*,
109)[122] can be seen as a further echo of the midrashic motif of
"Isaac's ashes." In the same way, the legends discussed here,
especially those dealing with the motif of slaughter and resurrection, suggest a covert meaning in the description of the people of
the city of Edirne, noted for the incision in their necks, and
the scar on Shoeblack's neck ("Soldier," 11f.), as well as in the
latter's stories of resurrection and the narrator's attempt to
"revive" him. Also, the fact that the narrator "arranged with
Izakino" during Passover, to work in the bakery ("Baker," 307),
is not accidental in view of the theory that sees a possible link
between Passover and the *Akedah*.[123]

The most radical departure from the biblical text is to be
found in the characterization of Sultana, a fascinating, grotesque
metamorphosis from the saintly Sarah to the diabolic Sultana.
Placed in the ominous setting of the bakery, and evoking in the
narrator a sense of the mysterious forces that rule the *shekhunah*,
she incorporates several symbols and archetypes from Jewish and
Greek myths that surface in Aloni's childhood stories.

The Various Facets of Sultana

The first time she is mentioned, Sultana is identified with
a creature that to the reader of these stories has connotations of
fear and fascination: the owl. When he arrives at the bakery for
the first time, the narrator sees her sitting on her stool "like
an embalmed owl" ("Baker," 306). Examining the links between the
owl (*Yanshuf* in Hebrew), as a symbol that gave its name to the
whole book, and Sultana, may shed light on the relation between
images and their masked emotional contents and on the personal
imagery versus the collective symbolism.

The bafflement over the grotesquely metamorphosed Sarah, in
the form of Sultana, is greatly reduced once one accepts that
these stories are a sort of "quest-romance" conforming to Frye's
definition.[124] In dream terms, according to Frye, the "quest-
romance" represents "the search of the libido or desiring self for
a fulfillment that will deliver it from the anxieties of reality
but will still contain that reality."[125] In trying to define "the
antagonists of the quest," Frye identifies them as being often
"sinister figures, giants, ogres, witches and magicians, that
clearly have a *parental* [italics added] origin."[126] As for the

witch, Frye says that she "is appropriately called by Jung the
'terrible mother', and he associates her with the fear of incest
and with such hags as Medusa[127] who seem to have a suggestion of
erotic perversion about them";[128] such "sinister parental figures"
abound in "the world of the ogre and the witch."[129] One instance
of this "terrible mother" could be seen in a European *Märchen* mentioned by Géza Róheim. This *Märchen* describes the meeting of the
hero and an old witch "whose jaws reach to the sky and who is
otherwise as hideous as she can be. He says, 'Good morning,
grandmother,' and the witch says, 'It's lucky you called me grandmother, otherwise I would have killed you.'"[130]

It has previously been suggested that the narrator's sexual
longing for his friend's mother ("Shmeel") represents a projection
of repressed incestuous feelings. To this hypothesis another may
be added: that Sultana, in the role of a "terrible mother," serves
as a means of overcoming an incestuous feeling based on a strong
maternal tie which might prevent the boy from growing up, and
which might create adolescent difficulties as a result of a failure to enter the adult world. Turning the mother figure into a
wicked, sinister creature could help him cut himself loose from
such a harmful tie. Aloni's remark about incest in the *Keshet*
interview can now be seen in a new light. Also, in this context,
his disclosure that in real life, at the age of thirteen (which
corresponds more or less to the age of the narrator in these
stories) he wrote a play called *Oedipus*, assumes a new significance. It foreshadows a persistent preoccupation with the Oedipal
theme and the theme of generational strife, which were later at the
core of his plays, and for which the childhood stories served as a
laboratory for thematic experimentation. Merely hinted at in *The
King is the Cruellest*, which antedated these stories, the Oedipal
pattern surfaces in *The American Princess*, written after them, in
which the Crown Prince is the bitter rival of his father, the King;
in a play-within-a-play the son acts the role of the father in his
youth, marries the queen, his mother, has a son, himself, then,
playing himself, shoots his father. This parricidal motif re-
appears in *Aunt Liza*, where the son kills his father, and in *The
Gypsies of Jaffa*, culminating in *Eddie King*, Aloni's modern and
grotesque version of Sophocles' *Oedipus Rex*. In the last play,
the setting of which is the New York underworld, the gangster
Eddie (Oedipus) kills his father, Don Laios, the Godfather, and
marries his mother.

In the childhood stories, the incestuous context may be seen
as a clue to the narrator's attraction to the owl, the mysterious
creature that causes blindness; the allusion to Oedipus blinding
himself after committing incest is clear. A subtle suggestion of
incest is introduced in the first encounter of the boy with the
blind Sultana, the "owl." When he sees the wrinkles in the old
woman's face he is reminded of *erva* (ערווה), which in Hebrew
stands for nakedness, genitals. The term *gilla erva* (גילה ערווה),
which literally means "he uncovered nakedness," is used with the
sense "he committed incest," just as *gilluy arayot*, as already
pointed out, is used to mean incest.

In the role of Sarah, Sultana is not just a mother, but "The
Mother," for Sarah was the wife of "The Father of the nation."
Her association with the owl and its totemistic implication can be
explained in line with Róheim's observation that "mythological ancestors are identified with an animal."[131] Throughout the stories
the owl assumes the role of an animal to be revered. Owls are
often associated with wisdom ("A wise old owl"[132]). To the ancient Greeks the owl represented intelligence because it was believed it presaged events; its large, wide-open, set forward
eyes,[133] which help it to perceive the whereabouts of its prey in
a three-dimensional manner, symbolized wisdom. It became the bird
of Athena, the goddess of wisdom, and appeared on the coins of
Athens. In relating to Sultana as a totem, the boy-narrator indicates his desire for knowledge, for a mentor who could guide his
spiritual growth. The thousand-year-old owl denotes accumulated
wisdom to which he would like to have access. But not only that.
The boy's attraction to Sultana could be better understood upon
defining her mystical resonance as a grotesque version of
Persephone.[134]

Greek mythology has it that Persephone, daughter of Zeus and
Demeter, was carried off by Hades (Pluto) while gathering flowers
in the vale of Enna, and was brought to the lower world as the
wife of Hades to become the queen of the world of death. The owl
serves as at least one direct link between the myth of Persephone
and Sultana. Answering Demeter's prayers, Zeus agreed to the return of Persephone on condition that she had eaten nothing in the
infernal world. But Ascalaphus, son of Acheron, revealed that she
had eaten some pomegranate seeds, and to punish him Demeter turned
him into an owl. Demeter's request to have her daughter back was
finally only partly fulfilled when Zeus allowed Persephone to spend
half of the year on earth[135] and half of the year with Hades as his

wife, the queen of death. There is a semantic analogy between
Persephone as a queen and Sultana (whose name in Hebrew can mean a
queen), and the element of darkness associated with Persephone is
analogous to Sultana's living in a world of darkness due to her
blindness; but the essential analogy is to be found in Aloni's
repeated association of Sultana with death, which introduces into
his story implicit chthonic overtones.

In the opening lines of Tennyson's poem "Demeter and Persephone" ("Faint as a climate-changing bird that flies / All night
across the darkness and at dawn / Falls on the threshold of her
native land"),[136] Persephone is portrayed as a nocturnal bird; so
is Aloni's Sultana as an owl. The boy-narrator's attraction to
the latter is his attraction to the mysteries of death. Talking
about Persephone, G. Robert Stange remarks: "In the fires of hell
she has seen revealed the secrets of death."[137] Indeed these are
the secrets Aloni's neophyte expects to learn from Sultana, as he
does from Shoeblack. For this boy-narrator (the artist-as-a-young-
man), the Persephonic element of Sultana conveys what the legend of
Persephone conveyed for Tennyson, the "sense of the poet's penetra-
tion of the realm of the imagination, of the forbidden region of
shadows which must be entered before the highest beauty or the
highest meaning of experience may be perceived."[138]

Tennyson's poem does not dwell on the erotic aspect of the
goddess of death as does Swinburne's "The Garden of Proserpine."
In Swinburne's poem:

> Her languid lips are sweeter
> Than Love's who fears to greet her
> To men that mix and meet her
> From many times and lands.[139]

And she is described as a woman hungry for men:

> She waits for each and other
> She waits for all men born.[140]

There is in her, in this respect, an element of a Circe,
which may well be applied to Sultana as the sinister temptress who
casts a spell on the boy, acts as a demonic counterpart to his
mother, and embodies his death-wish; "Circe, who is symbolic of
both the love-death and the eternal round of womb and tomb."[141]
Unlike Odysseus, the boy in Aloni's childhood stories stands no
chance of escaping this siren. For Sultana is also Lilit, a female demon featured lavishly in Jewish demonology. Lilit's role
as the queen of the demons is not dissimilar to that of Persephone
who reigns over the spirits of the underworld; introducing her

into the study of Sultana necessitates a closer look at myths
concerning this female demon.

As noted, Sultana is symbolized by the owl, *Yanshuf*--one of
at least eleven names for the owl mentioned in the Bible. *Yanshuf*
[this Hebrew name has been connected with *neshef* (night) or with
neshifah (hooting)] appears in Lev 11:17, Deut 14:16, Isa 34:11,
and is identified with the long-eared owl *Asio Otus*. Another name
is *Lilit*, the *Strix Aluco*, also mentioned in Isa 34:11. The
similarity of this name to *laylah* (night) denotes a nocturnal
bird.[142]

There is apparently an early connection between *Lilit* the owl
and Lilit the queen of the demons in Jewish folklore. The superstitions connected with owls are universal. Because of their
solitary nocturnal existence owls became creatures of ill-repute
and were associated with the occult and the otherworldly. In the
Bible, because they inhabit ruins and their hooting sounds like
mourning, they are a symbol of destruction and devastation. One
species of owl, *Tyto Alba*, was particularly looked upon as a symbol of disgrace. It is a bad omen to see an owl by daylight, and
an owl flying around the house hooting at night signals death.[143]
Similarly, one who looks into an owl's nest "will thereafter be a
sad and morose soul."[144] The hooting sound of the owl could provide an additional semantic clue to the connection between the owl
and Lilit, also known as *Meyallelet* (the howling one).[145] Jewish
myths have it that Lilit, who had been one of Samael's[146] wives,
left him for Adam.[147] *Alpha Beth de-Ben Sira* (a midrash written
in the East after the rise of Islam), identifies her with the
"first Eve" who was created from the earth simultaneously with
Adam. Their union produced the demons, *shedim*.[148] Ben Sira's
description of Lilit as a demon who murders infants may have been
indebted to Greek mythology where night is said to have given birth
to death, and also to the myth of Juno and Lamia.[149] When Juno discovered that Lamia had had intimate relations with her husband,
Jupiter, she grew furious and devoured all the little children she
came across.[150] In *Alpha Beth de-Ben Sira*, Lilit is quoted as
saying:

> I have been created for the purpose of weakening and
> punishing little children, infants and babies. I have
> power over them from the day they are born until they
> are eight days old if they are boys, and until the
> twentieth day if they are girls.[151]

To some extent, one can find an allusion to Lilit as a demon
who inflicts suffering on women in childbirth and strangles

infants[152] in the information Sylvan gives the narrator about
Sultana's mysterious activity as a "midwife": "When she was a midwife she made a lot of money. With that money she built this oven.
Haven't you heard the screams coming out of the walls at night?"[153]
("Baker," 311). This cryptic remark suggests that Sultana was not
a conventional midwife; presumably she was called to perform
abortions. The boy-narrator, too young to understand what sort
of "a midwife" Sylvan meant, senses though the sinister aspect of
Sultana's activity when he repeats before his friends what Sylvan
has told him and adds in a thrill: "She brought terrible suffering
upon women who had given birth" (316).

Apart from her role as the murderess of infants, Lilit is
known in Kabbalistic demonology also as a seducer, a Jewish version of Circe.[154] In this respect Shmeel's mother, as a seducer,
could be identified with Lilit as well; which might explain why
the narrator's mother tells him to recite "Hear O Israel!" (a traditional formula to ward off demons) before going to sleep, as he
sees her in his dreams. In the role of the seducer, Lilit is also
recognizable as the Queen of Sheba.[155] For a long time the Queen
of Sheba's role in Jewish folklore was that of "a snatcher of
children and a demonic witch."[156]

On a symbolic level the myth of Lilit as a child murderess
conveys initiatory significance. Eckert speaks about boys who are
"frequently removed secretly and at night, and the mothers are
told that the gods have stolen them and may kill them."[157] The
idea behind it is that it helps effect a break with the maternal
world, since the boy's "death" is to a large degree the death of
childhood and of the "effeminizing influence." When the narrator
(in "Baker") tells his parents about his wish to work in the
bakery, his apprehensive mother refuses to let him, as though she
senses that she may lose him to Lilit-Sultana. In her maternal
premonition she is reduced to the pathetic role of a Cassandra who
foresees tragedy but is unable to prevent it. She thus calls to
mind the midrashic treatment of the biblical Sarah when her son is
taken to the *Akedah*, and going to work in the bakery is thus
viewed as an initiatory experience, somewhat reminiscent of going
to the *Akedah*. Aloni seems to infer that the boy's initiation
will succeed if he can defend himself against dangers which Sultana represents as a Lilit, a Circe, and a Sarah--if one accepts
that Aloni's use of heroic archetypes is often ironic. The open
hostility between Sultana and Avramino, which in Aloni's story
appears to be rooted in a long-standing bitterness, may be

elucidated by a legend that describes how Abraham deceived Sarah
when he took Isaac to the *Akedah*. Not daring to reveal the truth,
he told her: "I will go and bring him to Shem and Eber his son and
there he will learn the ways of the Lord, for they will teach him
to know the Lord."[158] The otherwise unexplained malevolence
towards men of the Sarah-Sultana figure suddenly makes sense, when
viewed in the face of such deceit.[159] So too does her attempt, in
her grotesque metamorphosis into Lilit, to kill them at birth or
at least to bring about their destruction when they are about to
be initiated into manhood.

The Killing of the Sun

     At the first encounter of the narrator with Sultana, when she
hears that he wants to be a baker, "she turns her head *toward the
sun* [italics added] and walks to the entrance of the bakery"
(*Tarmil*, 116).[160] Indeed, there is in these stories a constant
juxtaposition of day and night, light and darkness. Sultana, as
an entity incorporating elements of Lilit and Persephone the queen
of darkness, is the adversary of the sun. The book is named after
a nocturnal predator. The narrator is extensively described roaming, as though in a labyrinth, the alleys of the *shekhunah* in the
hours of darkness (intensified by the wartime blackout), and he is
drawn to Sultana. But the fact that his perspective is truly solar
in essence, that he really identifies with the sun, emerges strongly in "Shmeel" when he gets up early every morning to watch the
sunrise, and when he opposes Shmeel's regicidal-deicidal wish to
"kill" the sun.
     The apocalyptic notion that associates the end of the world
with damage to the sun is as old as humanity. Frye mentions the
fear of the ancients at the sun's nightly "mysterious passage
through a dark underworld, sometimes conceived as the belly of a
devouring monster."[161] Frankfort points out that "the dramatic
quality of the Sun's course is acknowledged by the stories of
battles which he has to fight....Every sunrise is a victory over
the darkness, every sunset a forcible entrance into the Nether-
world where dangers crowd in upon the sun-god."[162] And Kirk talks
about the prayers that were said each night in the temples of ancient Egypt to avert the dangers of the sun-god's enemy, the ser-
pent Apophis, as the boat of the sun-god Re passes under the
earth.[163] The Aztecs maintained that there had already been three
or four destructions of the world, and that another one was ex-
pected; the sun ruled each one of these worlds and its

disappearance marked the end. The *Mahābhārata*'s concept of the
cosmic cataclysm is of an horizon bursting into flames with seven
or twelve suns drying up the seas and burning the earth.

The narrator's naïve belief in Shmeel's ability to perform a
miracle more astounding than that of the biblical Joshua (see Josh
10:12-13) has a faint echo of the dragon-fight motif. Aloni's
mythopoesis, as expressed here, is grounded in the ancient pattern
of thought that man could control the universe for his own purpose,
a belief that placed in his hands the lever whereby he could exercise that control. Aloni seems to go along with Chase's observation that "myth must always discover and accept preternatural
forces; it must always reaffirm the efficacy of the preternatural
and insulate it from the ordinary world."[164] Simultaneously, Aloni
is aware that he has to "accept the supernatural as operating
within nature."[165]

In the ancient Graeco-Oriental world the sun came to represent the intelligence of the world; in Aloni's stories when its
counterpart, the "Sultanesque" element, is to the fore the boy
Shmeel is given to destructiveness. In the case of "Shmeel," a
story dense with Oedipal nuances, the act of holding a mirror up
to the sun in order to kill it means, on an allegorical level,
bringing about a sacrificial death of the god-father. Such a
parricidal act symbolically puts the boy Shmeel in the role of
avenger for the countless youths sacrificed to the sun-god.[166]
Because the mythological role of the sun is that of the "Primal
Father"[167] (the ancient Egyptians viewed Re as "the source of life
and generation...a divine king and the self-created Creator,"[168]
and the Incas worshipped the sun as a revered Father), Shmeel's
act may be interpreted as a symbolic allusion to a revolt of a son
against his father, of an "Isaac" against an "Abraham."

Holding a mirror up to the sun is for Shmeel as cathartic as
the "breakfast-table witchcraft" is for the narrator. The two
deeds are similar. In the latter an attempt is made to pierce
Goldberg's eyes then slay him.[169] Goldberg, the only Ashkenazi in
these stories (i.e., the only fair-skinned person), suggests in
this context a personification of the sun.[170] Since the sun was
considered in various cultures as the eye of a celestial supreme
being,[171] it seems plausible to regard the "breakfast-table witchcraft" against Goldberg as an affront against God, as well as an
initiatory rite which, to quote Eckert, "usually includes killing
an enemy or performing a sacrifice or both."[172] Goldberg is
the enemy--he is the lover of the woman whom the narrator

desires. The sun, it follows, is given here a carnal connotation
as well. This is nothing new in Jewish folklore, as Rappoport
points out: "In Jewish folklore the sun is often compared to a
bridegroom,[173] for crowned like a bridegroom and accompanied by
ministering angels, it rides forth every day in a chariot."[174]
In Jewish folklore the sun, not in its masculine self *shemesh* but
in its dainty anima *ḥamah*, serves also as a model of beauty.
And it is perhaps appropriate after a lengthy exploration of the
dark side of Sultana, to end the discussion of the sun in Aloni's
stories with a legend that links it with the biblical personality
to whom Sultana is related as a grotesque foil--Sarah; a legend
which stresses Sarah's luminous side.

> On his journey from Canaan to Egypt, Abraham first observed
> the beauty of Sarah. Chaste as he was, he had never before
> looked at her, but now, when they were wading through a
> stream, he saw the reflection of her beauty in the water
> like the brilliance of the sun.[175]

Calamitous Water

Paradoxically, despite his use of the myth that singles out
the sun in relation to the destruction of the universe, Aloni does
not associate cataclysm with fire but rather with water. In the
intricate network of his symbolism, water as a destructive element
belongs to the same category as the owl and Sultana, and would be
found at the chthonic pole; fire and sun would be found at the opposing, creative and celestial pole. As in the Bororo myths which
Lévi-Strauss analyzes in *The Raw and the Cooked*, water and death
are often connected in Aloni's thought. Frye's observation that
"the world of water is the world of death" (for which he finds an
illustration in "Dante's symbolic figure of history"[176] and which
can be verified in Swinburne's poems of Persephone[177]), is applicable
to Aloni's childhood stories. In at least two places in these
stories it is possible to detect traces of undeveloped attempts to
associate water as a malevolent element with the myth of Sirens.
In both, Aloni prefers not to elaborate, but to shroud the narrative in mystery. The first instance is the mention of the drowned
horses that neigh beguilingly every night in the rivers ("Soldier");
the other is the mention of the laughing, mysterious, beautiful boy
who drowned in the pond ("Baker"). The concept of the water of death
in these stories calls to mind the biblical tale of the flood
(Genesis 6-8). An echo of this tale reverberates in the imaginary
description of the water covering the *shekhunah*, as a result of
torrential rains ("Owl," 36). Aloni even uses here the same biblical word for flood: *mabbul*.

When Aloni describes a sea-monster he draws his inspiration
from Hollywood monster films.

> I saw the sea suddenly bursting into the town like a huge
> animal rearing on its legs and its body falling on the
> street, and the sky crumbling on the roofs of the houses
> and the wind whirling and tearing the skin off my face
> and people fleeing to the hills. ("Shmeel," 192)

Later in the same story, the image of the sea highlights
another version of destruction.

> I saw the street gape open in the morning and the houses
> crouching on my mother's hair and chunks of concrete
> falling on my father's face and crushing it all...and
> Shmeel and I sitting on the parapet in the terrible
> darkness and looking as if at a sea with nothing around
> us. (202)

On almost every occasion when the sea is mentioned in these
stories it is associated with death. In the first story the boy
follows Shoeblack to the beach, where the sea smells of drowned
horses. There Shoeblack tells him about his imminent death, and
about "the secret of the dying people" ("Soldier," 20-22). But
since Thanatos is closely linked to Eros in these stories, just as
retribution is to sin, and since water is also a prime symbol
of fertility from time immemorial,[178] the image of the sea is
also associated with Shmeel's mother. She is twice described as
staring at the street as if it were a sea ("Shmeel," 176, 184).
Feeling sinful for his erotic feelings about her, the narrator's
awareness of the sea here is that of punishment.

The sea is mentioned three times in the context of his erotic
dream: his body rolls between the sheets in the sea of darkness;
the balcony of Shmeel's mother stands out like a white bone in the
sea; Shmeel's mother's sea of yellow hair rises to choke him (184,
186).

Finally, the sea as an image of foreboding is linked with the
mirror, the instrument of destruction in "Shmeel." The boy Shmeel
is described as he "trapped a sea of sparks in a cracked mirror,
turned his sharpened nail up to the sun, and twisted his mouth"
(206).

The Glorious Desert, The Girls From Jaffa

In contrast to the sea, the desert in Aloni's imagery is not
viewed with fear, although it, too, is associated with death and
destruction as the place where fierce battles are raging at the
time; in the romantic imagination of the boy-narrator it becomes
synonymous with a much desired objective.

Ever since the days of the Bible one of the principal
connotations of the word desert in Hebrew is that of heroism
(another is, naturally, desolation). In the formative years
of the Jewish nation the desert fulfilled an initiatory function:
that was the place where the nation was forged over a period of
forty years. The desert stands for a place where one retreats for
meditation, to incubate new ideas, have new insights, and come
back into the world. The generation of slavery that Moses led out
of Egypt was found unfit to enter the promised land and was doomed
to perish in the desert, to be replaced by a new generation of
free, fierce, and fearless people, better equipped to conquer a
homeland.

In Yizhar's "Runaway," the desert is associated with the idea
of freedom--it is the destination of the horse in his liberating
gallop. In Aloni's stories the desert is not associated so much
with freedom per se as it is with heroism. The desert, in this
case the Western desert and not the Sinai, is the place the narrator and his friends wish to reach in their fantasies described at
the very beginning of the first story ("Soldier," 8), the place
the glorious fighters, including Shmeel's father, are to be found.
When the girl ("Owl") tells the narrator that her brother has
joined the army he is thrilled. In his mind's eye he sees himself
in the sands of the desert with her brother, and the mental picture is so vivid and palpable that the glare dazzles him (52).

While the desert is associated with soldiers, its most typical tree, the palm--particularly its fruit, the date--is associated
with prostitutes, "the girls from Jaffa." By and large, the role
of Aloni's palm tree is that of a theatrical accessory aimed at
providing local color. It is not an element of pastoral, which it
would have become had it been a story by Yizhar. Aloni's narrator,
unlike Yizhar's, is not a Rousseauistic child of nature, but a
city boy with no interest in the zoological or botanical aspects
of his milieu. The animals or insects mentioned are used as a
subordinated component of a metaphor or a simile, devoid of independent existence: "he hops up and down like a grasshopper," "his
eyes glitter like the eyes of a frog," "Shmeel's face is like a
gecko," "the cars screech by like angry chameleons."

When Aloni introduces elements with pastoral potency such as
the uncle's vineyard, eucalyptus groves, the pond in the orange
grove, and the night heavy with the scent of jasmine--all in
"Baker"--he does so superficially, unlike Yizhar who would have
gone to great lengths to charge each of these details with

overflowing feelings of nostalgia and pastoral. The village's
simplicity has no appeal for him. When presented with a choice,
his boy-narrator would rather stay in the *shekhunah* with its
labyrinthine intricacy, preferring the dry cistern surrounded by
scorched trunks and thistles to the pond in his uncle's orange
grove. This dry cistern is a much more thrilling place: it is
rumored that at night "the girls from Jaffa" come there. At any
rate, he feels more at home with scorched trees, fire being his
true element.

Promethean in spirit, what he is really after throughout the
stories is contact with fire, achieving his greatest satisfaction
when allowed it openly, in the bakery. His tragedy lies in being
robbed of the chance to become a fulfilled "baker," in being de-
feated by the "witch" Sultana. Unlike Hansel and Gretel, he does
not burn the witch in the oven and does not rid himself of this
persecuting figure of his imagination. Referring to this issue in
a different context, Bettelheim says: "A witch as created by the
child's anxious fantasies will haunt him; but a witch he can push
into her own oven and burn to death is a witch the child can believe himself rid of."[179] Aloni's boy-narrator could not bring
himself to push his witch into her own oven, hence his fall.

We leave Aloni's stories with a conception of a pubertal boy
whose rite of passage was thwarted by his frailty and consequently
marred by a sense of defeat. The triumphal sensation which would
have marked them had they been fairy tales such as "Hansel and
Gretel" is noticeably missing. There is no guarantee, one feels,
that when this boy-narrator grows up he will be fully rid of his
childhood anxieties, even when tackled by the boy grown into artist, and dealt with by being transmuted into art; which is indeed
what Aloni's subsequent writings--for the stage and not for the
page--bore out.

CHAPTER III

REMEMBRANCE OF THINGS PAST IN JERUSALEM: DAVID SHAHAR

David Shahar, born in Jerusalem in 1926, is a fifth generation
Sabra on his mother's side and a fourth on his father's, unlike
Yizhar and Aloni, first generation *Sabra*s. Both his parents origi-
nated from the Jerusalem old *Yishuv*. On his father's side[1] he is
a descendant of the followers and relatives of the "Ḥatam Sofer."[2]
His great-great-grandfather was one of the founders of the
Hungarian Houses,[3] in the Mea Shearim quarter.[4]

Of his own father, Shahar says in his story "First Lesson":

> Father himself, like most of his generation who had aban-
> doned orthodoxy at an early age, had commenced his educa-
> tion in the *ḥeder* and the *yeshiva*[5] in the Old City, but
> soon transferred to the Alliance School, where he learned
> French, and then to the Ezra Seminary for teachers, where
> he learned German. At the end of the First World War,
> under the influence of Jabotinsky,[6] he left the seminary
> before graduation and joined the Jewish Legion in the
> British army, although for some unknown reason he ac-
> tually spent most of his military service not in the
> Jewish Legion but in an English battalion.[7]

Upon leaving the army, Shahar's father returned to Jerusalem
and opened a language school. Because of financial difficulties
Shahar's parents moved in with his grandmother who lived in Mea
Shearim. The ten years the young boy spent in Mea Shearim became
the period which provided material for his childhood stories. His
life moved in two conflicting worlds simultaneously. With his
modern, Zionist parents he communicated in Hebrew, but with his
grandmother, who was fanatically Orthodox in her extreme adherence
to the old way of life and who regarded Zionists as heretics--a
view common to most other inhabitants of Mea Shearim--he had to
speak Yiddish. It was during that period that an ambivalent attitude to the old *Yishuv* developed in him: a son of his ancestors
he descended from it; belonging to the new generation he stood at
its opposite pole.[8]

After finishing elementary school he was sent to a non-
religious high school in Beit Hakerem, another quarter of
Jerusalem, and upon graduation attended the Hebrew University
studying psychology. His first stories were published in the
Jerusalem weekly *Ha-Galgal* in 1946, his first collection of short
stories, *Al ha-Ḥalomot (Of Dreams)*, came out nine years later.[9]

87

The characters who populate these stories are old-time Jerusalemites who abandoned religion and uprooted themselves from the old
Yishuv without being able to complete their integration into the
new, consequently finding themselves dangling in a cultural-
psychological limbo, forever at odds with their provincial society.
The stories' predominant feature is nostalgic reminiscence; they
have the quality of an old chronicle, of faded photographs in an
old family album. Achieving this effect is more important for
Shahar than depicting the childhood experience per se. Childhood
is of interest to him mostly as a means of reproducing a bygone
era, that of the mid-1930s, when he himself was nine or ten years
old. The myth of the *Sabra* is foreign to him and figures very
little in his stories; when he does use it, as is the case in his
first novel, it is chiefly for satirical purposes. His typical
protagonist, an embodiment of the antihero, is a member of a de-
clining, proud Jerusalemite aristocracy of the old *Yishuv* ousted
by dynamic newcomers who, through their Zionist activities,
assumed positions of leadership in the new *Yishuv*.[10]

   In his second book, the novel *Yerah ha-Devash ve-ha-Zahav*
(*Honeymoon and Gold*),[11] Shahar turns from a lyrical depiction of
the intimate dark corners of the old *Yishuv* to a satirical reflection of the modern society of the new State in pursuit of materialism, pragmatism and hedonism. His criticism lacks the fury,
bitterness and denunciatory tone which characterize Yizhar's rejection of the present; he prefers instead to satirize. The protagonist is a young Israeli who has spent three months in a kibbutz before leaving for Jerusalem to study at the university.
Along the way, he proves to be a swindler and a fraud, whose
corruption mirrors the moral standards of the society in which he
moves.

   Shahar's third book, *Keisar* (*Caesar*),[12] comprises additional
stories about the Jerusalemites from the milieu with which his
readers became acquainted in *Dreams:* people who no longer belong
to the old *Yishuv* but are not yet part of the new, and who could
be accurately described as incurable outsiders.

   It was followed by a children's book, *Harpatkotav Shel Riki
Maoz* (*The Adventures of Riki Maoz*),[13] a long story told in the
first person by a boy-narrator about his adventures during the
final phase of the British Mandate, and the siege of Jerusalem
during the War of Independence. Its narrative contains elements
which the author subsequently developed in his later childhood
stories.

Maggid ha-Atidot (*The Fortune Teller*)[14] is a collection of
six stories which begins with "The Fortune Teller" and ends with
"First Lesson." All of them deal with the same Jerusalem milieu
of the earlier stories. The characters are mostly members of one
big old family. The atmosphere is that of Jerusalem in the 1930s.
The scenery, background, and ambience are reproduced in retrospect,
with much warmth, empathy and longing. The dynamics of the stories is determined by a carefully attained harmony between the
metaphysical inclinations of the characters and their realistic
portrayal; and by a wish to disrupt the chronology of the characters, while juxtaposing as many events as possible.

Stories which appeared in these three collections were subsequently included in the following two collections: *Moto Shel ha-
Elohim ha-Katan* (*The Death of the Little God*)[15] and *Sefamo Shel
ha-Apifior* (*The Pope's Mustache*).[16] Altogether they can be viewed
as a laboratory in which Shahar experimented with his attitudes to
Jerusalem and its residents, and with his narrative technique,
before embarking on the ambitious project which he began in 1964:
a five-volume novel termed by him "Lurianic Novel," after its main
protagonist--the mysterious Gabriel Luria, whom "Mustache" first
introduced.

The novel is entitled *Heikhal ha-Kelim ha-Shevurim* (*The Palace
of Broken Vessels*) (hereafter: *Palace*). In terms of time and place it
corresponds to the short stories, but its human panorama is larger
in scope, the relationships more entangled, the narrative more
complicated, and the author's mysticism brought more to the fore.
The narrator, a young adolescent with a keen observation of people
and situations, whose biography greatly resembles that of the author, describes Gabriel Luria, his family, and other local characters, mostly on the eccentric side, through a series of inter-
twining vignettes in which the protagonists can be seen from
different angles. The emphasis is on atmosphere rather than plot.
The rich gallery of characters include Gabriel's father, the old
Bey, Yehuda Prosper Luria, a Sephardi remnant of the Ottoman
period, who maintains two wives and two families; his servant
Señor Moïse; his Ashkenazi wife, the narrator's landlady, Gabriel's
mother, who towers above all other characters with her individuality and life force. Other characters featured here are a Jewish
librarian from the old *Yishuv* who becomes a Christian missionary,
Jewish Orthodox fanatics and many non-Jews of various denominations.
Throughout, the mysterious and mystical interlace with realistic
detail. The first three volumes of this novel have appeared in the

following order: *Kayitz be-Derekh ha-Neviim* (*Summer on Prophets Street*),[17] *Ha-Massa le-Ur Kasdim* (*Journey to Ur of the Chaldees*),[18] and *Yom ha-Rozenet* (*The Day of the Countess*).[19]

While at work on the "Lurianic Novel," Shahar published another novel which has little to do with the subject matter of the "Lurianic," *Sokhen Hod Malkhuto* (*His Majesty's Agent*).[20] Set at the end of the Mandatory period, its protagonist is a double agent who works for the British as well as for one of the Jewish underground organizations.

In form and technique, Shahar's childhood stories are not as true to the genre as are Aloni's. Because they are reminiscent and retrospective in nature, a large number of them contain visions of childhood even when purporting to be dealing with the immediate present. These will be included in this study within the framework of discussion connecting the theme of childhood with other major themes in Shahar's works.

Of the stories to be discussed here, the following are available in English: "Ha-Rofe ha-Katan mi-Rehov ha-Habashim" ("The Little Doctor"), "Al ha-Halomot" ("Uncle Zemach"), "Ma'aseh be-Roke'ah u-bi-Geulat ha-Olam" ("The Pharmacist and the Salvation of the World"), "Sefamo Shel ha-Apifior" ("The Pope's Mustache"), "Maggid ha-Atidot" ("The Fortune Teller"), "Eshet Ba'alat ha-Ov" ("The Woman with the Familiar Spirit"), "Shi'ur Rishon" ("First Lesson").[21] Of the stories not available in English translation, the following are also pertinent to the study: "Al ha-Tzlalim ve-ha-Tzelem" ("Of Shadows and the Image"), and "Ha-Metziah" ("The Find").[22]

Of the stories listed above, only the following were first published in the 1960s: "The Fortune Teller,"[23] "The Find,"[24] "The Woman with the Familiar Spirit,"[25] "The Pope's Mustache"[26] and "First Lesson."[27] However, failure to discuss them in the context of earlier childhood stories would leave this study incomplete.

The Theme of Jerusalem

Because Shahar's stories often give the impression that Jerusalem is much more than mere background, it is appropriate to begin a review of his work by examining his treatment of it as both setting and theme. It is immediately clear that apart from its landscape, he is eager to capture its inscape--the distinctive and intrinsic attributes of a place which became a universal symbol charged with emotional, religious, spiritual and historical

connotations. As with any other Jewish writer who attempts an
artistic rendering of his experience of Jerusalem, Shahar is constantly aware of the magnitude of the challenge superimposed on
him by such a theme. It is often thought that for a Jewish author
the image of Jerusalem is a dominant "pre-existent" form which he
is not free to treat arbitrarily as though it was his own design.[28]
This assertion is only partly true with regard to Shahar, an author
who was privileged to enjoy an advantage denied to some other major
Israeli authors writing about Jerusalem, such as Agnon (1887-1970),
Reuveni (1886-1971), and Hazaz (1898-1973). They arrived on the
scene as immigrants, he was born and raised there. For him Jerusalem was not a conceptualized romantic myth,[29] but a natural
habitat which he had known ever since he had known himself. "I
don't accept the schmaltzy idealization of the city. It is a
tough reality," he contends.[30]

The Jerusalem he portrays is a schizo-scenic, provincial city,
in which Jews, Arabs and British commingle in a precarious coexistence. Admitting his ambivalence about it, Shahar says: "I feel
about Jerusalem the way a man feels about his family. Hating it,
loving it. Only what is very close to you can you hate, be angry
with, be hurt by, and love."[31] And he goes on to say in the same
breath:

> Jerusalem is a very intense city. The contrasts in it
> are sharp and so are the mutual hatreds. Things essen-
> tially opposed to each other exist there in an inevitable
> tension....In order to write about this complex theme--
> I have to get away from it, to immerse myself in a world
> which is the Jerusalem I once knew and to reconstruct its
> rhythms on paper.

Still, the reproduction of the city in his stories cannot be
regarded as an exact replica of the authentic model, much as it
strives to resemble it. It is more likely to be a stylized, fictitious treatment of childhood memories as perceived by his senses,
imagination and consciousness, after these memories have been fil-
tered through the comprehension of an adult who has come to terms
with his conflicting sentiments about the city. This reproduction
is rendered by means of the interaction of fictitious characters
and authentic scenery, bringing to life a panorama of idiosyncratic
figures from the back streets of Jerusalem's past.[32]

There is a gradual change in Shahar's approach to the Jerusalem scenery. While in his early works it functions mostly as a
complementary element, a setting and an illustration to the plot,
in the later works it strives to be inseparable from the ideo-
metaphysical context.[33]

The autobiographical narratives which constitute a reconstruction of childhood are set, on the whole, in the environment
of the old *Yishuv*, where the boy Shahar spent his childhood. As a
rule, the places are mentioned by their genuine names, without the
author trying to disguise them; moreover, he takes great pains to
provide the reader with detailed topographical data. In "First
Lesson" (hereafter: "Lesson"), the story which has as its climax
an inevitable confrontation between the boy-narrator and his
grandmother, the place of action, the old woman's home, is identified as being "in the Mea Shearim marketplace opposite the syna-
gogue and the big yeshiva" (*News*, 220). The same applies to the
narrator's description of his first home, in the same story: it
was in the Beit Israel quarter, the last house in the street from
which a "track continued up to the tombs of the Sanhedrin," com-
manding a view of the mountains of Nebi Samwil, Sheikh Jarrah and
Mount Scopus (210). Outside the claustrophobic confines of Mea
Shearim, this home is still within the periphery of the old *Yishuv*,
as are other well-known sites of the period mentioned in these
stories, such as the Bukharans quarter, Abyssinian Road, Edison
Cinema and the Lemel School. In "Uncle Zemach" (hereafter:
"Zemach"), the narrative's territory is extended to include places
outside the immediate boundary of the old *Yishuv* such as the
Bezalel School of Art where Zemach studies painting before deciding
to switch to law, and the Café Tamar, where his brother Lippa plays
his violin to entertain English soldiers, and the Government Land
Administration Department which is in Mamilla Road, next to Zemach's
office (32). And further on towards the center of the new Jerusalem is the municipal park, stretching between King George Street
and the Naḥlat Shivah quarter, where Uncle Zemach teaches the narrator drawing (63). "Mustache" enlarges the geographical, as well
as the ethnic scope by including a part of old Jerusalem which is
not generally known as a place where Jews used to live. Here the
narrator's home is "at the bottom of Mamilla Road opposite the
Jaffa gate and the walls of the Old City" (189).

By contrast, in stories lacking time gap between the actual
period in which they were written and the period they depict, such
as "The Woman with the Familiar Spirit," the scene is that of
present-day Jerusalem. This story's map contains places much removed from the old *Yishuv* and the author's childhood. Nevertheless, once a flashback is introduced, the scene automatically
switches to old Jerusalem, as is the case when the narrator recalls
a childhood episode associated with his classmate, Saul Haimjan
("Mustache," 116).

The childhood environment of these stories, unlike Aloni's
shekhunah and Yizhar's *moshavah*, is, much to the narrator's exasperation, strictly Orthodox. Detesting religious dogma and coer-
cion, Shahar can hardly disguise his antipathy to Mea Shearim.
The constant feeling of Ephraim, the protagonist in "Of Shadows
and the Image" (hereafter: "Image"), is one of suffocation. The
place is lacking in sanctity and spirituality;[34] it is an extension of the ghetto. Zeraḥ, the protagonist of the story "Of Little
Sins," an owner of a bookstore in Mea Shearim, confesses:

> In this stinking swamp I spent my life and here I raised
> my sons. And the stench...it's now chasing Yoḥanan, my
> second son, except that he calls it a new name *gallutiut*,[35]
> and this Jerusalem which in all generations gave light
> to the Jews in their darkness...is the worst of all
> exiles to my son who was born here.[36]

Although there is no artistic description of Mea Shearim,
Shahar devotes much energy to ridiculing its typical representative, the old grandmother. In his stories she comes to be an
antithesis of yet another old woman in Hebrew letters who is the
incarnation of all that is noble, graceful, saintly and beloved
of the old *Yishuv*, Tehilah, the eponymous heroine of Agnon's
story,[37] who lived in the poverty-stricken Jewish community of the
old walled city. The ideological difference of attitudes between
Agnon and Shahar derives, in this context, from opposing sentiments towards religion and the religious meaning of Jerusalem.
Whereas the immigrant Agnon, the superior artist, was able to keep
the right distance to conceptualize Jerusalem in accordance with
the tradition of dispersed Jews down the centuries, the Jerusalem-
born Shahar was incapable of transcending personal grievances and
relating to Old Jerusalem beyond his own confining experience. And
yet, his aversion to the ultra-Orthodox Jerusalem is matched with
his nostalgia for the other Jerusalem. This nostalgia is more
easily understood in the light of Shahar's fascination with the
Levantine ambience, one of the prime features of this city in the
pre-State era.

Under a British Umbrella

Unlike that of Yizhar, Shahar's nostalgia is devoid of the
element of pastoral. As with Aloni, the city boy, Shahar's longings are not for an open country but for city-scapes and urban
situations. In "Lesson" he openly admits to an inadequacy in an
area where Yizhar's forte lies: "This business of the naming of
plants after their kinds has always been one of the weak spots in

my life; there are very few plants which I know by name" (*News*,
216). Nonetheless, an element of pastoral does crop up in "Image"
and, as is the case in Yizhar's stories, it is linked with the
theme of rebellion and freedom: the boy Ephraim escapes to nature
to get away from the coercive Orthodox society and his authoritarian father (*Dreams*, 20, 23). But nature itself holds no interest for the boy; once in the fields he immerses himself in reading
a book which allows his imaginary escape to faraway places.
Earlier, when he was six, while going for a walk with his mother
in Jerusalem's main street, he saw a painting of horses in a display window of a picture gallery. He was fascinated, but--in
contrast to the boy in Yizhar's "Runaway"--not by the horses as
much as by their colors (12).

Shahar's nostalgia is fuelled by memories of an era in which
the effervescent mix of Christians, Moslems and Jews produced a
unique blend of the Levant in a unique setting, with Jerusalem
serving as a cosmopolitan meeting-ground of east and west, old and
new, holy and secular. Such an ambience is recaptured in "Mustache" in a detailed description of a street scene as seen by the
boy-narrator from the terrace in his home. The participants of
this colorful scene are nuns from the nearby convent, *narghile*
smokers, effendis of a local Arab café, an itinerant tamar hindi
vendor, tarbooshed coachmen, Armenian pedlars, arrogant British
officials and mustached Irish policemen (*News*, 189f.). The multi-
ethnic interaction is felt also in the narrator's home. Whenever
Sarah, the Moslem maid, hears the bells or the singing of the nuns
floating into the house from the convent she "would stop washing
the floor or beating the mattresses and stand stock-still, frozen
in holy awe" (192). Conversely, the other Moslem maid in the
narrator's home is quite indifferent to the music of Christian
liturgy. But this maid, Jamilla, becomes very animated when
Gabriel Luria, "the most regular and welcome of all the visitors
to our house" (192), calls in.

Gabriel Luria is probably Shahar's most engaging character.
The narrator of "Mustache" who delights in describing this suave,
debonair figure, savors every detail in depicting him as a Jerusalem dandy who carries himself with panache. Whenever he appears
Jamilla comes "running from the kitchen to take his silver-knobbed
cane and his white hat banded with a black ribbon--a stiff hat
made of woven white fibres which he called a 'Panama hat'" (193),
then she hurries to place the wicker armchair and the round, three-
legged folding table on the balcony, and rushes to the kitchen to

bring him Turkish coffee and "sweetmeats like raḥat lakum" and
"savory pastries like bureka" (194). The adjective "lordly" is
several times used of him. He is described dressed "in white
flannel trousers, called by him 'tennis trousers,' and in a blue
blazer with gold buttons, lording it over our balcony" (194). His
"lordliness" is demonstrated by the way he sits: "solemnly reclin-
ing upon the fullness of the harmony that existed between him and
all the world surrounding him" (194).

    Shahar takes great pains in such descriptions to introduce
his own concept of the paradigm of the native Eretz-Israel Jew.
His Gabriel Luria is the furthest one can get from the stereotyped
Sabra, as presented in the works of the "Generation of 1948." He
is not characterized by the features that have come to typify the
tough, "prickly" *Sabra*, a member of a pioneering youth movement
and kibbutz orientated, who demonstrated ingenuity, patriotism and
self-sacrifice in volunteering to be instrumental in the operation
of illegal immigration, or as a glorious fighter. This Gabriel
Luria is an offspring of a respectable family of the old *Yishuv*;
his father Yehuda Prosper, the old Jerusalem-born Sephardi, held
the Turkish honorary title Bey, while his mother was a daughter of
a very poor Ashkenazi family from the Old City.[38] There is clearly
an attempt to show Gabriel not only as a deep-rooted Jerusalemite
whose family's presence in the city goes back to the Ottoman era,
but also as a refined gentleman who has acquired European sophistication. From information given about him in the "Lurianic Novel"
we learn that he was "sent off like a prince" to study medicine in
Paris, but instead of finishing his studies he wandered around
"like a tramp," squandering his father's money (*News*, 159). His
mother bitterly blames this on the "Oriental fantasies" derived
from his father. But this "Oriental" (Middle Eastern) streak in
Gabriel's personality is precisely what makes him so endearing to
the narrator, as well as an authentic product of the Levant. Like
the elder brother in Yizhar's childhood stories, he is intimately
familiar with Arab customs and folklore, earning the esteem of
Arabs from all walks of life. The description of him negotiating
a business deal with Boulos Effendi bears a resemblance to the description of the elder brother's dealings with Arabs in Yizhar's
"Dunghill"--except that in Shahar's "Mustache" the customer is a
sophisticated, rich Arab who evokes the narrator's delight, whereas
in Yizhar's story it is the poor, ignorant Bedouin who evokes the
narrator's compassion. This may be attributable to the difference
in approach of the two writers towards the Arab motif. For Yizhar

it serves the purpose of pastoral, for Shahar it is a device to
recall the days in which the Jewish-Arab coexistence in Palestine
produced some sort of harmony.

"Mustache" skilfully portrays the slow, lengthy procedure that
acts as ritual prologue to the actual negotiation and is very much
part of it. Although the Arab has come solely for the purpose of
purchasing building material which he needs urgently "since his
workers were already sitting idle at his expense and every hour
that passed took its toll of his purse" (*News*, 195), he is in no
hurry to conclude the deal. Both he and Gabriel Luria, the sales-
man, lounge in upholstered armchairs at the rear of the shop "with
a comprehensive and noncommittal sigh at the hardship of the times"
(195), while the messenger boy is sent to a nearby café to bring
Turkish coffee and sherbet and biscuits and a bubbling *narghile*.
Before getting down to business, the two men begin by praising "the
lovely ladies of the metropolis of Beirut, who could perform and
make you perform in the Occidental or the Oriental, the Italian or
the French manner," and who are "so marvelously various and subtle
and exotic that they could supply everything needed to satisfy the
dearest wishes of a civilized and discriminating man" (195). The
ritual of the meal in the Arab restaurant, later in the same story,
is described while dwelling on numerous obligatory post-meal
practices. Only after Boulos Effendi "hiccupped once and then
twice" and "gave vent to one last, loud, comprehensive belch," and
sighed "a sigh of melancholy satisfaction" (201), does he proceed
to give his account of what happened between Gabriel Luria and the
English nun.

To this category of cordial descriptions of Arabs one may add
the Arab judge in "Teller" before whom Uncle Kalman is brought for
not paying his debts, who relishes his conversations with Kalman
about "matters of the spirit" so much that he finds "mitigating
circumstances for all Kalman's transgressions of the law" (*News*, 7).
This, however, is not the only attitude to Arabs in Shahar's stories. When referring to the ethnic mentality of the Arabs as a
group, he regards them as a dangerous and hostile entity. In one
of his early stories, "Be-Erev ha-Kayitz" ("On a Summer Evening"),[39]
he reports the apprehensions of Shulamit, a member of a Jewish underground movement in whose mind "the Arabs seemed manipulated by
forces which could not be grasped by the human mind; by their very
existence they were undermining her and endangering her being."[40]
To remove doubts from the readers of "Mustache" about the precarious nature of a state of harmony between Jews and Arabs, Shahar

makes clear at the beginning of the story that it took place
"before the troubles between Arabs and Jews broke out in 1936"
(*News*, 189). In "Zemach," the protagonist, at that time a student
in the Bezalel Art School, is described as single-handedly fighting
off the Arab marauders who attacked Mea Shearim in the riots of
1921 (23f.). Years later, as a successful lawyer, Zemach finds
himself involved in an altercation with an Arab official in the
Land Administration offices. Looking at the Arab's chin, he observes that this chin "embodies the rootedness of the Arabs, their
profound and all-embracing arrogance, and their hatred and contempt
for the Jews" (43).

The Levantine ambience in Palestine was greatly affected by
the presence of the British who, in their capacity as colonial
rulers, set standards for Western elegance in the region. As with
his attitude towards the Arabs, when Shahar relates to the British
influence in Jerusalem his ambivalence comes to the fore. In
their pursuit of things English, his characters reflect the mentality of the provincial middle-class aspirants. The culture with
which they came in touch through the Mandatory administration
served as a model for imitation, representing worldliness and
sophistication. However, quite often what these Anglophiles borrowed from English culture was the shadow, not the substance. A
typical example is Zemach, who after graduating from law school
decides to continue his studies in England so that he can come
back and be "the most famous and distinguished lawyer in the country" (25). To acquaint himself with the right manners he purchases
a book called *Etiquette*, and a silver-knobbed cane, presumably to
project the image of a respectable, prospective lawyer. In the
process of calculated social climbing, Zemach befriends an English
judge, William Benton, and takes an English wife. Stella, the
daughter of a wealthy Jewish family from Liverpool, loves Zemach
no less even when she realizes that he has married her for her
family's fortune. While Zemach is seeking social success--the
shell, Stella looks for what he had left behind--the quintessence,
loving in him not the sycophant prosperous lawyer, but the artist
which he has repressed.

As for the young women aspirants, their Anglophile snobbery
has its source in their formal education at the Evelina de Roth-
schild School for Girls, founded on religious principles by the
Rothschilds of London, in 1864, with the aim of introducing its
pupils to English culture. One former pupil is Aunt Pnina ("The
Find"; hereafter "Find"), who is fond of interlarding her Hebrew

speech with English words (*Mustache*, 187). Another is Esther
("The Old Man and His Daughter"[41]). Shahar's sarcasm about this
school is evident: "Perhaps in England such a school could have
managed to turn its graduates into 'English girls of the Hebrew
persuasion,' but here, in Jerusalem, they didn't become English,
nor did religion become their forte. Most of them ended up as
successful secretaries in the Mandatory administration" (82).

In contrast with the girls from good families who have re-
ceived an English-style education, in "Find," Shahar mentions the
Jewish prostitutes who wait for English soldiers in a Jerusalem
café (*Mustache*, 182). He refrains from passing judgment, although
he puts pejorative remarks about them into Pnina's mouth.

Considerable space is dedicated to the admiration of the
narrator's father for things English, an admiration acquired while
he was serving in the British army. Of all the photographs of his
father in this period, the narrator especially likes the one in
which he stands "rigidly erect in puttees and short trousers, the
uniform of the English soldiers of the time but without the hat,
holding a baton under his arm" (*News*, 223). Certain things which
the father procured during his service in the British army he
retained all his life:

> ...the always erect posture, the smooth shave every day,
> even on the days of his deepest depression, and above all
> the love of what he used to call "the character of the
> English people"--the patience and the tolerance, the
> British sense of humour, dislike of comprehensive prin-
> ciples and rigid world views, hatred of dogmatic theories
> of life, and above all, respect for the personal inclina-
> tions unique to each and every man. (224)

In contrast to this pro-British sentiment, the attitude of
some of the protagonists in stories written in the 1950s, when
memories of the struggle against the British were still vivid, is
marked by hostility. Shulamit ("Evening") participates in an
attack on the British, and Ephraim ("Image") strikes a British
policeman shortly after his mother is killed by a drunken British
soldier in a hit-and-run accident.[42] However, as an antithesis to
the "bad" Englishman in the second of these stories, the first
introduces the "good" one. Milford knows about Shulamit's involvement with the underground, and yet, instead of arresting her, he
courteously escorts her to safety during the curfew. For Shahar,
the humane Milford (or Benton in "Zemach") represents the British
more than the drunken soldier who killed Ephraim's mother. The
portrayal of Milford affirms the fact that by and large the pro-
British sentiments of Shahar's father were not wasted on the son.

When discussing the various components responsible for the
redolence of the Levant in Shahar's stories, it is instructive to
consider his treatment of the Oriental Jew, the Sephardi. In the
1930s Jewish Jerusalem was made up of various neighborhoods, each
inhabited by a different ethnic group which wished to preserve its
old traditional customs, patterns of life, folklore. While the
vitality of this kaleidoscopic multitude emerges from Shahar's
stories, in the Jerusalem which he reproduces the hegemony is that
of the Ashkenazim,[43] which is natural since the author of this
autobiographical prose originated from an Ashkenazi background.
When he writes about the Sephardim, it is as an outsider to add
local color and social dimension, whereas Aloni, the Sephardi,
writes about them as an insider, and Yizhar, the Ashkenazi, ignores them altogether.

Shahar, who from an early age had ample opportunity to become
acquainted with Sephardim--in the elementary school he was the
only Ashkenazi in the class[44]--always felt that the Sephardim have
more vitality and spontaneity than the Ashkenazim.[45] The portrayal of Saul Haimjan, the narrator's classmate who is mentioned in
several stories, is along these lines. An attempt to present his
herculean streak is given in "The Woman with the Familiar Spirit"
(hereafter "Spirit").

> He was the strongest boy in the whole school and he grew
> up to be the strongest man I know. He was the man who
> broke out of the old prison in Jerusalem and escaped
> with the other four members of the Irgun Zvai Leumi[46]
> who were caught with him. On the very night that he
> was arrested he dismantled the iron bed in his cell,
> broke the locks of the door with a bar from one of its
> posts, and escaped. (*News*, 115)

Haimjan is not an intellectual but rather more of Aloni's
virile ideal. He is also a practical man who was clever enough to
move out of the slum to the prestigious Jerusalem, mostly Ashkenazi
neighborhood, Rehavia.

The Sephardi characters are treated with the same humorous,
sometimes sardonic, tone with which the author treats their Ashkenazi counterparts. His Sephardi gallery includes the old Bukharan
woman and Rahamim the old stonecutter, the two peculiar customers
of the fortune teller (*News*, 2); the landlord Mr. Arajun, a Persian
Jew who has a vegetable shop in the market in the Bukharan quarter
(213); Bulbul, another Persian Jew (227); Levi, the drunken
Georgian porter who speaks Yiddish (69); Mr. Avisar, the teacher
(217); and hakham Shvilli, the café owner (*Mustache*, 191f.). Although all of these are woven into the tapestry of the stories as

marginal characters, each demonstrates Shahar's ability to infuse
individuality, at the same time as ensuring that they all blend
harmoniously into the panoramic view of the Jerusalem society that
these stories reconstruct.

The Family Saga

The attempt to reconstruct a panoramic view of the old Jerusalem society is, however, secondary to the wish to put together a
family saga. The protagonists may be misfits and dropouts, but
they are not dissociated from their clan.[47] Where in Aloni the
tendency is to mythicize the *shekhunah*, in Shahar it is to mythicize the family group, the *mishpaḥah*. The family and its past is
the source of the vitality of Shahar's characters as well as of
their destiny.[48] One can detect in these stories the sort of atmosphere one meets in a gallery of a portrait artist who undertakes
to record family trees with all their divergences.[49] The clan is
depicted with its apparent decadence. Yet, despite the great attention given its "black sheep" and nonconformists, the story is
more interested in showing how the family works than how it falls
apart.

The conflict between the individual and the collective is
manifested within the family dynamics in the rebellion of a member
of the clan against its authority and conventions, which, in this
case, correspond to those of the old *Yishuv*. The family serves as
a microcosm of Jerusalem society. Almost every one of its members
is eccentric, but they are all interconnected by some obscure inner
bond and share a common fate.[50]

It is as if the family were hooked up to a time machine, its
memory reaching back through three generations--a dimension missing
in the stories of Yizhar and Aloni. The narrative goes back in
time by way of retrospection. The narrator's own memories are
confined to Mandatory times, but some of his characters--especially
the grandmother--return in their memories to the Turkish era.[51]
These layers of time suggest a deep-rooted family whose chronicle
reflects the history of the old *Yishuv* in Jerusalem from the beginning of the century, unravelled in an intimate manner of family
gossip.

In sharp contrast to Aloni, Shahar is not concerned with the
interaction of the boy-narrator and his coevals. "Image" and
"Lesson" present the boy as a misfit in school; his solitude being
that of the outsider, the artist-as-a-young-man.[52] His interaction
is mostly with his "uncles," or with family friends, on whom he

spies incessantly. Aloni's boy-narrator is very much the same
voyeur, but while the men on whom he eavesdrops are, for him, the
paradigm of virility, the men with whom Shahar's boy-narrator is
fascinated are the epitome of "immature" adults, in whom he tries
to discover himself. Understanding them is understanding himself,
for he is destined to end up like them, as Uncle Zemach notices at
the end of the story named after him: "The boy's getting more like
me every day" (News, 62).

The old grandmother at the head of the family is not just a
figurehead. In the absence of a grandfather, she plays the active
part of the defender of the faith; an obstinate, tyrannical, nagging and devious manipulator[53]--despite frail health. She appears
in several roles: mother ("Old Man"), grandmother ("Lesson,"
"Little Doctor"), aunt (Honeymoon), and landlady (Palace). Like
Aloni's Sultana, her eyes are diseased. However, while Sultana is
completely blind, Shahar's grandmother only suffers from trachoma.
Another element of similarity is the motif of the mummy, which
identifies the two old women as symbols of the ancient, ancestral
world. In Aloni's stories, Sultana is depicted as "an embalmed
owl"; in Shahar's "Little Doctor," the grandmother's face is described as being "ancient like the faces of mummies thousands of
years old" (News, 95). Shahar takes pains to point out that his defiance of "grandmother" reflects only the rejection of the particular Jewish world she stands for (the world of Mea Shearim), and
not the rejection of the ancestral world in .toto. He stresses:
"Already as a child I sensed that Judaism as represented by my
grandmother has nothing to do with the God of the Bible. The God
of Israel could not have spoken Yiddish."[54]

Much as Shahar enjoys giving a graphic description of the
elegant attire of Gabriel Luria ("Mustache"), the Jerusalemite he
likes, he equally enjoys ridiculing the clothes of the old woman
("Lesson"), the Jerusalemite he dislikes.

> Grandmother's bloomers spread out on the table in front
> of the stove in all their tremendous breadth were a
> source of constant amazement to me. Respectable cloth
> bloomers decorated with lace frills, they were wider
> than any other pair of panties that I have ever seen,
> althouth Grandmother herself was the smallest and most
> shrunken of women. (News, 225)

As was the case with Sultana, casting the grandmother in the
role of a "sinister parental figure," or a "terrible mother," carries initiatory overtones; it helps overcome maternal ties. On a
symbolic level, these maternal ties apply to old Jerusalem just as

they do to the world of the grandmother. Shahar makes no secret
of his complex involvement with Jerusalem: "I was born in Jerusalem, and I feel a part of it. I love it, hate it, fight it, but
I can't dissociate myself from it." "Image" clearly displays
Oedipal overtones in relation to Jerusalem: the boy Ephraim is
thinking that "she, Jerusalem, was his mother" (Dreams, 22).[55]
Since, metaphorically, the old grandmother is tantamount to Jerusalem, the boy's struggle with his grandmother in "Lesson" might
well reflect also the artist's fears of being dominated by this
city, and his wish to preserve his artistic freedom and integrity.
In the breaking of the matricidal taboo which the boy experiences
when he wishes for her death (News, 240), he communicates a subtle
wish to liberate himself from the clutches of the old world; an
essential prerequisite for him to obtain individuation.

      A similar wish is manifested also in the boy's attraction to
the family rebel: the uncle. All uncles in Shahar's stories--Kalman
("Teller," "Find"), Lippa and Zemach ("Zemach"), Pinik ("The Proposal"),[56] Abie ("Things in the Nature of Man"),[57] Zerach ("Of
Little Sins")--are one persona revealed in its multifarious nature.
Their persistent desire to find their inner truth and follow it
turns them, in most cases, into misfits. Defying the system, their
withdrawal is, in a way, a continuation of the grandfather's escape.
Similarly maladjusted, they cannot partake of ordinary family life,[58]
and remain dreamers who do not mind their image as "losers." Uncle
Zemach, it appears, is the only one who tries to escape this fate.
Being "endowed with a practical turn of mind" (News, 22), he decides to repress his artistic impulse, "keep his talents under control and direct them into the channels of material profit" (22).
His decision results largely from his embarrassment that his
brother Lippa, with a BA in economic studies from an American university, gave up an academic career and respectable position in
society, to become an obscure musician in a Jerusalem café. The
evening his brother makes his musical début, Zemach makes up his
mind to leave Bezalel Art School, where he has been studying
painting, and go to study law. "Better, he said, to be a second-
rate lawyer than a fourth-rate artist" (24). But, as it turns out,
even clever Zemach can not outmanoeuvre destiny; the inextricable
fate of the "gifted members" of his family, upon whom "for some
reason fortune failed to smile" (21), catches up with him, too.

      In narrating Zemach's tale, Shahar does not manage to escape
the traps of romantic clichés associated with the art/bourgeoisie
conflict. In fact, his stories tend to convey a sense that the

love of money and social success, and the love of art cannot coexist in the artist.[59] His opinion is stated clearly: "The world
of reality and activity is for me merely a passing illusion, and
whoever lives in this world leads a life of a lie."[60] He further
elaborates his rejection of the cult of success: "External success
does not attract me. I am trying to trace the inner success. To
map the spiritual exaltation."[61] It is precisely this idea that
seems to lie behind the epitome of the "uncle" in Shahar's stories
--the unworldly, tragi-comic loafer, Uncle Kalman, the most typical anti-hero in Shahar's works.

Uncle Kalman's background is similar to that of other offspring of the old *Yishuv* in these stories. The narrator humorously
recapitulates it by associating it with Kalman's rich repertoire
of songs.

> ...he used to sing all kinds of songs--Yiddish songs from
> the days when he was a Yeshiva student, and German songs
> from the days when he was a student at the "Lemel"
> School, and French songs from his schooldays at the
> "Alliance Israelite" and the records of Maurice Chevalier,
> and even Turkish songs which had somehow remained in his
> memory from the days of his early childhood. (*News*, 3)

The reader's first encounter with Uncle Kalman takes place in
"Teller" soon after his release from prison, where he was held for
neglecting to pay debts to his creditors and alimony to his wife.
In his denial of material things, his estrangement, his negligent
appearance and ineffectuality, Kalman contrasts with the "lordly"
debonair Gabriel Luria, and with the robust Haimjan. Yet, his
unworldliness is precisely what makes him so endearing to the boy-
narrator, who informs the reader: "I loved my Uncle Kalman more
than anyone in the world."

In another context, Shahar proclaimed:

> In my opinion an artist must try to make his art first
> and foremost an expression of life that has beauty...the
> beauty I mean is something beyond the daily reality...
> literature must express a truth which is beyond truth,
> a reality which is beyond reality, a dream which is
> beyond dream.[62]

The task of attempting to reach the "reality beyond reality"
is assigned to Uncle Kalman in his explorations of the esoteric;
in this respect Kalman is comparable to Yizhar's Ḥabakuk. Acting
as the actual initiator, he leads the boy-narrator into the cave
of the tombs of the Sanhedrin, where the two come upon the magic
stone ("Find"). Descending into the dark cave is a symbolic en-
actment of the rite of initiation. While the initiator is leading

the initiate into the depths, the latter experiences a complex
feeling: on the one hand he is curious to unveil the cave's secrets; on the other, he is apprehensive of what they may hold for
him. This ambivalence could be regarded as analogous to the sensation of one who embarks upon a journey of discovery of the
irrational and the subconscious of his psyche.

The discovery of the stone is a moment of revelation shrouded
with religious overtones, as "a stroke of light, like a blade of a
thin spear burst in from the entrance, cut through Kalman's body
and stuck in a small, smooth stone hidden on the floor of the
cave" (Mustache, 184). For the young initiate it functions as the
key to the domain of mysticism, since the stone has an amazing
quality: "Everything was seen through it as though rolled up in it
and originated from it." Looking through this magic object on
his surroundings, he experiences a mystical sensation: "All of
Jerusalem, including the mountains around it, the whole space surrounding the mountains and the sky, all these were inside me, and
it was my body that was encircling them, and from it they originated and within it they existed" (185).[63]

Introducing the boy to this "miracle," Uncle Kalman reacti-
vates an in-built marvelling mechanism with which the boy first
made contact at the age of three, as we are told at the beginning
of "Lesson," when his father first takes him outside to show him
the night sky. Thirty-six years after that night, as he sits down
to write "Lesson," he is still responsive to the stimulus of a
sensation of awe and fear that had accompanied the first time in
his life that he was "smitten with the terror of the great miracle"
(News, 209). Moreover, he admits, "today there is nothing at all
in the whole world that does not arouse my wonder and amazement,
and the more I concentrate my attention on anything the more intense the wonder and amazement grow" (212). This trait, which
Shahar claims to have been a focal point of his response to the
world, is given overt expression in the mysticism which is first
apparent in "Teller"--the story that introduces Uncle Kalman--
and becomes a prominent feature of his art in the ensuing stories,
culminating in the "Lurianic Novel."

Shahar's Mysticism

Even though Shahar defies institutional religion and narrow
dogmatism, he is far from being agnostic. He truly believes that
"if there is a reality--it is the reality of God."[64] He advocates
the liberation of the individual from subordination to theological

dogma, to enable him to grasp the supreme reality through an intense spiritual experience, deploying the mystical experience as a
counterbalance to the methods institutional religion uses to approach God. This is also an essential element of his *ars poetica*,
in accord with his belief that the business of good literature is
to deal with "what is beyond reality." This principle which
guides his stories written in the 1960s--with "Teller" as their
forerunner--gives rise to the opinion that they "aim towards a
moment of illumination. The anecdotal aspect, the wish to tell a
story, is significant, but the main thing is the moment that contains the cosmic meaning."[65]

Often, the intuitive illumination is depicted by the metaphor
of light. "Teller" ends with "a stroke of a beam of light" (*News*,
19), which marks Uncle Kalman's moment of insight. And "Find"
(which follows it in both *Teller* and *Mustache*) opens with the mention of the "stroke of a beam of light" which marks the moment
Uncle Kalman and the boy-narrator find the magic stone in the cave.
Other stories introduce several objects that reflect or emit light:
the diamond brooch pinned to the bodice of Clarissa, the medium,
in "Spirit" (139); the glass button on the blouse of Mrs. Green-
feld in "Teller" (17); the stove on which Grandmother's giant
bloomers were drying in "Lesson" (232); and the stars at the beginning of this last story.

While moments of illumination happen spontaneously in childhood, the adult has frequently to resort to various practices to
bring about such an effect. Uncle Kalman's practice of medita-
tion--reminiscent of the philosophy of Zen-Buddhism[66]--leads him
at the end of "Teller" to a nirvana-like state of bliss, as a
result of the negation of the Self.[67] In "Spirit" the people who
come to a seance at Clarissa Oberlander's house practice meditation as well as spiritualism. The same story introduces the concept of *gilgul* (the kabbalist term for transmigration of souls,
reincarnation, or metempsychosis).[68] The instance of an "out-of-
body experience"[69]--the possibility of the soul leaving its body
for a brief period to travel out of it, before returning to it--
is suggested in "Spirit" in a comic-erotic fashion: Saul Haimjan
reveals that when he had intercourse with a prostitute he felt as
if her soul was outside her body (*News*, 116), and the narrator
himself experiences the same sensation: "I felt that my soul was
outside my body, that I was standing behind my body and seeing
myself from behind" (120). This concept becomes in "Mustache,"
again in a comic-erotic context, the central element of Boulos

Effendi's report of the bizarre intercourse between Gabriel Luria
and the nun. But here another peculiar twist is added: the transmigration of Luria's soul into a body of a dog during the intercourse (News, 204-6).

While never acknowledging the influence of Buddhist philoso-
phies, Shahar does, however, claim an affinity to the Kabbalah,
particularly to those mystical ideas associated with one of the
central figures of the Kabbalah, the "Ari," Isaac Luria Ashkenazi
(1534-1572).[70] Explaining in an interview how he came to realize
his attachment to the Lurianic mysticism, Shahar says:

> We had in our courtyard a cistern which was always inade-
> quate. In a dry year it was empty and therefore evoked
> a feeling of disappointment. In a rainy year it was
> overflowing and flooding the courtyard. There was never
> harmony between the vessel and the abundance. The same
> applied to the light. My eyes in my childhood could not
> contain the strong, dazzling light that was coming down
> harshly on the barren mountains. I would stand on the
> rooftops and my eyes would be dazzled, unable to contain
> the light. When I grew up and read the Kabbalah of the
> "Ari," it was like a revelation to me. Suddenly I dis-
> covered a native Jerusalemite who felt like me and found
> suitable symbols for this feeling. I was very much in-
> fluenced by the Kabbalah of the "Ari" and came to see
> our world as a world of broken vessels that the divine
> abundance had broken.[71]

One way in which Shahar suggests his affinity with the
Lurianic Kabbalah is his choice of Luria as the name of the chief
protagonist of his "Lurianic Novel," the title of which--The Palace
of Broken Vessels[72]--carries clear connotations of the Lurianic
mysticism.[73]

Of all the protagonists introduced in his 1960s childhood
stories, Uncle Kalman is the most persistently mystical. It seems
as though Shahar, in portraying him, had in mind the observation
that the mystic way "involved the ascent of the soul to a state of
ecstatic rapture through a process of concentrated thought and
meditation."[74] There is, however, a discrepancy between Kalman's
way and the way of the Kabbalah. As Scholem sees it: "The practical application of mystical meditation in the Kabbalah is connected mainly, if not exclusively, with the moment of prayer."[75]
This moment is excluded from Kalman's mysticism, prayer being
another instance of institutional religion which Shahar can do
without.

The mystical sensation that Shahar intends to convey throughout his writings involves a sense of union with a transcendental
reality. In "Find," the boy-narrator experiences what might suggest it when looking at Jerusalem through the magic stone. This

stone allows him also another mystical experience: "seeing the
aura" of individuals, in his case that of his Uncles Pinik and
Kalman and of his Aunt Pnina (*Mustache*, 186f.). Seeing the aura,
as Scholem points out, is an aspect of the occult phenomenon in
practical Kabbalah called *gilluy einayim*: "whereby a man might be
granted a vision of something that, generally speaking, only the
rare mystic was permitted to see. Such visions included a glimpse
of the "sapphiric ether" (*ha-avir ha-sappiri*) that surrounds all
men and in which their movements are recorded."[76] The kabbalists
believed that this ethereal garment served as an intermediary between man's material body and his soul. In celestial paradise,
before descending to earth and following their reascent after
physical death, souls clothe themselves with this "garment." Only
a kabbalist's eye could discern it during their sojourn on earth.[77]
The title "Al ha-Tzlalim ve-ha-Tzelem" ("Of Shadows and the
Image"), which Shahar gave to one of his stories, is influenced by
this concept. The *Tzelem* ("Image," on the basis of Gen 1:26) is,
according to this concept, "the principle of individuality with
which every single human being is endowed, the spiritual configu-
ration or essence, that is unique to him and him only."[78] The aura
is the ether of the *Tzelem*.[79] Shahar's title is based on a play on
words the kabbalists used to draw a parallel between man's *Tzelem*
and his *Tzel* ("shadow"), which they considered to be a projection
of the inner *Tzelem*.[80]

The concept of the *gilgul* is central to the teaching of the
Kabbalah, as is, to a lesser degree, the concept of "out-of-body
experience." Talking about a similar phenomenon in the Kabbalah,
Scholem says: "In a number of places prophecy is defined as the
experience wherein a man 'sees the form of his own self standing
before him and relating the future to him.'"[81]

In his attempts to give literary expression to a mystical
experience, Shahar faces a contradiction in terms. Mysticism is
knowledge that cannot be transmitted directly (although it can be
conveyed through symbol and metaphor); and while in theory esoteric knowledge can be communicated, "those who possess it are either
forbidden to pass it on or do not wish to do so."[82] Aware of this
shortcoming, when he describes in "Spirit" a mystical experience
which he terms "attack," Shahar apologizes: "I call it an 'attack'
for lack of any apter word" (*News*, 111). In the Hebrew text of
"Spirit" this sentence is followed by an elaborating remark which
for some reason was omitted in the English translation: "This
'attack' cannot be captured by words and everything which could be

said about it is merely a symbol understandable only to those who
experienced it" (*Mustache*, 25). And yet, Shahar does not refrain
from attempting to recapture such experiences in words, betraying
in so doing a peculiar ambivalence towards his own mysticism, the
outcome of the tension in his narrative between scepticism and
mysticism.

Whenever the narrator describes his own mystical experience
his tone is serious, but when he relates somebody else's, particularly Kalman's, the tone becomes humorous, sardonic.[83] He makes a
farce of the seance in "Spirit" and the mystical intercourse in
"Mustache"; yet when in "Find" he relates his feelings when looking at Jerusalem through the stone, and his oneness with it, the
tone is solemn, obviously seeking to convince the reader of the
authenticity of the experience.

Shahar's indulgence in mysticism has aroused critical reservations. It has been suggested that his affinity to kabbalist
mysticism, the position of the narrator and the characters in the
moments of "illumination," are merely a literary pose,[84] and that
in clinging to old clichés, he falls for a basic misconception
which is that stories about Jerusalem ought to be imbued with an
air of holiness or mysticism.[85] It has also been suggested that
his smugness and insistence on flirting with mysticism curb his
aptitude.[86]

Indeed, one of Shahar's presuppositions is that his characters' involvement with Jerusalem is made clear on a mystic level;
however, this tendency often results in a contrived, or over-
simplified mysticism beneath the veneer of a mannered style. The
element of transmutation is missing. At times, mysticism is
superimposed on the narrative with verbosity where the sensation
defies description and requires silence. The portrayal of Kalman
as the innocent who engages in introspection and meditation to
attain "direct human communication with God through annihilation
of individuality (*bittul ha-yesh*, in ḥasidic terminology),"[87]
aims more at amusing the reader rather than at presenting an in-
spiring paradigm. The author seems to be satisfied with type-
casting Kalman in the comic role of a *schlemiel* who tries to evade
responsibility and remain an eternal juvenile. The narrative
never manages to convince the reader altogether that Kalman's
"mysticism" is anything more than a pretext for leading such a way
of life.

The Comic Effect

Shahar recounts his childhood events as though addressing a
person close to him. In time the memory of these events has become merged with layers of mature knowledge. The distance from
which this knowledge reacts to the actual tale accounts for
the narrative's humor. This ingredient has undergone a distinct
development. Whereas in the childhood stories written in the
1950s the humor is innocent, earthy, and artless, in those written
in the 1960s, in keeping with the development of Shahar's mannered
style, it becomes affected, calculated from the outset to exhibit
wit. The author goes to great lengths to bring out the comic aspect of the characters and the situation, by organizing the events
in combinations that expose the ridiculous in human nature and its
judgment, and by humorous manipulation of word-combinations, puns,
slang, and ethnic dialect.

On several occasions[88] Shahar mentions his admiration for
Shalom Aleichem and Agnon, in whose writings humor is frequently
employed. Often humor functions in his stories as "a life-buoy
in a tragic world."[89] Thus, at the ending of both "Zemach" and
"Little Doctor," humor helps the tragic character overcome the
pain of loss and readjust to life. In the former it is Lippa whom
"every small event reminded...of a joke" (*News*, 66); in the latter
it is the little doctor who overcomes the sorrow of losing his
wife with the help of books by Shalom Aleichem, Mendele Mocher
Sefarim, Mark Twain, Cervantes and Dickens (98).

Uncle Kalman in the role of *Schlemiel* is a figure with whom
the author is clearly intrigued. The *schlemiel*, according to one
possible definition, "inhabits the shadowy margin between the
comedy of errors and a comedy of terrors."[90] Above all, "as a
chronic loser he is indestructible, the kind of man no society can
do without: he'll go on losing forever. And as a figure of fun
he's a threat to no one."[91] Almost every situation in which Uncle
Kalman is involved automatically turns comic. In "Teller," after
running away from his wife he takes refuge in the cellar of Levi
the porter, hiding from the court clerk who tries to deliver the
summons, from the law enforcement officer who tries to serve him
warnings, and from the Jewish policeman who has been ordered to
arrest him and who lives right above this cellar (*News*, 6). After
his release from jail he is described as taking a bath in a big
washtub which was "doing double duty as a bathtub when the occasion arose" (10), scrubbing himself while singing Maurice Cheva-
lier's "Beneath the Roofs of Paris" at the top of his voice; then

emerging, "wrapped in mother's dressing gown," to inquire if there
were sardines in the house, the only meal he had craved during his
twenty-one days in jail (10). The chain of comic events in
"Teller" culminates in Kalman's having to play the role of a fortune teller as a result of his failure to remove the sign from the
little room into which he had moved, and which had previously
accommodated the fly-by-night fortune teller.

In "Find," the stone Uncle Kalman comes upon in the cave
evokes the narrator's linguistic wit. He intends a pun when,
wondering how to name it and after running through a list of biblical precious stones (*Mustache*, 185), he comes up with *soḥeret*
(Esth 1:6), which in Hebrew also means "a trader," or "a dealer"
in the feminine gender, in line with the Hebrew feminine gender of
stones. The latter meaning becomes pertinent at the end of the
story when Kalman tries to negotiate a deal, in which this stone
is the merchandise he has to offer, with another comic character--
Shatz.

Shatz (שץ), whose name is an acronym of *shliaḥ tzibbur* (Hebrew
for leader in prayer, or a community representative), is a Zionist
public figure whose speeches are filled with empty rhetorical
phrases which the boy-narrator has learned by heart and inserted
in his school essays without quite understanding them, and earned
high marks. The situation in which Shatz as a suitor comes to
court Aunt Pnina, the spinster, is intended to be a comic one as
Shahar invests it with his natural instinct for satire. Shatz,
who in his capacity as a Zionist public figure used to wear khaki
shorts and an open shirt, shows up for his rendezvous in a brown
striped suit and a top hat. During his conversation with Pnina he
does not once mention his favorite topic: "The redemption of the
masses and the common weal of the *Yishuv*." Quite the contrary:
the topic is America and it turns out that this Zionist public
figure is contemplating settling in America. In this context, the
name Shatz, which is also an acronym of Shabbetai Tzvi, the false
Messiah (1626-1676), highlights the farcical aspect of Shahar's
fictional character. In addition, the comic effect also draws on
an allusion to the German *Schatz* ("treasure," a pet name). The
falseness of Shatz thus gains a new dimension: he (the "treasure")
courts Pnina (Hebrew for "pearl," "gem"), who, as portrayed in the
story, is far from being a gem, while being blind to the real gem,
the treasure which Kalman offers him: the magic stone.

By turning Shatz into a satirical figure, Shahar illustrates
his criticism of certain aspects of the "Zionist renaissance" and

the condescension of a son of an old Jerusalem family toward such
upstarts. To stretch the satire further, Shatz is associated with
Satan by the use of a biblical phrase. In the Book of Job, when
Satan is asked by God,"Whence comest thou?" Satan answers, "From
going to and fro in the earth" (משוט בארץ ומהתהלך בה, Job 1:7).
This is the phrase the narrator uses to describe Shatz on his way
to Pnina for their Tuesday night date (Mustache, 187). By associating Shatz with Satan on this particular occasion the narrator has a joke in mind; shortly before, he has described how Pnina
decided to meet Shatz on Tuesday, a day which according to Jewish
superstition is protected from Satan (187).[92] The Shatz-Satan
analogy introduces into the negotiation between Uncle Kalman and
Shatz an element of farcical innuendo faintly reminiscent of the
theme of Faust. When Uncle Kalman offers to trade the stone with
Shatz he calls it *yeḥidati* (my *yeḥidah*) (195). The term *yeḥidah*
was used by kabbalists to describe one of the two higher parts of
the soul (the other one being *ḥayyah*), and it was considered to
represent "the sublimest level of intuitive apprehension and to be
within the grasp of only a few chosen individuals."[93] According
to Lurianic Kabbalah, the soul having its source in the *yeḥidah* of
the *Sefirah keter* of the world of *atzilut*[94] was believed to be
that of the Messiah. It is not unlikely that on a subtle level
the narrator is implying that Kalman had noble intentions when he
prepared to entrust this *yeḥidah* to a representative of the Jewish
Agency, the body which, at the time, was in charge of the process
of "the redemption of the Jews." However, carried away by his
satirical bent, all Shahar managed to construct was a burlesque
scene. The introduction of a demonic dimension into this scene
is suggested by the peculiar reaction of the streetlight to the
presence of Shatz. It "lit up, flickered a few seconds; for a
moment it seemed to overcome an obscure obstacle, but suddenly it
went out" (190). This reaction of the streetlight in "Find"
brings to mind the lamppost in Aloni's "Soldier," in which, as the
boy-narrator believes, Death is located. In Aloni the allusion is
to the angel of death, who is synonymous with Satan-Samael. However, one can find little resemblance between Aloni's Satan, the
habitué of the local café, and Shatz, in the role of Satan, as an
habitué of ḥakham[95] Shvilli's café. While the café in both stories is where soldiers meet Jewish girls, Shvilli's café, unlike
the café in Aloni's stories, holds no erotic mystery for the narrator;[96] instead, it stimulates his sense of the comic. The pa-
trons of Shvilli's establishment, a kosher café-restaurant, are

not religious Jews but English soldiers and their prostitutes.
Shvilli, a religious Jew, makes his wife sew a hat on the head of
Herzl which is woven in the tapestry hanging on the wall of his
café. Giving his rationale, he says: "How is it possible that he
[Herzl] has a beard but is bareheaded like a priest or a Christian
monk?" (*Mustache*, 192).

Focusing on the funny aspects in the character and situation,
Shahar aims at an immediate effect. In Uncle Kalman's case, that
means paying almost no attention to the other facets of his personality, his tragic side. Had Shahar done this he might have
created what E. M. Forster defines as a "round character."[97]
Instead, when the story ends the reader is left untouched; Uncle
Kalman's situation may be desperate but not serious.

In the case of Gabriel Luria, another character in which the
comic is a major component, Shahar introduces an antithesis to
Uncle Kalman. Luria is a complex figure whose contrasts and contradictions are fully developed only later, in the "Lurianic
Novel." In "Mustache," however, where the emphasis is on his
"lordly" side, it is mostly in order to stress the dramatic change
that takes place in him after the "nun episode." The comic effect
is linked to the fantastic report of this episode by Boulos
Effendi and to the zany version of the Arab restaurant-owner.
But this relates to another aspect of Shahar, the erotic.

Art and Eros, Eros and Art

It is consistent with the unpretentious nature of Shahar's
writing in his early stories that the rendering of the erotic in
them is simple, innocent, and unaffected. Some of the stories of
the 1950s contain potential for explicit erotic description--the
character of Nicole,[98] the doctor's wife in "Little Doctor," for
example, and the impulses of Zemach in the story of that name--but
Shahar refrained from developing this potential. At that time his
purpose was to make the boy's innocence and not the adult's cynicism the prevailing factor in the narrator's viewpoint.

In "Image," the erotic elements, implicitly Oedipal, are rendered in carefully restrained language. What Ephraim does not
dare confront in reality emerges in his two Freudian dreams, both
of which expose the strong association in his mind of Art and Eros.
In the first dream (*Dreams*, 33), he sees himself painting his
father, who is standing on the wall of the Old City with his
tefillin and *tallit*. Suddenly his father climbs down from the
wall, tears the painting, curses him and accuses him of fornicating

with a married woman. Just then Varda (a married painter who has
befriended the boy) appears and picks up the torn painting.
Ephraim's father begins hitting her, but it turns out that she is
not Varda but Ephraim's mother, who Ephraim's father calls adul-
teress. In the other dream, which Ephraim has the night after his
mother's death, he sees himself going out to the fields to paint
with Varda. Suddenly she removes her blouse and says to him,
"Come sleep with me" (*Dreams*, 38). When he begins to undress her
he wakes up and the first thought that crosses his mind is that
his mother is dead.

     For the dreamer, in both dreams Eros and Art--"forbidden
fruit"--are associated on the one hand with sin, and on the other
with the rebellion against the religious dogma of the old *Yishuv*,
as symbolized by the wall of the Old City on which the father
stands. In destroying the painting the father is paralleled to
the grandmother of "Lesson," who in her attempt to stop the boy
from painting is regarded by the narrator as an agent of the
tyranny of obscurantist theology. [99]   In the second dream, Eros
and Art are associated with another element which is again regarded as a sin, by the standards of ultra-Orthodoxy, the pastoral:
the fields where the dream takes place.

     Erotically, Ephraim's dreams are less graphic and more re-
strained than the Oedipal dreams of the boy-narrator in Aloni's
"Shmeel"; but this restraint does not carry over to the fiction
Shahar published in the 1960s. As his confidence and his desire
to demonstrate authority grew, so did his tendency to explore more
explicitly the erotic-pornographic dimension. The novella "Caesar"
contains a monologue of an Arab jailed in a Jerusalem prison, who
fantasizes with explicit details a week-long sexual orgy with two
Jewish women. But at that point in Shahar's writing sex was not
yet linked with mysticism. The latter element did not begin to
assume significance until "Teller." In "Spirit" the erotic is
already closely linked with the mystical. This process culminated
in a story published four years later, "Mustache," in which an
interplay of the elements of mysticism and Eros was devised to
produce an amusing, grotesque tale.

     The link between Eros and a monastery--so vivid in the men-
tality of the boy-narrator in Aloni's stories--is enlivened in the
narrator of "Mustache" as he describes a womanizer Gabriel Luria
sitting on the balcony, deriving "the utmost possible pleasure
from the sight of the convent and its nuns" (*News*, 194), whom he
watches with "a gloating smile of lascivious satisfaction" (192).

The fact that Luria's curiosity about nuns is that of a voyeur
rather than of an innocent spectator becomes even more evident as
the story unfolds. A behavior that the Shahar protagonist cannot
allow himself with regard to religious Jewish women--who lack any
appeal for him--he allows himself with regard to a religious
Christian woman. The young nun, sensing the phallocratic male in
him, confronts him: "Do you know, Mr. Luria, there are two kinds
of women who are accustomed to being asked, 'what made you choose
this path?'--nuns and prostitutes" (199). In Boulos' humorous
narrative the nun represents a blend of two of the three proto-
types of women in Shahar's stories: the "madonna" and the "prostitute" (the third prototype being the "terrible mother" as embodied
in the grandmother).

The image of the prostitute in Shahar's tales has undergone a
change consistent with the development of his mystical approach.
If in "Find" the prostitute Malka is no more than a stupid, ugly
girl (*Mustache*, 182), and Agnes of "Spirit" is spiritually pro-
moted by describing the intercourse with her as instrumental in
separating the soul from the body, Mary Anne the nun, in "Mustache,"
is at the center of a most transcendental coition. Because of her,
Luria's body "split open" and his "naked soul" is left "quivering
in eternity, which is like a ring of radiance" (*News*, 204). But
here the grotesque begins. When Luria's soul "took fright at the
supreme radiance," it "went hither and thither seeking shelter in
the material world" before reaching the nun's dress, "which was
waving from the summit of the cypress and hid inside it" (204).
Luria's empty body is invaded by the soul of the dog Latif who begins making "vigorous use" of it, "penetrating the body of the nun
to great depths," while Luria's eyes that were "peeping out of the
folds of the nun's habit looked and longed" (205). Gabriel cannot
return to his body as long as it is held captive by the dog; his
suffering "multiplied exceedingly" and he is in an urgent need for
help. As for what happens next, opinions are divided. While
Boulos, the Christian Arab who was born in Bethlehem, maintains
that "Our Lord Jesus of Nazareth saw the suffering and distress of
this soul and in his infinite mercy and his great love, he came to
save it" (205), the Moslem restaurant-owner claims that Luria's
savior is no one but "Our Lord Mohammed the Apostle of Allah," who
in his "bounteous mercy" remembered that Luria was named after the
angel Gabriel, who appeared to Mohammed "when he was living as a
recluse in the city of Mecca and its environs, and called him
"Apostle of Allah'" (208).

Technically, the story suffers from a sudden switch in the narrator's viewpoint, shifting from the limited perspective of a boy to that of an omniscient adult-narrator. The boy-narrator, who gives his account as an eyewitness in the first half of the story, goes out of the picture the moment the nun enters it. From that moment on the author prefers to entrust the narrative to an adult narrator, as he cannot find a way of having the "mystical" intercourse related directly by a young boy. This shortcoming deprives the boy-narrator of an initiatory experience, to which he is introduced four years later in "Spirit," at the age of fourteen, when Haimjan tells him about his intercourse with Agnes the prostitute, a tale which made such an impact on the erotic growth of the narrator that he reminisces about it as a significant episode of his childhood.

It is noteworthy that Shahar links initiatory moments of the revelation of erotic and mystical secrets with sexual symbols, such as the cistern near which the two boys stand "looking together into its mouth" (*News*, 116), when Haimjan tells him about his experience with the prostitute, and the cave where Uncle Kalman takes the boy to introduce him to the world of mysticism through the stone found there. Cisterns and caves were not uncommon in Jerusalem at the period described. Although the cistern as a place associated with prostitutes and connected with the boy-narrator's state of awakening sexuality appears also in Aloni's "Shmeel," on the whole, in comparison with Aloni's childhood stories, Shahar's contain considerably fewer symbols of this kind.

The Manifold Raconteur

While Shahar's narrator struggles with his childhood environment, the author struggles with two forces inside himself; he is torn between the burden of childhood memories and the wish to give them artistic expression and expose their meaning.[100] By and large, Shahar manages better with the shorter stories, which impose a stricter management of memories, forgoing irrelevant materials. And yet, each of his short stories bears witness to the tension between the narrator and the element of reminiscence, the writing self and the remembered self, the present and the past.

In "Mustache," for instance, this unresolved tension results in a loose structure, with each part of the story striving to become autonomous. The element of reminiscence dominates the first part as the narrator attempts to recapture an earlier era and its heady ambience. As a memoir it conveys a private chronicle by a

first-person narrator, whose presence is vigorously felt, although,
as in the majority of Shahar's stories, he is just an eyewitness.
In the second part, an unidentified omniscient narrator--an adult
by his tone and perceptions--takes over, and although he does not
establish himself as an eyewitness he quotes at great length the
words of Boulos Effendi and the Arab restaurant-owner. The previous realistic and spontaneous narrative is replaced by a surrealis-
tic, improbable and well-mannered mystical-erotic parody. Feigning
folksiness, this omniscient narrator, through Boulos and the restaurant-owner, rhapsodizes and editorializes in a labored manner
that underestimates his readers. This narrator serves as a foil
when juxtaposed with the narrator of the first part of the story,
thus turning the latter into a dramatic persona whose own character, despite remaining a bystander throughout, becomes vital to
the story. His naïveté, his incomprehension, his susceptibility
to childish fascination, emerge when he observes the old nun
greedily drinking tamar hindi. He tells the reader:

> Strange, conflicting feelings rose within me at the sight
> of the eagerness with which she drank. She fell in my
> estimation to the level of common humanity, if not lower.
> For what could be forgiven ordinary flesh and blood
> could not be forgiven an exalted being, and it was as
> exalted beings that I saw them, these nuns. (*News*, 190)

In contrast to this voice of a marvelling boy who admits:
"the convent in all its aspects had cast a spell of enchantment on
me" (192), the story, in its first part, also brings the narrating
voice of an experienced and cynical adult. This narrator, who
skilfully delineates the idiosyncrasies of the two Moslem maids
and the nuances of the business neogtiations of Gabriel Luria and
Boulos Effendi, is also responsible for the observation that when
the former watches the nuns he has "a gloating smile of lascivious
satisfaction" (192).

The narrator is mentioned by name as David in "Lesson," "Mustache" and "Spirit." The fact that his name is identical with the
author's suggests a wish to introduce genuine autobiographical
tonality. To follow Booth, a narrator is "*reliable* when he speaks
for or acts in accordance with the norms of the work (which is to
say, the implied author's norms), *unreliable* when he does not."[101]
In other words, the reliability of the narrator depends on the
author's approval of the persona which he has created. In applying this theory to "Mustache," one is aware that in the first part
of the story the author approves of the boy-narrator, whose reliability even gains weight from the fact that the author excludes

him from the second part, when the tale turns fantastic. The author thus indicates the line of demarcation between fact and
fancy, and the reader is advised that, once that line has been
crossed he ought to be dubious about the information the story
provides: from now on he is no longer travelling with a reliable
source.

The author's wish to make the boy-narrator likeable and engaging is felt throughout other stories as well. Occasionally,
he directs the reader's attention to the boy's moral qualities.
In "Zemach," when the boy catches his uncle lying, he is shocked:
"All my respect for Zemach vanished in an instant. His childish-
ness I forgave him, but not his lie" (*News*, 27). And in "Lesson,"
the only story in which the boy plays an active part, he is portrayed in his conflict with his grandmother as one who is ready to
fight for his integrity and his right to express himself.

Employing the device of a boy-narrator as an innocent eyewitness, ostensibly helps the stories to achieve narrative objec-
tivity based on the fallacy that a young boy would not invent such
reports, and therefore their accuracy must be beyond doubt.[102]
The boy-narrator's function is to illuminate the hero from the
standpoint of a child, thus enabling the author to express his
sympathy for his hero without running the risk of sentimentality.
In this manner the distance between the adult "implied author" and
the "boy-narrator" decreases, and the reader's empathy with the
latter increases. Whenever the boy-narrator appears in Shahar's
stories it is supposed that he is the young persona of the author,
which explains the ease with which Shahar switches from the young
to the mature narrator (the persona of the mature author) within
the same narrative.

The intrusions of the omniscient adult-narrator are often
calculated to introduce ironic effects; they indicate a gap between the naïve account of the boy-narrator and the concealed
meaning of his narrative, of which he may not be aware. These
instrusions and digressions, which often slow down the narrative,
are a manifestation of the loose structure and the circular pattern of many of Shahar's works. His average story begins at a
certain point of time, goes back in time, as the plot, through a
transposed exposition, unfolds in a constant associative movement
back and forth, moving through the stages of conflict, climax,
dénouement, and coming full circle.[103]

The calm, leisurely style of Shahar as a raconteur differs
vastly from the restless, nervous style of Aloni, whose limited-

perspective narrator is not equipped with an adult's hindsight,
but is hermetically sealed in the time capsule of childhood.
Another basic difference between the two concerns the rhetoric of
their fiction: while Aloni refrains from explaining, Shahar has
difficulty in suppressing his predilection for overstatement and
overinterpretation. In his approach he seems to have little regard for an important principle in the art of storytelling, widely
acknowledged, and summarized succinctly by Walter Benjamin.

> Actually, it is half the art of storytelling to keep a
> story free from explanation as one reproduces it....The
> most extraordinary things, marvellous things, are related
> with the greatest accuracy, but the psychological connec-
> tion of the events is not forced on the reader. It is
> left up to him to interpret things the way he understands
> them, and thus the narrative achieves an amplitude that
> information lacks.[104]

The unique resonance of Shahar's language originates in his
intense sensitivity "to the soft cadence peculiar to the speech of
those who were born in this country and started speaking Hebrew in
the days of the Turk."[105] It is a deep-rooted, intimate Hebrew,
spoken approximately in the 1930s and 1940s by sons of veteran
Jerusalem Ashkenazi families, well-versed in the old layers of the
language as well as the latest colloquialisms.[106] It is rich with
old idioms, and at the same time close to the emerging vernacular.
The aroma of words counts very much with Shahar, who uses his
lingual acumen to capture the ethnic, educational, or occupational
background of his characters, as well as to finding Hebrew equiva-
lents for the linguistic idiosyncrasies of those of his characters
who speak Yiddish, Arabic, or English.

A repressed aspiration to become a painter may shed light on
the visual quality of Shahar's fiction. The childhood experiences
which left the deepest impression on him were those connected with
painting;[107] they were recorded in "Image," "Zemach" and "Lesson."
In the latter story he relates that when he saw paintings by
Toulouse-Lautrec he was "pierced by an intense, throbbing joy, as
if encountering fragments of memories from a previous incarnation"
(*News*, 226). And in "Image" the boy-protagonist declares: "If I
were painting Jerusalem, I would use oil-colors and not watercolors"
(*Dreams*, 28). In fact, in his stories, particularly in passages
aimed at reproducing local atmosphere, Shahar is fond of exhibiting
in equipotent verbal expressions his penchant for strong colors,
every detail of the composition contributing to a unity of color
and design.

The medium, however, is secondary to the message; mysticism
infuses his writing with a sense of mission. Asked why he writes,
he resorts to kabbalistic terminology: writing helps him return to
the "abundance and the vessels which cannot contain it, to the
broken vessels." To elaborate further, he adds: "I want to gather
the broken vessels to make a reconstruction. To restore in my way
the broken vessels."[108] His statement alludes to the concept of
tikkun (restoration), and its central place in the kabbalistic
doctrine. It implies both the restoration of the original world
harmony and the ultimate redemption heralded by the coming of the
Messiah. It was Adam's sin that broke off the communion, which
was the goal of creation, between God and man, and it is the
tikkun's goal to bring about "the reunification of the divine and
the human wills," so that creation will be "restored to its former
grandeur."[109]

It might be argued that in declaring that his writing aims at
attaining something tantamount to a *tikkun*, Shahar exhibits a pre-
tentiousness and self-aggrandizement which could cause his readers
to react to him with some unease. But such declarations, in line
with his mystical thinking, can also be viewed as subconsciously
counter-balancing the incipient sense of sin or guilt associated
for him with engaging in writing, or in any other form of art.
For a man who grew up in Mea Shearim, to become an artist meant
not only being at odds with ultra-Orthodox dogma (as described in
"Image" and "Lesson"), but also defying the conventions of pragmatic upbringing. The latter seemed to disturb him most, as he ad-
mitted while speaking about his attraction to artistic pursuits,
such as painting and writing.

> These occupations seemed impractical and unproductive to
> me. I tried to steer clear of them also out of a sense
> of self-preservation. I was afraid that by immersing
> myself too much in introspection I would become a
> *schlemiel*. So I tried to find myself in the world of
> action.[110]

Having the same misgivings, Uncle Zemach, the prospective
painter, resolved to repress his artistic inclinations and to study
law; Shahar, his creator, went to study psychology. However, just
like Uncle Lippa, when he had finished his academic studies, Shahar
realized that he could not escape his calling, even if it meant
submitting to the stigma of *schlemiel*. In this respect, the portrait of Uncle Kalman, a comical alter ego, is a projection of the
conflict within the author between the anxiety of becoming a
schlemiel, and fascination with the nonconformity of the misfit.

The adoption of the kabbalistic idea of the *tikkun* as a justification for an artistic pursuit furnishes a sort of alibi: if he is a
schlemiel, he is one for a noble cause.

   This line of thought became rooted in Shahar's *ars poetica* in
the 1960s. Prior to that, in the 1950s, before mysticism was integrated into his writing, the crisis of the artist's self-
fulfillment was embodied in the dichotomy of the two brothers
Lippa and Zemach. These two, and the other "uncles," personify
various aspects of the mentor from whom the boy, the artist-as-a-
young-man, draws the courage not to succumb to conventional no-
tions that might obstruct his self-fulfillment when facing the
responsibility of accepting himself as an artist. The subsequent
application of mystical concepts to define artistic individuation,
and the use of mysticism as a catalytic vehicle represent a more
sophisticated stage in Shahar's development. But this stage is
not without its hazards. Shahar's move over the years from the
simple, spontaneous expression of childhood visions towards a
mannered, Proustian realm of sensibility is centrifugal, leaving
him no option but that of travelling off and away from that innocent and primary source of his creative impulse, in his endless
pursuit of things past in Jerusalem.

CHAPTER IV

THE TRAGIC AND THE TRIVIAL: AMALIA KAHANA-CARMON

Amalia Kahana-Carmon was born in 1926 in the kibbutz Ein Harod,[1] a fact that seems to have had little bearing on her writing; the kibbutz is not mentioned in her stories. Furthermore, unlike Yizhar, Aloni and Shahar, her childhood stories contain no overt chronological elements which might be interpreted as autobiographical. Not only in her fiction but also in her essays, interviews and similar sources, she does not divulge any information about her formative years apart from the fact that she graduated from the Gymnasia Herzlia, a Tel Aviv institution, the first Hebrew secondary school in Palestine. Her first published story, "Be'er Sheva Birat ha-Negev" ("Beer Sheba the Capital of the Negev"),[2] drew on her experience as a radio operator in the military unit that conquered this city in 1948. But in her subsequent works she tended to skirt the theme of the 1948 war, the major theme of the "Dor ba-Aretz" writers in the first decade of the State. The fact that she entered the literary scene a decade after her coevals accounts in great measure for her being out of step with their writing in her style and themes.[3] For this reason she is frequently regarded in the context of the second generation Sabra writers such as A. B. Yehoshua (b. 1936) and Amos Oz (b. 1939), whose early publications coincided with hers.

Her first book was a volume of previously published short stories, Bi-Kfifah Ahat (Under One Roof).[4] It was followed by the novel Ve-Yareah be-Emek Ayyalon (And Moon in the Valley of Ajalon).[5] Her third book, Sadot Magnetim (Magnetic Fields),[6] consists of two stories and a short novel, hence the subtitle which describes it as a "triptych."

All of her stories, including those narrated by a man, express the standpoint of a woman;[7] the central characters in her fiction are women, perhaps one woman in different stages of development. Each one of these heroines responds to an incessant urge to seek the father image in the (always) older man to whom she is attracted. Her tragedy originates from the fact that this man, the "father-lover," remains forever unattainable; their "affair" cannot be brought to fruition.

121

The childhood stories under discussion are "N'ima Sassoon
Kotevet Shirim" ("N'ima Sassoon Writes Poems"),[8] "Lev ha-Kayitz,
Lev ha-Or" ("Heart of Summer, Heart of Light"),[9] and "Hinumah"
("Bridal Veil").[10] Their setting is the period in which they were
actually written, the 1960s. Unlike Yizhar's, Aloni's and Shahar's,
their locale, as well as their social milieu, vary from story to
story, as do the cast of characters, their cultural background and
the duration of the plot. The narrative comprises either one central episode, focal to the life of the protagonist, or a series of
vignettes that expose a certain development in the protagonist's
life; and it is pictorial rather than dramatic. "N'ima" is an
account of a sensitive Sephardi girl with a touch of a poet, in
her last year of a Jerusalem religious primary school for girls,
and her infatuation with her teacher Ezekiel. "Heart" is the
story of Ronen Sokolow, a Tel Aviv Ashkenazi boy, who records the
sad family life of his parents, and the infatuation of his mother,
Hulda, with Baruchin, a pediatrician who treats his younger
brother. "Bridal Veil" deals with the infatuation of Shoshana, a
teenage girl from a semi-rural and underprivileged immigrants'
settlement with a Canadian UN soldier whom she meets on an evening
bus while returning home from a trip to the town where her father
works.

Basically, the visions of childhood that interest Kahana-
Carmon are not those involving children among themselves, as much
as children in relation to adults. But, while her precocious
child-protagonists do not interact with their peers, they are
nevertheless unable to distance themselves from the context of
childhood. These stories are about a developing awareness. In
each one of them a discovery is being made which is brought about
by a recurrent pattern: the encounter.

The Pattern of the Encounter

Synchronicity, as formulated by Jung,[11] is a term used to
describe a "meaningful coincidence" of "outer and inner events
that are not themselves causally connected." The emphasis is on
"meaningful," for this coincidence generally happens because "certain types of event 'like' to cluster together at certain times."
In Kahana-Carmon's stories the mechanism of the encounter is set
in motion when the characters are acting out, in their minds or in
reality, an attempt to break away from crippling circumstances.
The encounter is always with a man who, in the heroine's fantasies,
assumes unreal dimensions and who, again as perceived in her

fantasies, could help rescue her from drowning in ennui. At the
moment of observation and through the rich emotions of the female
observer, this man, who is essentially a grey character, is endowed with "magical" powers.[12] In "N'ima" he is teacher Ezekiel;
in "Heart," Doctor Baruchin; and in "Bridal Veil," a UN soldier.

    The third story introduces the formula boy-meets-girl most
effectively. The meeting may be just coincidental but it would
not have made such an impact had it not been a "meaningful coincidence." Whatever strength they may have had initially, when N'ima,
Shoshana and Hulda stumble into the "magnetic field" of a man,
they become utterly dependent on him. In that respect there is no
difference between the two thirteen-year-olds, N'ima and Shoshana,
and Hulda--the woman in her thirties. Their weakness leads no
where, their assertiveness guarantees no success.

    The encounter can be a "one night stand" ("Bridal Veil"), or
longer ("N'ima" and "Heart"). In her confessional story, N'ima
does not reveal when exactly her obsession with teacher Ezekiel
began. When her account starts to unfold, her infatuation has
reached its zenith. During midmorning break at school when her
classmates leave, she alone remains in class because he is there.
She intentionally takes the wrong bus home because it is his bus,
or goes by his house to catch a glimpse of him. When he avoids
her attempts at verbal communication, she tries the ploy of wearing dresses that she hopes will attract him. But all in vain.
On the bus he ignores her; when she takes the seat near him he
stands up; when she gets off at his stop, he remains on the bus.
That her monomania is erotic rather than platonic is never proven;
at any rate it is lacking in the elements of warmth and sensual-
ity.[13] The encapsulation of a piece of madness within an otherwise sane--though fragile--personality,is the source of her behavior. She confesses that she was "sick all year. With a kind
of blind determination I have brought on myself, let us say, a
certain type of cold. A cold with a high fever. And I don't want
to be cured" ("N'ima," 228).[14] The tone of her story, which is an
account of the dizzy escalation of this "illness," and her way of
relating it, attest to her feverishness. She keeps approaching
the teacher to involve him in intimate conversation, but he keeps
avoiding her. As a last resort, she gives him her poems about him.
His reaction: "Your poems. I started to read them. I must have
read about two pages and then I fell asleep" (242). The shock is
not sufficient to open her eyes. When she desperately corners him
and he can no longer avoid the issue, he blurts out: "You keep

pressing me to tell you something. You must see that I can't"
("N'ima," 246). A few lines later he elaborates:

> Today, it's school. Tomorrow, life. Listen, and bear
> this in mind. Limits are set. We are not living in
> the days when there was no King in Israel, and every man
> did that which was right in his own eyes.

As one follows the course of N'ima's obsession, the ending is
never quite unpredictable. Reading Ronen's story, on the other
hand, one can never be categorically sure about the possible consequences of Hulda's romantic involvement with Baruchin. Although
they are both married, he is not as unattainable to her as is the
adult Ezekiel to the minor N'ima. Dispirited Hulda, unhappily
married and leading a withdrawn life, experiences a sudden awakening the moment Baruchin enters her life. For her astonished son,
the inexorable eyewitness, a Pandora's box of discoveries is
opened. Eavesdropping on her telephone conversation with Baruchin,
he hears her laughing--she who seldom laughs--and "it sounded won-
derful over the phone." On the face of it there is nothing special
about this conversation--his mother is making an appointment for
the doctor to see her sick child. But the intuitive boy perceives
the real meaning of the emotional change in his mother even before
she herself is aware of it. Something vital and essential, dormant
in her and untouched by his father, is awakened, threatening the
fragile status quo of his family. Henceforward, the son cannot
stop spying on his mother to find out if his fears are justified.
He follows her in the street and observes a random encounter between her and the doctor; he watches her reacting to the doctor in
the doctor's clinic and at the party she gives at home, all the
while tormented by unspoken anxieties: will she find the strength
to resist the doctor, overcome *her* attraction to him? Or will she
succumb to the urge to deliver herself to him? Hulda's vulnerability is emphasized time and time again. When she meets Baruchin
in the street by chance she informs him that she is on her way to
see him. He wants to know why and they embark on an allusive dialogue, centered on two of the meanings of the Hebrew word *ishur*
(אישור): "certificate" and "assurance" ("Heart," 592).[15] The doctor realizes that while she uses the former meaning as a pretext
(a medical certificate for her sick child), she really means the
latter. She seeks an assurance of his interest in *her*. Later, at
the party, she and Baruchin find themselves briefly tête-à-tête on
the balcony,[16] unaware of Ronen who hides under the table. Baruchin
utters a polite remark about the apartment and Hulda asks him play-
fully whether he wants to buy it. His reply: "Are you included in

the sale? I'll buy with both hands" ("Heart," 603). Hulda does
not answer but stands "twirling ceaselessly her ring, her thin
wedding ring," signalling that she cannot discard her marital
commitments. When Baruchin inquires whether she wants to see
him again, she tells him: "I don't know anymore what I want and
what I don't want." Neither does the boy, for that matter, nor
the reader. The ambiguity remains when the story ends. The boy's
ambivalence mirrors his mother's impasse: he wants her to be happy,
but her happiness means the destruction of the family unit. For a
while it seems as though Hulda has made up her mind to stay with
her husband--she offers to work in his shop. Taking place soon
after the balcony scene, her move may indicate that the wedding
ring, the silent participant in that scene, wins. This impression,
however, fades as the reader observes that when she tells her husband that she wants to help him, she utters it in a "choked voice,"
and while "turning her face to the wall" (605), her suppressed re-
sentment and lack of enthusiasm thus revealed.

By contrast, Shoshana does experience a relatively more ful-
filling liaison, perhaps because her escapade is made possible on
a temporary basis only--a chance encounter of two strangers meeting on a journey. As she is sexually ripe to explore the path of
eroticism, the timing is right for the principle of synchronicity
to catapult her into this path. The encounter mechanism is acti-
vated the moment her father puts her on the bus, freeing her to
enter the magnetic field of the UN soldier. Unlike its manifestation in Aloni's stories, the romantic image of the soldier here is
devoid of glorification. It is marked instead by a sentimental
yearning for a foreigner perceived as Prince Charming. In the
girl's imagination he looks like a film star from the moment she
first lays eyes on him, triggering a chain reaction of admiration,
a desire to succumb to him, and a hope of being rescued through
his intervention--an archetypal situation common in fairy tales.

The discernible presence of a fairy tale's motif is apparent
not only in this story; it is constantly at work in the background
of each of Kahana-Carmon's other stories. This will be illustrated
next.

The Fairy Tale Motif

Examining the meaning and importance of fairy tales in his
book *The Uses of Enchantment*, Bruno Bettelheim offers his explanation of why the literature of fairy tales, with its special
genius for speaking directly to children, has fed the child's

imagination and stimulated his fantasizing through most of man's
history. Fairy tales answer the child's most important questions
although they do not pretend to describe the world as it is, nor
prescribe what one ought to do. They are not concerned with im-
parting useful information about the external world, but with the
inner processes of an individual: In a fairy tale internal processes are externalized. They make sense as represented by the
figures of the story and its events. The significance of fairy
tales for a child lies in the fact that they are most meaningful
to him at the age when his major problem is "to bring some order
into the inner chaos of his mind so that he can understand himself better--a necessary preliminary for achieving some congruence
between his perceptions and the external world."[17] The fantasy
materials which the fairy tale offers to the child suggest in
symbolic form what the struggle to achieve self-realization is
all about; they also guarantee a happy ending. The child
perceives that while these tales may be *unreal*, they are not
untrue, and that while what they describe does not happen in
fact, it must happen as inner experience and personal development. Trusting the truth of the tales gives the child solace,
and enables him to work out unconscious pressures. From the
standpoint of initiation, the fairy tale, like myth, is highly
significant because it gives symbolic expression to initiation
rites or other *rites de passage*--such as a metaphoric death of
an old, inadequate self so that one can be reborn on a higher
plane of consciousness.

A A fairy tale motif conspicuous in Kahana-Carmon's stories is

The inner world of the Kahana-Carmon heroine is fed by elements subterraneanly drawn from fairy tales. In a paradoxical
manner, the author is assisted by these elements in sustaining two
conflicting tendencies which coexist at the core of these stories:
the tendency to escape to a world of fantasy, that is, to remain a
child forever; and the tendency to undergo a symbolic initiation
rite, that is, to leave childhood behind and achieve maturity.

A fairy tale motif conspicuous in Kahana-Carmon's stories is
that of "Sleeping Beauty." Unlike many fairy tales which stress
great deeds that the heroes must perform in order to attain self-
realization, this one stresses the long quiet concentration on
oneself which is needed as well. The process of "turning inward,
which...looks like passivity (or sleeping one's life away)" takes
place "when internal mental processes" leave a person in a position in which "he has no energy for outwardly directed action."[18]

The long sleep can symbolize a withdrawal which is a "natural reaction to the threat of having to grow up."[19] However, while the narcissistic withdrawal is a tempting reaction to the stresses of adolescence, this fairy tale warns that such a withdrawal leads to "a dangerous, death-like existence when it is embraced as an escape from the vagaries of life. The entire world then becomes dead to the person."[20] The function of the Prince's kiss is breaking the spell and awakening "a womanhood which up to then has remained undeveloped," because "only if the maiden grows into woman can life go on."[21]

"Heart" is the story of a "maiden" (although she is the mother of two) who sleeps her life away. The story suggests that she is awakened by a potential lover, but it does not answer the question: does she or does she not want the spell broken? The fact that she remains unkissed by the "Prince" indicates that their meeting is not harmonious, that their "affair" cannot be "consummated," and that her womanhood remains dormant. Much the same can be said about N'ima and her "Prince"--teacher Ezekiel.

As for the theme of sleep itself, it is brought up several times throughout Ronen's account of his mother's withdrawal. When she takes a nap "she locks herself in the bedroom [in the Hebrew ḥadar shena (חדר-שנה) "sleeping room"] for long hours. All sounds stop at her door. Sometimes she does not go out for a whole week" ("Heart," 577). Her mother-in-law complains in her flawed Hebrew: "All day long she is locked in bedroom. All day long she sleeps in bed" (581). She alone uses the bedroom. Her snoring husband sleeps on the sofa in another room. There is an echo of Snow White's sleep in the beds of the dwarfs, or of Goldilocks' sleep in the bed of Baby Bear, when Ronen describes her going to sleep in one of her children's beds, after being disturbed by her husband's snoring: "I remember clearly how she used to squeeze herself in the bed which was smaller than her size" (578). In relating this memory, the subtle irony, of which the child-narrator may not be aware, lies in portraying his father--the man who cannot (symbolically) "wake her up"--also as the man who does not let her fall asleep. Only Baruchin can wake her up. At her party, when Baruchin takes out his cigarette case, Ḥulda "rose like a sleepwalker, hovering towards him" (598), to light his cigarette. Trying not to bump into her guests, she trips over the rug, and if Baruchin had not hurried to catch her, she would have fallen down "like a rag doll."

128   Israeli Childhood Stories

The Sleeping Beauty motif is fundamental in "Bridal Veil" too.
For the unsophisticated Shoshana, the UN soldier has an aura of a
glamorous, foreign world. He is larger than life. She can picture
him only in a romanticized and idealized version. She sees herself
going to visit him in his barracks where, as befitting fairy tales
in which prince and horse go together, he will be grooming his
horse, and upon seeing her will take her in his arms and make her
"the regiment's girl" ("Bridal Veil," 25).

The Sleeping Beauty motif is given a peculiar twist in "N'ima."
Here the role of Sleeping Beauty is played not by a female but by
a male, teacher Ezekiel; or rather it becomes commingled with the
themes of Prince Frog,[22] and Beauty and the Beast.[23] The two
themes are often identical: a handsome prince has been enchanted
by a witch and turned into a frog or a beast. The spell is or-
dained to last until a beautiful girl should love Beast for his
goodness, or kiss Frog. Throughout her story, N'ima seems to feel
that teacher Ezekiel is under a spell and that it is up to her to
rescue him. At home he is trapped with an older wife, sarcasti-
cally described as wearing a locket with a photograph set in it,
which could be teacher Ezekiel's photo, or that of her pet dog
("N'ima," 230). Was she the witch who cast the spell over him?[24]
At school the headmistress humiliates him; he sits at his desk all
day "and never raises his eyes from his worksheets, his books, and
his registers" (227). But she, N'ima, detects the Prince in him,
"the most handsomely dressed young man of his day...a ballet
prince" (228). An allusion to the Prince Frog motif is implied in
describing him squatting to slip "a wedge of folded wastepaper
under one of the legs of the desk, to stop it wobbling" (234); in
the Hebrew text his squat is termed yeshivat tzfardea (ישיבת צפרדע)
"a frog-like squat." When N'ima watches him, "that which I have
discovered in him flashes out and pierces me afresh" (234); what
she discovered in him is the Prince within the Frog.

The theme of people under a spell is recurrent in N'ima's
story. Teacher Ezekiel is "moving with the conviction of a sleepwalker" (233). When N'ima approaches him at the bus stop she feels
"possessed" (237), and as they stand talking she wonders what the
"spell" cast over them is (238). She cannot help feeling that
both of them are governed by mysterious powers as though they were
marionettes on strings. In his discussion of archetypal patterns
in literature, Arthur Koestler describes the pattern of Puppet on
Strings, or Volition against Fate, as "one of the most powerful
archetypes, which appears in countless variations in the history

of literature."[25]   Reading Kahana-Carmon's three childhood stories,
one comes across this pattern in all of them. Observing the
strange pas de deux of herself and teacher Ezekiel, N'ima ponders:

> What are the strings that keep tugging at us. He walked.
> I hurried towards him. He walked. Stopped. Walked.
> I did not stir. Hurried toward him. He stopped. He
> walked again. I stood still. He walked, then spun round
> again. Started coming back. What is the flute we dance
> to? (247f.)

Aware though she is of being manipulated by this mysterious
flute, she cannot make sense of it, nor know what its purpose is.
The sense of mystery lingers with her even as the story draws to
its end. "The spirit strives to follow, comprehend, the melody"
(249) she admits, while knowing at the same time that this melody
is not to be comprehended, and that "the spirit can only yearn."

In "Heart," the theme of lovers as marionettes surfaces
whenever Hulda and Baruchin meet or talk. Unaware, they too obey
a melody played by a mysterious flute which only the two of them
can hear. Much the same thing could be said about Shoshana and
the UN soldier.

In each of these stories the heroine under the spell of love
becomes ecstatic and dangerously frail and, like Little Red Riding
Hood, "helplessly incapacitated by the consequences of her encounter with the wolf."[26] But since in her case the "wolf" is not
eager to play his role and refuses to "devour" her, their encounter
is incomplete. In the fairy tale when devoured by the wolf, Little
Red Riding Hood undergoes a significant process of transition, at
the end of which she loses her childish innocence. As Bettelheim
puts it: "When she is cut out of the wolf's belly, she is reborn
on a higher plane of existence."[27] In the case of the Kahana-
Carmon heroine in the role of Little Red Riding Hood, not being
devoured by the "wolf" means an arrested development, a thwarted
rite de passage.

Reflecting on "Little Red Riding Hood," Bettelheim maintains
that this tale projects the girl, in a symbolic form, "into the
dangers of her Oedipal conflicts during puberty, and then saves
her from them, so that she will be able to mature conflict-free."[28]
Such a psychoanalytic approach regards the wolf as symbolizing the
father, and the tale as symbolizing a state in which "with the
reactivation in puberty of early Oedipal longings, the girl's wish
for her father, her inclination to seduce him, and her desire to
be seduced by him, also become reactivated."[29] While acknowledging
the need for caution in applying the methodology of psychoanalysis

to literary research, the possibility should not be overlooked
that in the three Kahana-Carmon childhood stories the man with
whom each of the female protagonists is infatuated embodies for
her also a father-image. In "Bridal Veil" the age gap is relatively small, but in the other stories the men to whom N'ima and
Ḥulda[30] are attracted are old enough to be surrogate fathers. In
the case of Baruchin, the author's wish to age him is apparent not
only in making him a son of a writer from "the period of the
Revival,"[31] but also in describing him as "an old man. And perhaps not old. Only a mummy, a fossil" ("Heart," 587).[32] As for
the young girls N'ima and Shoshana, in addition to the romantic
involvement, the teacher and the soldier fill a vacuum created by
the absence of a father, either because of sickness, or because of
working away from home. "Bridal Veil" symbolically implies it by
describing the UN soldier taking the seat in the bus near Shoshana
immediately after its being vacated by her father. This instance
coincides with a central motif of "Beauty and the Beast" and of
"Prince Frog"; in both fairy tales the father is the person who
brings his daughter and her future husband together.[33]

       In his psychoanalytic interpretation of the theme of Beauty
and the Beast, Joseph L. Henderson suggests that it indicates a
woman's "need to find the answer to a personal father fixation or
to release a sexual inhibition."[34] Accordingly, "Beauty is any
young girl or woman who has entered into an emotional bond with
her father, no less binding because of its spiritual nature."[35]
As Beauty learns to love Beast, she opens up to the power of human
love concealed in its animal (and therefore imperfect), but
genuinely erotic, form. This, Henderson presumes, represents an
awakening of her true function of relatedness, enabling her to
accept the erotic component of Oedipal feelings which had to be
repressed for fear of incest. A similar view is expressed by
Bettelheim, who maintains that "the Oedipal love of Beauty for her
father, when transferred to her future husband, is wonderfully
healing."[36]

       If these psychoanalytic observations can serve as guidelines
to Kahana-Carmon's stories, the incessant romantic fascination of
her heroines with men who represent for them a father-image indicates an unresolved father fixation which the author seeks to work
out in her stories. Because her heroines exhibit inability to
redeem themselves and their image of the masculine from the forces
of repression, their initiation is not followed through and their
encounters with men remain incomplete. This basic situation is,
however, less so in Shoshana's case.

The symbolic pattern of Shoshana's initiation is the "Night
Journey." As a result of an accident, the bus aboard which she
meets the soldier suddenly stops in the midst of what was supposed
to have been a short evening journey, subsequently causing her own
"journey" with the soldier to continue into the night and end at
dawn. The metaphorical role of both night and dawn is well recog-
nized. Both represent a "time when the threshold of consciousness
is lowered and the impulses and images of the unconscious can pass
across it."[37] Discussing the archetype of Night Journey,
Koestler defines it as "the meeting of the Tragic and the Trivial
Planes."[38] He finds this motif in countless guises and describes
its basic pattern as follows:

> Under the effect of some overwhelming experience, the
> hero is made to realize the shallowness of his life, the
> futility and frivolity of the daily pursuits of man in
> the trivial routines of existence. This realization may
> come to him as a sudden shock caused by some catastrophic
> event, or as the cumulative effect of a slow inner de-
> velopment, or through the trigger action of some appar-
> ently banal experience which assumes an unexpected sig-
> nificance. The hero then suffers a crisis which involves
> the very foundations of his being; he embarks on the
> Night Journey, is suddenly transferred to the Tragic
> Plane--from which he emerges purified, enriched by new
> insight, regenerated on a higher level of integration.[39]

Such a Journey symbolizes a plunge to the sources and tragic
undercurrents of existence, "into the fluid magma, of which the
Trivial Plane of everyday life is merely the thin crust."[40]
Koestler's contention is that in most tribal societies the plunge
is symbolically enacted in the initiation rites just before a
turning point in the life of the initiate, such as puberty or mar-
riage. The initiate is made to undertake a minor Night Journey
segregated from the community, to experience the essential solitude of man, and establish contact with the Tragic Plane.

As a catalyst, Shoshana's night journey accelerates a process
which otherwise might have taken a longer period. Banal as it is,
her encounter with the UN soldier is interpreted by the unworldly
girl as an overwhelming, transformative experience. As the name
of the story and her fantasy of becoming "the regiment's girl"
suggest, she feels nubile. The child in her died that night so
that something new, her womanhood, could be born. Undergoing
pubescence, she gains a new awareness of her self-being, that
taste of herself above all and in all things.

No, She is Not a Anna Karenin

The sense of family is not elaborated in Shoshana's or N'ima's
stories as it is in Ronen's. "Heart" is intended by its scope to
be a family portrait, revolving around the mother. We slowly enter
the world of the Sokolows, a world deficient in verbal communication, introduced to the taciturnity of this family through the
opening sentence of the story: "The mute things are the talking
ones, this everyone knows." Because of Hulda's withdrawal, there
is little communication of emotions among the members of the family, and the domestic atmosphere reminds one of "the deathlike
sleep into which everybody surrounding Sleeping Beauty falls."[41]
The necessary things are said in the most laconic manner. "At
first sight, a family like all families," Ronen muses ironically
("Heart," 576), bringing to mind the opening sentence of Tolstoy's
Anna Karenin: "All families are alike but an unhappy family is unhappy after its own fashion." Ronen's tone leaves no doubt that
the family machine is malfunctioning. At breakfast Hulda sits at
the edge of the dining table "like a guest," and this theme,
her being a guest in her own home, runs throughout the story. The
family is fenced in, unwilling to face problems. The father gets
up from the breakfast table--not one word having been exchanged
between him and his wife or sons--walking over to the terrace to
smoke a cigarette, returning "as though loading on his back a
heavy burden." Ronen notices that his father's lips are tight
and that one corner of his mouth seems more tense than the other
"as though his nose is constantly prepared for a bad smell."
Observing the strained silence between his parents, he wonders:
"What did these two people find in each other to get married?"
They are "two people who didn't strike roots in each other,"
and who have learned to coexist because "two horses hitched to
one shaft had better not kick one another." Referring to his
mother, Ronen muses: "Does she really love us? Is her soul
really attached to the souls of the people with whom she spends
her life?" Hulda has created for herself a machinery of denial:
"Mother had no connection with anyone. Even her parents she
almost never sees." Her husband will forever remain the immigrant he was when they first met, while she, a *Sabra*, regards
herself as a member of the Israeli elite. Dr. Baruchin, a *Sabra*
of prominent social status, naturally appeals more to the "princess"
in her. She does not try to conceal her contempt for her mother-
in-law. In fact, Ronen has inherited her scorn for the paternal
grandmother with his vitriolic descriptions of her and his

nicknaming her "the witch,"[42] or "Silvia the Czardas Baroness"
("Heart," 597).[43] Her loud loquaciousness--in contrast to Ronen's
taciturn family--and her bad Hebrew, contribute towards the comic
effects of this otherwise sad story. Full of little snobberies,
she cannot stop animadverting and grumbling. "In her own eyes,"
Ronen says, "she is the white missionary, sacrificing her life
while black Africa doesn't know how to appreciate it. But even
Africa, there is this Africa and there is that Africa. Mother
and her sons are the blackest Africa" (581). As she attempts to
incite her son Pesaḥ against Ḥulda, Pesaḥ, trying to keep his
neutrality, finds himself between the devil and the deep blue sea.
By letting Ḥulda have her way he makes it all the harder for her
to leave him. Not being the narrator, Ḥulda does not transmit
sufficient information to us about herself. Ronen's not very reliable account depicts her as alienated and engrossed in herself
to the point of being oblivious to her husband and sons. When she
runs into Baruchin on the street she is not even aware of her son
Ronen standing so close to her that he can easily eavesdrop[44] on
her conversation (592). Ronen is twice nicknamed "an old child"
(577, 613). Indeed, younger than N'ima and Shoshana, his narrative appears to be more mature. In his spying he is guarding the
interests of his father, as well as masochistically nourishing his
own jealousy. To the extent that his narrative represents an initiatory experience, it does mark the death of his innocence, his
bitter bite from the fruit of the Tree of Knowledge; he senses
this the first time he overhears his mother's telephone conversation with Baruchin. He is, in Henderson's words, "experiencing a
rite of death and rebirth that marks his passage from youth to
maturity."[45] Paradoxically, his own initiation reflects his
mother's thwarted initiatory attempts. She remains throughout
blocked, inhibited, never really capable of properly waking up
from her "sleep," as her abortive affair with Baruchin demonstrates.

"A Whip Decked with Roses"

It appears that none of the three female protagonists can di-
vorce the issue of her "sin" from the issue of retribution. Juvenile N'ima knows that her efforts to impose her monomaniacal obsession on her teacher are wrong. She wonders: "Why does he never
reprove me for my impertinence?" ("N'ima," 231). Her tale about
a mad woman she meets on the street, who points at her declaring
that she, N'ima, is mad too (235), is an expression of self-
admonition, an intimation that her compulsion is destructive.

The love-hate she harbors for her teacher surfaces when she wishes
bad things to happen to him: "Have you managed to get home all
right, teacher Ezekiel? You deserved to break a leg on the way,
teacher Ezekiel" ("N'ima," 230). Or: "A hard man. Even in hell
you would not burn" (246). Throughout she is aware of the dis-
comfort she causes him. Her covert wish to be tamed emerges when
after one of her painful confrontations with him she relates to
the reader: "The title of a play I had once seen advertised on a
hoarding came back to me, *The Taming of the Shrew*. And a sleeve
of a record album in a shop window, a picture of a whip decked
with roses" (247). Her only self-justification is the theory of
the marionettes. Believing that she is under a spell, or that she
is a marionette on a string, frees her from taking responsibility
for her conduct.

Shoshana's coping with the problem of Sin and Retribution is
apparent at the end of her story when she recalls her mother's
tale about a brother who killed his adulterous sister ("Bridal
Veil," 26). The fact that her mother had praised the killer does
not seem to discourage Shoshana, although she is the only one
among the three female protagonists to have physical contact with
the man she desires and her "sin" is not just a thought as is the
case with N'ima and Ḥulda.

As for the adult Ḥulda, in addition to being deprived of the
excuse of ignorance, or innocence, with regard to sin, she has
more at stake than the two girls. However, she is not cut out to
be an Anna Karenin. She will not elope. Her offer to work in her
husband's shop is a self-imposed mortification; the ordeal of
working in this shop, in which she never cared to set foot before,
is her way of atonement.

Although by and large Kahana-Carmon allows her narrative to
unfold avoiding an explicit moral judgment, her stories tend to
associate illicit love with death, the inference being that death
is a form of punishment. In "Bridal Veil," in addition to the
mention of a brother who kills his adulterous sister, we are told
that on one of Shoshana's bus trips a student who sat near her and
made a pass at her was reading a paperback called *It Was a Murder
in the Moonlight* (15).

"N'ima" is concentrically structured around the concept of
death, the death of the love expectation.[46] The mood of the story
is set by its motto:

Do tears know who sheds them?
And hearts know who tills them?
They are tilled by light entering the turf
And the turf does not know what's within.[47]

Borrowed from an epitaph written by the Hebrew poet Judah
Halevi (before 1075-1141),[48] this lament reverberates several
times throughout the story when N'ima tries to communicate to
teacher Ezekiel her desperate love for him. In a quasi-mystical
vision, she sees teacher Ezekiel "ascending into the space that is
between the heavens and the earth" ("N'ima," 233); he is "cloaked
in a blazing garment," before vanishing "behind the curtain of the
sky." Immediately after teacher Ezekiel stuns her by telling
her that her poems put him to sleep, she experiences an apocalyptic
hallucination drawing on unconscious material, a vision abounding
with thanatic overtones (243).[49] Later she sees teacher Ezekiel
"like a man carved out of chalk, like a pillar of salt" (246).
The biblical association of Lot's wife who turned to look back
when escaping the scene of destruction and was turned into a pillar of salt is textually appropriate, following the previous
apocalyptic vision.[50]

In "Heart," almost every image connected with Hulda's relationship to Baruchin is dense with intimations of death or destruction. When she speaks to him over the phone, she has two
voices: the ordinary one and another voice that is "buried" in the
former ("Heart," 585). Taking her sick child to Baruchin's clinic,
she looks "as though she were going to the gallows" (590). In the
hospital, when Baruchin leaves her, she looks "as though her world
was destroyed." Mentioning the cakes and sandwiches that she
prepares for the party at which Baruchin is guest of honor, the
narrator muses in an image pertaining to the Eucharist: "To eat
them is like eating her flesh" (604).

Some of the abovementioned symbols and metaphors represent a
deliberate attempt on the part of the author to spoon-feed the
reader with contrived implications, while others are generated
naturally and spontaneously from the narrative. The abundance of
imagery prompts a close inspection of Kahana-Carmon's handling of
it, for her symbols and metaphors provide more insights into her
creative mind than any of her other narrative devices.

Kahana-Carmon's Imagery

In a long essay entitled "A Passage for the Stage in the
Grand Manner," Kahana-Carmon argues that the artist's function is

"to add new life to the collective consciousness," and "to hit the
vein of symbols that express contents which embody the answers to
the needs of a living reality and are specific to it."[51] The symbols she has in mind are those "that brush aside the old set of
symbols which belong to a bygone reality"; when an artist achieves
this "he manages to isolate an element of eternity."[52]

Such a credo, which considers the possibility of a conscious
effort on the part of an author to use symbols in a premeditated
manner, is incompatible with Jung's approach despite Kahana-
Carmon's apparent acceptance of his theory of the collective
unconscious. Jung emphasizes that

> symbols...are natural and spontaneous products. No
> genius has ever sat down with a pen or a brush in his
> hand and said: "Now I am going to invent a symbol."
> No one can take a more or less rational thought,
> reached as a logical conclusion or by deliberate intent,
> and then give it "symbolic" form.[53]

Jung's position, however, does not rule out various degrees
of the artist's awareness of the symbol he uses, from the first
moment that it germinates in his subconscious, before being formulated by consciousness, as well as various ways in which he can
manipulate it. Wimsatt invokes Shelley's view that the language
of poets "is vitally metaphorical: that is, it marks the before
unapprehended relations of things and perpetuates their apprehension."[54] D. W. Harding, in his essay "The Hinterland of Thought,"[55]
asserts that "emergent impulses" undergo "evaluation and perhaps
modification" by value systems before reaching "conscious formula-
tion,"[56] before imaging or verbal thinking occurs. "By the time
an impulse has flowed over into imagery or words, there has been
ample opportunity for it to be checked, facilitated or modified by
processes outside consciousness."[57] Thus, the literary image
carries with it the results of extensive organization occurring
before it made its appearnace. Like Jung, Harding assumes that a
writer conveys meanings which he cannot be said to have intended
before writing, and which he may not observe even when he reads
over what he has written. An accidental turn of phrase may satisfy
him for it conveys a part of his total state of mind of which he
was unaware.

Kahana-Carmon's usage of imagery indicates that quite often
hers are natural symbols that derive spontaneously from the unconscious strata of the psyche, and represent variations on the
essential archetypal image. However, because she is a meticulous,
calculating writer by nature, her similes and metaphors sometimes

seem laborious, as though fabricated with great diligence to achieve by industry what could otherwise only come about by a miracle. One gets the impression that if she could help it, she would be unlikely to allow an impulse to flow over into her imagery without being "checked, facilitated or modified" first. The following list comprises a number of these symbols and images: the "chick," reminiscent of Ibsen's *The Wild Duck*, twice mentioned in "Bridal Veil" (13, 25) in an indirect reference to Shoshana; the oxymoron "black swan," borrowed from the legend which inspired the ballet *Swan Lake*, referring to Hulda ("Heart," 600); the image "white missionary" referring to Hulda's mother-in-law; the "mummy," referring to Dr. Baruchin whose clinic, that looks like "a lair of wild beasts," represents the fauna to which Hulda is drawn, in contrast to her husband, "the patient animal" (581).[58] The setting and events symbolically reinforce one another in "Bridal Veil," in keeping with the theme of Night Journey, and ironically so in "Heart of Summer, Heart of Light" which in contrast to its name takes place in winter and describes a family living "in the shadow of a cloud" ("Heart," 577). However, most of Kahana-Carmon's symbols and images are spontaneous and natural in the Jungian sense. Quite often these are symbols of transcendence. The mountain pass which appears in N'ima's hallucination ("N'ima," 243) denotes transition from an old attitude to a new one.[59] The mountain itself, the nucleus of Ronen's recurrent dream, is a common dream symbol for a place of revelation where transformation and change take place.[60] The "lonely journey," such as N'ima takes in her hallucination, and Ronen in his dream, is another symbol for a release through transcendence, which is required as an initiatory experience.[61] The theme of a true inner liberation through transcendence is represented also by the flight of birds. A bird represents initiation working through a "medium"--someone able to obtain cognition of distant events of which one consciously has no knowledge, by going into a trancelike state.[62] Such a concept could lie behind the description of Hulda as a "black swan" and of Shoshana as a "chick." Horses, often wild ones, represent as noted above[63] "the uncontrollable, instinctive drives that can erupt from the unconscious." This may account for the metaphoric stallions that N'ima sees in her hallucination immediately after her distressing meeting with teacher Ezekiel.[64]

Kahana-Carmon's use of metaphor follows the theory of Richards who regards this device as "a semi-surreptitious method by which a greater variety of elements can be wrought into the fabric of the

experience."[65] Many of her metaphors are cross-references from
one of the senses to another; a combination of different sensory
matrices designed to lend multidimensionality. N'ima's story, in
line with the persona of the juvenile narrator and her feverish
poetic imagination, is interspersed with incandescent metaphors.
The lights in the street are "an alien scarlet of wanton jubila-
tion and thriving prosperity smelted into a red river, in untempered orange of sulphur and gold ore, in untempered green, in
pellucid sapphire which shone like the terrible ice" ("N'ima,"
231). The evening is "pearly," the air is "filled with a slow
poison" (232), and the night is "lukewarm" (232).

        Less flamboyant and abundant are metaphors in the story with
the metaphoric name "Heart of Summer, Heart of Light," where the
emotional state of the child-narrator is not the same as that of
his counterpart in "N'ima." Ronen is not a poet madly in love,
nor is he directly involved. Instead, rather like the narrator in
Shahar's stories he is basically a bystander, an observer. His
narrative, therefore, is more detached and controlled; it feels
more at home with the simile, which does not require a highly
charged emotive language, but through which, in Koestler's words,
"the felicitous image unfolds in the mind--the only one which can
'explain' by symbols the rationally unexplainable--and express the
inexpressible."[66] Silberschlag points out this aspect in his
definition of Kahana-Carmon's writing technique as "a studious
exercise in the unusual simile."[67] In Ronen's case the simile is
an aid to the conveying of moods, interpretations, anxieties, and
a release from tension. Most of his similes lean toward the pic-
turesque and pertain to materials from his primary school text-
books. Some express a gloomy ambience, but on the whole they tend
to convey a light, jocular mood. Drawing on *Alice's Adventures in
Wonderland*, his dream is full of happiness "like a grin of a
Cheshire cat" ("Heart," 577);[68] and drawing on the Bible (Gen
39:12), his grandmother catches his sleeve in the street "like
Potiphar's wife catching Joseph by his garment" (579). Lipschitz, who is "like a thin lion" (597), has a way of talking
"as though picking grapes from a bunch" (601). Mrs. Baruchin
sits "like a judge," while her husband leans over his armchair
"like a bodyguard" (598). When Ronen, the taciturn child,
interrupts his parents' conversation, they stare at him as
though he were "Balaam's Ass" (589). When Hulda is ill and her
mother-in-law takes over the household chores, the latter makes
her two grandchildren wear their scarves in a funny way so that
both of them "looked like illustrations to Krylov's fables" (593).

The simile as a device for sardonic effects is overworked in "N'ima," whenever associated with the description of teacher Ezekiel: "Reflected in him, sitting there, I see the most handsomely dressed young man of his day, languid, a ballet prince, with the profile of Ivor Novello" ("N'ima," 228). And: "He is like a boxing champion who wouldn't hurt a fly" (229). And: "He is moving with...the astonishing trust of a piece of seaweed flung around by the flow" (233). And: "I watched him going out, striding, as he did, rather like a sailor" (237). And: "Since morning some of his hair has shifted to the wrong side, and he looks as though he's playing one of the early pioneers of the American West" (244).

Such similes are one way of conveying humor and irony in Kahana-Carmon's stories; another is contrast.

The Uses of Contrast

The systematic use of the contrast is apparent in almost every aspect of Kahana-Carmon's technique, as well as her themes. She is fond of the oxymoron: Ronen is "an old child," Ḥulda is a "black swan," teacher Ezekiel has the face of a "dark moon." When she begins one of her stories with a sentence such as "The mute things are the talking ones," the reader is conditioned to expect the two contrasting levels on which the story is going to unfold: the overt and the covert. Immediately following a crystal-clear passage written with precision, in minute detail and depicting a realistic situation, she introduces into the narrative an obscure, unelaborated passage as, for example, the hallucination episode in "N'ima" (243f.). In contrast to passages which show Kahana-Carmon's skill in handling the fundamental elements of a good short story--brevity, compression and distillation[69]--one finds in her stories passages which are overwritten, showy, filled with trivia and platitudinous sayings, interlarded with rare words.

She constantly arranges people, places, themes, in positions which contrast with one another. The child-protagonist is contrasted with the adults, and the adults among themselves, one serving as a foil to another. Pesaḥ Sokolow is contrasted on the one hand with Baruchin "the winner," and on the other hand with Alkalai, "the loser." Ḥulda is placed on the one hand in contrast to Mrs. Baruchin (when Ḥulda sat near her "she looked like her grandmother" ["Heart," 598]), and on the other hand, in contrast to her mother-in-law--"the Czardas Baroness." Mrs. Baruchin's hair is white (598), while the mother-in-law's is dyed "black like

a raven" ("Heart," 579)--but, in yet another contrast, "she is in
the mood of a blonde" (597). Phoney Mrs. Baruchin reads contemporary "high brow" fiction; phoney mother-in-law reads cheap best-
sellers. The mother-in-law's condescension towards Ḥulda is contrasted with Ḥulda's condescension toward this mother-in-law's
son, Pesaḥ. Lipschitz the "thin lion" has a temper of a "rotund
man" (597). Baruchin looks very old but his voice is young (587),
and his old wife has a young smile (598). All the descriptions of
Tel Aviv in "Heart" are scornful, while those of Jaffa are filled
with warmth and affection. Old Jaffa, as well as the Sephardi
Alkalai and his uncle, represents an empathy with the colorful and
exotic world of the Levant--recalling Aloni and Shahar--in contrast
with the dull, plastic reality of the modern-day Tel Aviv. Ronen's
recurrent symbolic dream is contrasted with a frustrating daily
reality, just as his mother's attraction to the imagined option,
the doctor, is contrasted with her domestic duties.

N'ima's serious attempt to communicate with her teacher
("Tell me, teacher Ezekiel, are you really singled out?" ["N'ima,"
238]) is contrasted with her classmates' silly babble about the
Tarzan film they saw; and, in yet another contrast their babble
is interspersed with quotations from the book of Psalms. The new
Jerusalem is contrasted with the old, the religious with the secular, soldiers with civilians (239-42). Mystical teacher Ezekiel
climbing the sky "cloaked in a blazing garment," is in contrast
with the ordinary teacher Ezekiel who is striding "rather like a
sailor."

In "Bridal Veil," the UN soldier is in contrast with Shoshana's father; the soldier is attentive, affectionate--the father
is not. When the soldier brings Shoshana home at four in the
morning, the contrast is between him and her peers, the boys who
return from an all-night party ("Bridal Veil," 21); the boys
represent Shoshana's real world, the soldier her fantasies.

And throughout one is constantly aware of the contrast between the voice and mentality of the child-narrator, or the child
from whose standpoint the story is narrated, and the voice and
mentality of the author herself.

Narrative, Narrator, Author

The technique employed in the three stories is that of selec-
tive omniscience,[70] which restricts the narrative to the consciousness of one of the characters in the story. "N'ima" and "Heart"
are narrated in the first-person. However, while N'ima's story can

be seen as an internal analysis of events,[71] whereby the main
character tells his or her own story, Ronen's story is an external
observation of events with the minor character telling the main
character's story. "Bridal Veil" is narrated in the third-person
but it too attempts to reflect as closely as possible its child-
protagonist's standpoint and can therefore be regarded as an internal analysis of events.

The plausibility of these stories depends on their loyalty to
the narrative convention adopted. The initial intention is to
make the reader relate to them as veracious and credible by judi-
cious use of techniques of selection, foreshortening, and summary.
As a rule, when the narrator is well-chosen, the deletions he
makes seem natural, and the selections significant. The author
then relinquishes his "'liberty of transcending the limits of the
immediate scene'--particularly the limits of that character he has
chosen as his mouthpiece."[72] This narrator can tell only what is
accessible to him through what he has heard or observed, or personally surmised, and the voice used must be his authentic voice,
suiting his background, perception and sensibility.

Depicting N'ima as a precocious minor, a poet, conditions the
reader from the outset to accept her flamboyant language as authentic. At the same time, her obsession with the teacher allows her
an extra adrenalized heartbeat, as expressed in her imagery. A
confessional writer, N'ima is addressing her story not homiletical-
ly to an audience but painfully to the self; it is private rather
than public, closer to the epistolary than to the oratorical.
Writing down her story is therapeutic, it helps her to overcome
the despairs of unrequited love. The reader has no difficulty in
accepting the desultory quality of the narrative sequence. Doubt
does arise, however, about whether a young girl of her age and
background, even if the reader were to make allowance for her pre-
cociousness, could be so sophisticated in her powers of reception
and perception. One of the passages that seems particularly im-
plausible is the one in which N'ima kaleidoscopically describes
nightfall in a Jerusalem street in an extempore tone of transcendence, based on free association ("N'ima," 231). Another conspicuous passage is her portrait of the city, after she has given
her poems to teacher Ezekiel (239-42). In this farraginous passage, which calls to mind musique concrète, she functions like an
itinerant photographer who seizes on every possibility in the
street, cataloguing data as in an album of snapshots, aimed at
showing in a combination of surface and symbol the trivialization

of life in a Jerusalem neighborhood.[73] All this is characteristic
of Kahana-Carmon's tendency to use landscape not just as a painted
backdrop, but as animated with feelings. Still, the questions
remain: is she indulging in scenic descriptions more than is
necessary or tolerable in a short story? Is this impromptu pho-
tography pertinent to N'ima's story, or is it contrived to show
off the author's connoisseurship? The rumination that sums up
this passage is hardly congruous with the mentality of a thirteen-
year-old girl.

> And I reflected: pick any street. Add some indefinable
> quality to it. Is it only by the power of sight--the
> vision of aspiration in eyeless things, humble things,
> struggling to be realized? I shall atone for them. And
> I reflected: an enchanted life. All in all, a mountain.
> Swarming with people, coming in and out like ants, making
> their living in the bowls of the earth. But each one
> of them knows: Jerusalem, thou that art builded as a
> city that is compact together--and it is Jerusalem where
> I am. How singular, how wondrous, how privileged. To
> be so close to the central pivot of things....

The child-narrator's voice is confused here with the mannered
voice of the adult author, invaded by it; in a sentimental way it
betrays the emergence of the author's sense of pathos. It is as
if the reader is intended to experience an intense emotion more
than is called for by the materials of the story; as if the author
tries to nudge the reader's response by poeticizing her literary
expression, quite apart from the dramatic issues involved in the
story.

Apart from the fact that her stories are sometimes excessively
clogged and burdened with extraneous detail in a way that cannot
fail to slow down the pace, Kahana-Carmon ignores the convention
of first-person narrative by having the child-narrator convey objective information of which this child cannot have knowledge.[74]
When N'ima says that she sees teacher Ezekiel with "the profile of
Ivor Novello" she expresses something quite outside of her experience. A young girl from a Jerusalem religious school in the
1960s could not know about the Cardiff-born (1893-1951) actor-
manager, dramatist and composer, with the "handsome smile and ex-
ceptional profile,"[75] who starred in films which young N'ima could
not possibly have seen (although the author herself could have
done so). Indeed, at the end of the story, apparently in an attempt to preempt the reader's reluctance to trust the account of
this obsessive, irrational narrator, the author makes the narrator
admit her flaws: "But I, with a faltering pen, scribble down and
stumble and start again" ("N'ima," 249).

The situation of a narrator whose veracity is similarly ques-
tionable is repeated in "Heart." Here the author wants to establish Ronen's authority and increase his credibility as a reliable
storyteller by an attempt to age him psychologically ("an old
child"), and by making us feel that he is knowledgeable and discriminating (the various encyclopaedias and newspapers that he
reads). This child-narrator functions as a combination of a
taperecorder and an interpreting camera. Although a boy and not
a girl, he is used as a mouthpiece for his mother, or the woman
Kahana-Carmon. This is particularly obvious in a passage in which
he envisages a possible beginning of the affair between Baruchin
and his wife before they got married ("Heart," 601f.): their meeting in Cairo's Shepherd's Hotel, to the music of Victor Sylvester's
orchestra, or in a ceremony headed by the British High Commissioner,
and characterized by an unmistakable Mandatory decor--again, things
undoubtedly out of the time province of a Tel Aviv child of his
age. He even demonstrates clairvoyant skills in recording a long
inner monologue of his mother as she looks out at the street in
what he takes to be a state of anxious expectancy for Baruchin
(610). In fact, this passage is a typical example of the many indirect authorial intrusions in Kahana-Carmon's stories which are
unlike the direct intrusions in Yizhar's and Shahar's stories,
where the author stops the narrative abruptly to interpolate his
own comments and commentary before allowing his narrator to resume
his narration.

When at the very beginning of his story Ronen says: "I don't
ridicule my parents' home. Here our life has to go on" (576), he
is implying that he does not regard his role as a narrator to pass
judgment. Nonetheless, he never misses a chance to ridicule his
grandmother, the Tel Aviv housewives or school children, and to
demonstrate his preference for Jaffa. His observations of reality
are often clouded by his reaction to the crisis of his mother. To
make things worse, he is constantly given to a strong inclination
to escape from reality into a dream, with the effect that from
time to time his narrative seems entirely delusory. He himself
doubts his sanity (610); and, admitting to being a profoundly confused, unreliable observer, he says at the end of the story: "Maybe
I was sick, hearing voices, seeing sights....What did I invent?
What didn't I invent? Hard to tell. What do I know at all?" (612).
And with this ambiguity his story ends.

Is it a calculated trick on the part of the author to employ
such a dubious narrator? Is it aimed at provoking suspense?

Kahana-Carmon is predisposed, in her writing, to the use of literary contrivances, but there is no evidence that a concern with
creating suspense is to be numbered among them. In this story,
the intention is rather to achieve what Brooks and Warren define
as "a shock of collision" between the narrator's attitude and the
reader's.[76] When this happens, the reader experiences a need to
reassess the narrator's attitude. The author's purpose in prompt-
ing the reader's participation in such a manner is to leave the
reader with the responsibility of doing some of the interpreting
himself, inventing an apparent meaning, or developing a meaning
beyond the point where the story actually comes to rest.

As noted earlier, "Bridal Veil" is the only one of the three
Kahana-Carmon stories which is not written in the first-person.
Because the characters lack a common language, Shoshana would not
be able to repeat to us what the Canadian UN soldier says; she
does not speak English and he does not speak Hebrew. If it were
not for that, this story too might well have been written in the
first-person, for the psychological perception transmitted is at
a level congruous with the sensibility of this particular child-
heroine. Unlike the other two stories, in "Bridal Veil" the author's presence is generally kept out of the narrative; it does,
however, invade the story when Shoshana begins to ruminate and
fantasize about the UN soldier at a level of perception inappro-
priate for her age and mentality. But this does not happen frequently in this story; generally the author is careful here to
avoid the "shock of collision" between the narrative and the
reader.

All three stories, narrated in the past tense, maintain the
illusion that there is no lapse of time from the moment the plot
ends and the moment its actual writing begins. This fallacy accounts for the absence of the element of nostalgia for childhood.
Ronen, N'ima and Shoshana are not satisfied with their present but
they do not look back; for them the present is only a period of
transition one has to put up with in order to be compensated later,
in some fantasized future. They are immersed in an inner time
which is in conflict with the actual time of the stories, the
1960s. Sometimes the narrative is made up of several layers of
time. The twelve-year-old Ronen describes a time "when I was
little" in terms of "long ago" ("Heart," 582). He also mentions
the ancient time of his dream with a seansation of déjà vu, and
refers to a symbolic antiquity which is represented in Baruchin,

the "mummy." As for the actual duration of the plot, the longest
story, Ronen's, stretches over a period of months (from Hanukkah
to Purim), N'ima's story covers the last days of school, while
Shoshana's--the purest in form and substance--describes only one
night. Timing, as expressed by selection and foreshortening which
enable the narrator to avoid irrelevant moments, is the least under control in Ronen's story, which contains superfluous descriptions of banal, tedious moments.

Ever since the earliest reviews of her stories,[77] Kahana-
Carmon's linguistic brilliance has been highly praised. This
brilliance can become an embarrassment of riches in the childhood
stories when, instead of using her hairsbreadth sensitivity to
words to create a literary counterpart of a child's language, she
tends to flaunt her undoubted talent as a verbal virtuoso. This
is often accentuated by an inclination to use rather unconvention-
al and arbitrary syntax which complicates her stories unduly.
Only in "Bridal Veil" does she come close to the childlike simplicity and innocence true to the essence of a childhood story.
The other two stories lose their veracity whenever the child-
narrator is made to sound like a sophisticated adult; they regain
it only when the child-narrators shed this pose and become what
they really are--children.

CONCLUSION

It has been said that writing about children is the next best thing to being a child. It can also be said that such an activity as a form of regression indicates a malaise that lurks beneath the facade of maturity, and an immanent escapist tendency. In the case of Yizhar, in particular, the escape is to that early period of his life, which had existed apart from, and uncontaminated by, the mechanical civilization that had produced a frustrating and unacceptable reality. In his nostalgic travelling back to childhood, Yizhar employs the vehicle of pastoral. Each of the other three authors discussed in this study--Aloni, Shahar, and Kahana-Carmon--utilizes, for the same purpose and more subtly so, a personally appropriate imaginative mode, drawn from the resources of, respectively, myth, mysticism and the fairy tale.

Written after the bite from the fruit of the Tree of Knowledge, the stories are motivated by not only a desire to dodge the present but also the author's retrospective wish to come to terms with his past. Searching for his quintessence in the fullness of childhood, the author manifests a strong need to reestablish contact with the natural, ingenuous individual he had once been, before the reality of growing up had compelled him to adapt to society and conform to mores imposed upon him.

The child within the adult author throughout these stories is seeking an outlet for the release of repressed emotions. In a considerable number of these stories, the evocation of childhood is associated with a failure of an initiatory process in which the neophyte should have learned how to bridge the gap between inner experience and the real world. The reenactment of this experience by a fictitious, but quasi-autobiographical character, may enable the author to confront inner conflicts which had thwarted his transition from childhood to maturity. Without such a confrontation and the new insights gained from it, a resolution of these conflicts is less likely to take place.

This cathartic by-product is, however, secondary to the more overt motivating force that leads an adult author to write autobiographical stories. Referring to this point, Gusdorf, in his essay "Conditions and Limits of Autobiography," has this to say:

> The man who takes the trouble to tell of himself knows
> that the present differs from the past and that it will
> not be repeated in the future; he has become more aware
> of the differences than of similarities; given the con-
> stant change, given the uncertainty of events and of men,
> he believes it a useful and valuable thing to fix his own
> image so that he can be certain it will not disappear
> like all things in the world.

Although the stories serve as manifestations of the "I", they
are not dissociated from the public context. While reflecting a
certain estrangement, they simultaneously attempt to recapture the
private and public moments of an earlier era, inspired by some
sort of identification between the individual and the collective.
With the exception of the Kahana-Carmon stories, beneath their
surface there is a tension between the materialistic cynicism of
the 1960s--the period in which they were written--and the idealistic innocence of the period in which they are set.

The inner world of the native-born Israeli which emerges in
these stories is devoid of glorification. Rather than looking for
protagonists in such activities previously regarded as focal
points of the committed *Sabra*'s way of life, the tendency in the
literature of the 1960s is to seek them among the misfits, on the
fringes of society. This trend corresponds on the one hand to the
deflation of the *Sabra* myth, and on the other to some features of
the contemporary cultural climate in the Western world. The 1960s,
particularly in America, were an age when the accent was on youth,
rejection of authority, eruption of protest movements, and the
cultivation of an introspective and quasi-mystical sense of self--
all of which may be seen in retrospect as adding up to a positive
celebration of the immaturity of youth. By and large, the childhood stories under discussion display a distinct assertion of the
child's sense of his own uniqueness, of his own isolation within
the group. The attributes made accessible by this reconstructed
"child-self"--innocence, spontaneity and freedom--enable the
author to experience and respond to the world with a degree of
nonconformity.

Each story is also instrumental in the author's attempt to
define his creative capability. In the stories written in the
first person, the narrative is revealed through the eyes of a
child who is either the chief protagonist or merely a bystander.
When the author intervenes it is to provide commentary or under-
score his own attitude to the characters, the situations, and
background. In the case of Yizhar and Shahar, authorial intrusions
are without disguise; in the case of Kahana-Carmon, the voice of

the author, carefully disguised, invades the voice of the narrator;
in the case of Aloni--whose stories are the most faithful to the
convention of childhood stories--the author is completely excluded
from the narrative leaving the stage in the hands of his innocent
narrator with his incomprehension, his fantasies, and his sense of
wonder.

Two conflicting tendencies determine the dynamics of the
childhood stories explored in this study: a reluctance and an im-
patience to grow up. The former, the Peter Pan syndrome, is particularly evident in Yizhar; the latter, in Aloni. The dichotomy
corresponds to the fundamentally contrasting approaches of these
authors. Whereas for Yizhar childhood is synonymous with freedom,
a state of being unencumbered, for Aloni it is a frustrating,
thwarting period of transition.

A pervasive element is the perception of the land, Eretz
Israel, as both a concrete phenomenon and a major metaphor, the
heightened response to which nourished the imagination of the
first generation *Sabra* writers. For the native-born Israelis,
more than for their immigrant parents, an affinity with the landscape was natural. Their writings demonstrate a strong attachment
to the land, and a fascination with its effervescent Mediterranean
features. There is a firm link between the spirit of time and the
spirit of place in the childhood world depicted. Yizhar's natural
setting is the pastoral habitat of the *moshavah* in the pre-State
era. The subject of his nostalgia is the primitive life and rural
landscape of the south; fields, wild patches, orange groves, the
open plain and the desert reaches. A significant role in his
Arcadia is reserved for the Arab, whether a villager or a Bedouin,
who symbolizes for him a lost exotic world. Aloni's milieu is the
Tel Aviv Sephardi *shekhunah* in the period of the second world war.
Its folklore stimulates the flamboyant imagination of the child-
narrator and reaches the reader colored by a residue of myth and
the author's leanings towards theatricality. The environment of
Shahar's stories is Mandatory Jerusalem, particularly its religious Ashkenazi neighborhoods. A provincial, yet cosmopolitan
city of contrasts, his Jerusalem is an exquisite souvenir of a
bygone era. By contrast, Kahana-Carmon's milieu varies from story
to story. It is present-day Jerusalem in one story, Tel Aviv in
a second, and an unspecified, semi-rural immigrant settlement in
a third.

It is noteworthy that nowhere in these stories is there any
reference to the principal tragedy of the Jewish people in our

time: the Holocaust. This is inevitable in the case of Yizhar and
Shahar, as the setting of their stories is that of the 1930s; and
perhaps also in the case of Aloni, whose stories take place--at
the latest--in 1942, when the *Yishuv* was not yet informed about
the Holocaust. However, there is no reference to it in the stories of Kahana-Carmon either, even though they are set in the
1960s. Moreover, of the four writers, only two (Shahar and
Kahana-Carmon) mention Jewish life in the diaspora, and even then
only peripherally. The egocentric mentality of the *Sabra* at the
time, and his condescending approach to the Jewry of the diaspora,
may well account for this lack of interest in the Jewish world
beyond his immediate Israeli experience.

        If the Holocaust is not mentioned, allusions can be found in
the three male writers to a tragedy more relevant to the *Sabra*:
the *Akedah*. This theme is reinterpreted in accordance with the
transformation of values in Israeli society in the post-War of
Independence era and the reexamination of the relationship of the
new generation to the old. In the literature of the 1960s, the
new "Isaac" (who, in these childhood stories, is striving to define his roots), is in many instances no longer the devoted son,
unhesitatingly ready to sacrifice his life for his father's
values; instead, he is the troubled, sceptical and embittered son.

        Often, the use of language in the stories with a first-person
child-narrator by Yizhar, Shahar and Kahana-Carmon, manifests a
striking incongruity between the narrative and its verbal expression. That is, in each, the linguistic register is not entirely
appropriate to a child or adolescent. Aloni, on the other hand,
does achieve something approximating to such sensitivity to the
external world inhabited by the child. His child-narrator engages
in dialogues that transmit the colloquial register of his peer
group, and the narrative incorporates games and other aspects of
behavior characteristic of the child-world within the *shekhunah*--
including the ploy of using the third-person singular pronoun
instead of the second-person, in dialogue between two children
("Shmeel") who are "not on speaking terms." Elsewhere, however,
in descriptive and contemplative passages, Aloni's child-narrator,
like those of the other three writers, tends to use the highly
sophisticated vocabulary and imagery of the mature author.

        What often emerges in these stories is a verbal intoxication
characteristic of Israeli writers in the 1950s and 1960s--an age
when literary modern Hebrew was still immersed in a search for a
linguistic identity. Writers were experimenting with old layers

of language, blending and synthesizing them with a new vernacular, giving rise to an odd variety of literary styles: quaint, affected, hybrid, often ornate and turgid.

The absence of authentic, contemporary children's language deprives the autobiographical narrative of what could have been an effective stylistic device to enhance the depicting of two contrasting layers of time: the time in which the story is set (the 1930s or 1940s), and the time in which it was written (the 1950s or 1960s). These two layers represent the objective, collective time of an era, as well as the subjective, personal time of the individual concerned. Hebrew underwent considerable changes in its growth from one period to another. Many nuances and variables of sense and register which could have been exploited to heighten the presence within the narrative of these changes are missing.

Although the short story is a form in which the four writers are gifted, and in which (in stories discussed here, and in others) they display considerable skill, none of them regarded it as the ultimate genre in their growth. It was employed by Aloni, Shahar and Kahana-Carmon as a laboratory in which to try out their themes and techniques, before moving on to what they considered more ambitious forms. Aloni switched to drama; Shahar and Kahana-Carmon to the novel. In the case of the last two, however, whatever their own preference and evaluation of their skills may have been, the short story rather than the novel seems to be their natural element. Despite a conspicuous difference of scale, their novels often remain more like collections of short stories. As for Yizhar, he had left the genre of the novel behind him by the time he wrote the childhood stories included in *Tales*. His last attempt to write a story ("A Story that Did Not Begin") produced a massive non-story, and he stopped publishing fiction altogether, turning instead to academic teaching and the writing of essays in the field of education.

For him, perhaps more than for the others, writing about childhood was a desperate attempt to make time stand still. The dread of growing up has to do with the realization that the further one gets away from the beginning, the nearer one gets to the end. In this sense, fear of death--which surfaces in many of the childhood stories explored in this study--may be seen as one of the primary factors in the act of writing stories with such a strong autobiographical element. It is as though for a while the storyteller makes believe that by some magic he can turn the clock back, stop the flow of time, and go back to "the Country of the

Ever-Young," thus denying decay and death. Unfortunately, though, any attempt to revisit this region, which one was forced to leave years before, is bound to end with the reaffirmation that Eden must be left behind. The acceptance of the loss of childhood through the process of coming of age is tantamount to an acceptance of the inevitability of death. When childhood dies, the corpses are called adults. This, more than anything else, accounts for the distinct poignancy of these stories.

NOTES

INTRODUCTION

[1]*Dor ba-Aretz*, ed. A. Ukhmani, S. Tanii and M. Shamir (Merhavia 1958) (H).

[2]Abbreviation for *peluggot mahatz* ("assault companies"), the permanent mobilized striking force of the *Haganah*, the most moderate among the Jewish underground movements in Palestine during the British Mandate.

[3]This literature is discussed in such works as: B. Kurzweil, *Sifrutenu ha-Hadashah Hemshekh O Mahpekhah? (Our Modern Literature - Continuation or Revolution?)* (Jerusalem/Tel Aviv 1965) (H); idem, *Bein Hazon le-Vein ha-Absurdi (Between Vision and the Absurd)* (Jerusalem/Tel Aviv 1966) (H); S. Kramer, *Hillufei Mishmarot be-Sifrutenu (Changing of the Guard in Our Literature)* (Tel Aviv 1959) (H); idem, *Realizm u-Shevirato (Realism and its Decline)* (Ramat Gan 1968) (H); Z. Luz, *Metziut ve-Adam ba-Sifrut ha-Ertzyisraelit (Existence and Man in Israeli Literature)* (Tel Aviv 1970) (H); B. Y. Michaly, *Pri ha-Aretz (Fruit of the Land)* (Tel Aviv 1966) (H); D. Miron, *Arba Panim ba-Sifrut ha-Ivrit Bat Yamenu (Four Faces in Contemporary Hebrew Literature)* (Jerusalem/Tel Aviv 1962) (H); E. Schweid, *Shalosh Ashmorot (Three Night Watches)* (Tel Aviv 1964) (H); G. Shaked, *Gal Hadash ba-Sipporet ha-Ivrit (A New Wave in Hebrew Fiction)* (Merhavia/Tel Aviv 1971) (H); E. Silberschlag, *From Renaissance to Renaissance: Hebrew Literature in the Land of Israel - 1870-1970*, Vol. 2 (New York 1977); R. Wallenrod, *The Literature of Modern Israel* (New York 1956); L. Yudkin, *Escape into Siege: A Survey of Israeli Literature Today* (London/Boston 1974).

[4]Cf. M. C. Bradbrook, "The Image of the Delinquent in Literature 1955-60," in *Metaphor and Symbol*, ed. L. C. Knights and B. Cottle (London 1960) 27.

[5]See I. Even-Zohar, "Israeli Hebrew Literature: A Historical Model," *Ha-Sifrut* 4 (1973) 433, 437 (H).

[6]P. Coveney, *The Image of Childhood*, rev. ed. (London 1967) (hereafter: Coveney) 31.

[7]Ibid.

[8]Ibid.

[9]Van Wyck Brooks, *The Ordeal of Mark Twain*, rev. ed. (London 1934) 215.

[10]Ibid.

[11]G. Gusdorf, "Conditions and Limits of Autobiography," in *Autobiography: Essays Theoretical and Critical*, ed. J. Olney (Princeton 1980) 47; see also J.-P. De Waele and R. Harré, "Autobiography as a Psychological Method," in *Emerging Strategies in Social Psychological Research*, ed. G. P. Ginsburg (Chichester/New York/Brisbane/Toronto 1979).

[12]In an introduction to a selection of stories from *Keshet*, published three years after the periodical ceased to appear, he reiterated this intention. See *Keshet Makor (The Best of Keshet)*, ed. A. Amir (Ramat Gan 1979) (H).

[13]For a discussion of the "Canaanim," or the "Young Hebrews" as they were also known, see Kurzweil, *Our Modern Literature*, 270-300.

[14]A. Koestler, *Promise and Fulfilment* (London 1949) 329.

[15]Cf. A. Elon, *The Israelis: Founders and Sons* (London 1971) 266.

[16]Gusdorf, "Conditions and Limits of Autobiography," 38.

[17]Its literary supplement is referred to throughout this study by its better known name: *Massa*.

NOTES

CHAPTER I

[1]See G. Kressel, *Leksikon ha-Sifrut ha-Ivrit ba-Dorot ha-Aḥronim (Cyclopaedia of Modern Hebrew Literature)* (Merḥavia 1967) 2.525-28.(H).

[2]Ibid., 525.

[3]Ibid., 523.

[4]First newspaper of the labor movement in Palestine, founded in 1907. It ceased publication in 1970.

[5]*Gilyonot* 6 (1938) (H). An English translation is included in *Midnight Convoy and Other Stories*.

[6]See D. Miron, "S. Yizhar: Some General Observations" (hereafter: "General Observations"), in *Midnight Convoy and Other Stories* (Jerusalem 1969) 260. Except for quotations from this essay, subsequent quotations from Hebrew essays and reviews of Yizhar's work were translated by the author of this study.

[7]Ibid., 258. Also see A. Kariv, "S. Yizhar" in *S. Yizhar-- A Selection of Critical Essays on His Writings*, ed. Ch. Nagid (Tel Aviv 1972) (hereafter: *Selection*) 41 (H); and E. Zussman, "Yizhar's *On the Edge of the Negev*," in *Selection*, 45.

[8]Miron, "General Observations," loc. cit.

[9]*Gilyonot* 7 (1938) (H).

[10]*Gilyonot* 9 (1940) (H).

[11]*Gilyonot* 12 (1941) (H).

[12]Tel Aviv 1945 (H).

[13]Merḥavia 1947 (H).

[14]Merḥavia 1949 (H). An excerpt of "The Story of Ḥirbet Ḥizah" in English translation appears in *Caravan: A Jewish Quarterly Omnibus*, ed. J. Sonntag (New York 1962). An English translation of "The Prisoner" is included in *The New Israeli Writers*, ed. D. Rabikovitz (New York 1969).

[15]Tel Aviv 1950 (H). Its English translation appears in *Midnight Convoy and Other Stories*.

[16]Cf. Shaked, "The Outsider and the Convoy," in *Selection*, 113-15.

[17]Tel Aviv 1958 (hereafter: *Ziklag*) (H).

155

[18]The debate in literary circles about its value and meaning lasted for a year. The book was awarded two major literary awards: the Brenner Prize and the Israel Prize for 1959. For a review of critical opinion on it, see Nagid's introduction in *Selection*, 25-32.

[19]Tel Aviv 1963 (H).

[20]His publications ever since show that his creative impulse has found its outlet in the writing of essays in the field of education rather than fiction. Some of these essays were published in book form, *Al Ḥinukh ve-Al Ḥinukh le-Arakhim* (*On Education and Education for Values*) (Tel Aviv 1974) (H).

[21]This English translation of the Hebrew title is used here in accordance with the introduction to the English translation of "The Runaway" in *Modern Hebrew Stories*, ed. E. Spicehandler (New York 1971) 79.

[22]First published in *Keshet* 4/1 (1961). It appears in Y. Schachter's English translation in *Modern Hebrew Stories*. All references to this story are to this translation.

[23]First published in *Mibbifnim* 23/1-2 (1961). This spelling of the title is used hereafter in accordance with the English translation of this story in *Midnight Convoy and Other Stories*.

[24]This English translation of the title is in accordance with *Midnight Convoy* (267). This story, as well as "The Dunghill," was not translated into English. All subsequent quotations from these two stories were translated by the author of this study. The page numbers of references to these two stories are from the Hebrew text of *Tales of the Plain* (1963 edition).

[25]Merḥavia 1950 (H).

[26]Cf. E. Schweid, "Perplexity on Perplexity," *Massa*, 1 Nov 1963 (H).

[27]See Y. Ha-Ephrati, "A Study in 'A Dip in the Pool,'" in *Selection*, 180-86.

[28]An English translation of this story, by C. Leviant, appears in *Jewish Frontier* 23/1 (1956).

[29]Cf. Schweid, "Perplexity on Perplexity," loc. cit.

[30]Kurzweil, *Between Vision and the Absurd*, 401.

[31]D. Kena'ani, "In the Convoy and Outside It," *Orlogin* 5 (1952); this essay appears also in *Selection*.

[32]Luz, *Existence and Man*, 55.

[33]Ibid.

[34]Shaked, "The Outsider and the Convoy," in *Selection*, 116.

[35]S. Sandbank, "Longing for the Open," *Ammot* 2/2 (1963) 94 (H).

[36]London 1972 (hereafter: Lerner).

[37]Ibid., 40.

[38]Ibid., 44.

[39]Ibid., 45.

[40]Ibid., 50-58.

[41]Cf. G. Poulet, "Proust and Human Time," in *Proust A Collection of Critical Essays*, ed. R. Girard (Englewood Cliffs 1962) 156-60; see also B. J. Bucknall, *The Religion of Art in Proust* (Urbana/Chicago/London 1969) 1-19; G. Stamboliani, *Marcel Proust and the Creative Encounter* (Chicago/London 1972) 200-29; M. Hindus, *The Proustian Vision* (London/Amsterdam 1954) 122-64.

[42]Lerner, 54.

[43]"A Psycho-Analytical Approach to Aesthetics," in *New Directions in Psycho-Analysis*, ed. M. Klein (London 1955) 390.

[44]Cf. Lerner, 211.

[45]All references are to the Hamish Hamilton edition (1951) (hereafter: Salinger).

[46]Ibid., 14.

[47]Bradbrook, "Image of the Delinquent," 32.

[48]Lerner, 136.

[49]Salinger, 205f.

[50]See above, p. 21.

[51]Cf. Holden's admission in his conversation with teacher Antolini: "The trouble with me is, I *like* it when somebody digresses. It's more interesting and all." Salinger, 218.

[52]Lerner, 72.

[53]Bradbrook, "Image of the Delinquent," 27.

[54]Ibid., 33.

[55]See M. Dickstein, *Gates of Eden* (New York 1977).

[56]Bradbrook, "Image of the Delinquent," 24.

[57]Published in *Hapoel Hatzair*, 18 Dec 1962, under the title: "In Commemoration of the Rishonim" (H).

[58]He uses the word *ruaḥ* (רוח) which in Hebrew means also spirit and morale.

[59]Rehovot was one of the first citrus *moshavot* in Palestine.

[60]Housing projects.

[61]Cf. Gen 19:17, the story of the destruction of Sodom and Gomorrah; see above p. 15 for another allusion to the "Lot's Wife" motif in Yizhar's story.

[62] P. Coveney, *The Image of Childhood*, 240.

[63] Quoted from Thomas Moult's eulogy of Barrie (ibid., 250).

[64] Lerner, 212.

[65] M. L. von Franz, "The Process of Individuation," in *Man and His Symbols*, ed. C. G. Jung and M. L. von Franz (London 1964) 174.

[66] B. Bettelheim, *The Uses of Enchantment* (London 1976) 290.

[67] Cf. D. W. Harding, "The Hinterland of Thought," in *Metaphor and Symbol*, 21: "The horse may serve as the symbol of a very complex mass of inarticulate potential experience, including a sense of delight, the danger, the power, the vulnerability, the wildness and the manageableness of animal vitality." For an additional attempt to interpret this horse, see below, n. 133.

[68] In his fascination with movement, speed, flight, fleeing from decisions and from oneself, and in his passion for departing and not arriving, Yizhar, the intellectual of the 1948 war, calls to mind not only the ideology of the beat and hip phenomena, but also that of the intellectuals of the 1914 war. Cf. R. Wohl, *The Generation of 1914* (London 1980) 226ff.

[69] The horse in the story "Hanoch's Bubkah," in *Six Summer Stories*.

[70] Cf. H. Barzel, "Yearning and Rebuke," *Yediot Ahronot*, 16 May 1973 (H).

[71] B. Kurzweil, "Comments on the State of Our Literature Today," *Haaretz*, 18 Sept 1963 (H); it is quoted also by B. Y. Michaly in "The Ethos that Failed," *Moznaim* 35/3-4 (1972) 251 (H).

[72] Schweid, "Perplexity on Perplexity," loc. cit.

[73] D. Miron, "On Yizhar's Last Two Stories," *Haaretz*, 1 Dec 1961 (H). For this aspect in Yizhar's stories, see also: D. Kena'ani, "In the Convoy and Outside It," in *Selection*, 64; Luz, *Existence and Man*, 57; E. Schweid, "Before Locked Gates," in *Selection*, 147; and idem, "Protest for the Sake of Conformity," *Massa*, 26 Sept 1965, and "Four Stories in a Different Light," *Massa*, 27 Mar 1959 (H).

[74] See *Tales*, 47.

[75] Van Wyck Brooks on Mark Twain, see above p. 3.

[76] Its version "Wild Flowers Also Want to Live," appears in *Davar*, 10 July 1964 (H).

[77] He uses this epithet in "Beyond the Boundary of the Story," *Haaretz*, 13 Dec 1963 (H).

[78] Cf. Miron, "General Observations," 267.

[79] Cf. Coveney's remarks, in this context, about Carroll, Barrie, Walpole and Forrest Reid; *Image of Childhood*, 272-74.

[80]Cf. D. Miron, "The Landscape in Yizhar's Stories," *Haaretz*, 28 Oct 1960 (H).

[81]H. Barzel, "Yizhar's New Stories," *Yediot Aḥronot*, 18 Oct 1963 (H).

[82]Miron, "General Observations," 262.

[83]See Y. Averbuch, "Days of Ziklag," in *Selection*, 135.

[84]Miron, "General Observations," 263.

[85]Ibid.

[86]S. Zemach, "Midnight Convoy," in *Selection*, 85.

[87]Shaked, "The Outsider and the Convoy," in *Selection*, 112.

[88]D. Patterson, "Some Aspects of the Transference of Hebrew Literature from Eastern Europe to Eretz Yisrael," in *Sefer Meir Wallenstein: Studies in the Bible and Hebrew Language Offered to Meir Wallenstein* (Jerusalem 1979) 62.

[89]Miron, "General Observations," 264.

[90]Lerner, 208.

[91]Gen 2:20.

[92]Segal, "A Psycho-Analytical Approach," 395.

[93]Lerner, 47.

[94]Virgil, *Eclogues, Georgics, Aeneid I-VI*, rev. ed., trans. H. R. Fairclough (London 1935) 1.9; cf. with the story "The Prisoner" in which Yizhar's sympathy is clearly with the Arab shepherd who is forcefully taken away from his home.

[95]Book 11, 268-86.

[96]Coveney, 241.

[97]Schweid, who points out such strivings in *Ziklag* (see "Before Locked Gates," 147), does not repeat it when reviewing *Tales*, which he regards as one small step short of "complete failure"; see "Perplexity on Perplexity," loc. cit.

[98]The first organized group of Jewish pioneers to emigrate to Palestine. They arrived in 1882. See S. Laskov, *Ha-Biluim (The Biluim)* (Jerusalem 1979) (H).

[99]*Keshet* 16/2 (1974) 9 (H).

[100]See Kena'ani, "In the Convoy and Outside It," in *Selection*, 74.

[101]See Y. Averbuch, "Days of Ziklag," in *Selection*, 139.

[102]M. Shalev, "Confusion and Sadism," in *Selection*, 50.

[103]Schweid, "Protest for the Sake of Conformity," loc. cit.

[104]Michaly, "The Ethos That Failed," loc. cit.

[105]Miron, "General Observations," 267f.

[106]U. Shoham, "The Open Plain, the Closed Orange Grove and the Arab Village," *Siman K'ria* 3-4 (1974) 336-46 (H).

[107]In this story he is not buying dung but land for the Jew-Jewish National Fund.

[108]W. Empson, *Some Versions of Pastoral* (London 1950) 17.

[109]*Davar*, 8 Feb 1978 (H).

[110]Lerner, 117.

[111]See Barzel, "Yizhar's New Stories," loc. cit.

[112]See Schweid, "Perplexity on Perplexity," loc. cit.

[113]Cf. Jolande Jacobi: "At ceremonies of initiation a youth must suffer a symbolic death before he can be reborn as a man and be taken into the tribe as a full member"; "Symbols in an Individual Analysis," in *Man and His Symbols*, 295.

[114]In *Tales* the death of Habakuk is linked with this war.

[115]Salinger, 223.

[116]These are surprisingly anemic curses: "Bandit" (186); "Thief" and "Son of a Bitch" (182).

[117]Cf. A. Green, "On Yizhar's New Stories," *Hapoel Hatzair*, 8 Oct 1963 (H).

[118]See Salinger, 47f.

[119]Cf. Miron, "Beyond the Boundary of the Story," loc. cit.

[120]Elon, *The Israelis*, 11.

[121]*Keshet* 16/2 (1974) 23 (H).

[122]Miron, "General Observations," 272.

[123]N. Alterman, *Ha-Tur ha Shevii (Column Seven)* (Tel Aviv 1948) 366f. (H).

[124]Cf. Kierkegaard's brilliant discussion of Abraham's filicidal disposition in *Fear and Trembling* (London/New York/Toronto 1939) 8, 24, 34, 102, 107, 111f.

[125]H. Gouri's book of poems, *Shoshanat Ruhot (Wind Rose)* (Tel Aviv 1960) (H).

[126]Translated for this study by Arthur Jacobs. For a commentary on this poem, see Y. Akavyahu, "The Father Image in New Poetry," *Meassef* 8-9 (1968) 348 (H); and H. Barzel, *Shirah u-Morashah (Poetry and Heritage)* (Tel Aviv 1971) 18 (H).

[127]S. Spiegel, *The Last Trial*, trans. J. Goldin (New York 1967) 45.

[128]Cf. G. Ofrat, "The Sacrifice of Isaac in Israeli Drama,"
Moznaim 49/6 (1979) 349 (H); see also I. Eliraz, "The *Akedah* as a
Theme in Israeli Drama," *Massa*, 9 Nov 1971 (H).

[129]The revue was staged by the *Cameri* Theater, Tel Aviv
(1970), but closed down after a short run because of strong public
protests. For the theatrical writings of Ḥ. Levin, see G.
Abramson, *Modern Hebrew Drama* (London 1979) 171-80.

[130]*Siaḥ Loḥamim (Seventh Day)* (Tel Aviv 1967) (H).

[131]*Shanah le-Aḥar ha-Milḥamah (A Year after the War)* (Ein
Shemer 1968) (H).

[132]Ibid., 7f.; see also U. Tal, "The Land and the State of
Israel in Israeli Religious Life," *Proceedings of the Rabbinical
Assembly* 38 (New York 1976) 21.

[133]On a symbolic level and in the context of this theme, it
is perhaps possible to interpret the motif of the runaway horse
in a new light. The horse may symbolize the sacrificed son, the
ne'ekad, to the extent that it connotes the "sacrificial horse"
described at the opening of the *Brihadâranyaka Upanishad*. See
The Sacred Books of the East, ed. M. F. Müller (Oxford 1884) 15.
73f. According to this *Upanishad*, the horse contains the whole
universe ("the dawn is the head of the horse which is fit for
sacrifice, the sun its eye, the wind its breath...Heaven is the
back, the sky the belly, the earth the chest," etc.). According
to Northrop Frye, this horse "is treated in the same way that a
Christian poet would treat the Lamb of God" (*Anatomy of Criticism*
[Princeton 1957] 143f.). For a comparison between the *Akedah* on
Mount Moriah and the Crucifixion on Golgotha, see Spiegel, *The
Last Trial*, 116f. The attempted escape of the horse in "Runaway"
may therefore symbolize an attempt to rebel against the *Akedah*,
an attempt that fails.

[134]*Ziklag*, 1024.

[135]Kurzweil, *Between Vision and the Absurd*, 401.

[136]Ibid., 399.

[137]See D. Miron, "The Hero in Yizhar's Stories," *Haaretz*,
16 Sept 1960 (H); and idem, *Four Faces in Contemporary Hebrew
Literature*, 212-15.

[138]See Y. Keshet, *Maskiyyot (Lockets)* (Tel Aviv 1953) 240 (H).

[139]See M. Breslawsky, "Musings on the Book of Perplexity,"
Mibbifnim 21/2-3 (1959) 347 (H).

[140]Barzel, "Yearning and Rebuke," loc. cit.

[141]W. C. Booth, *The Rhetoric of Fiction* (Chicago/London 1973)
28.

[142]H. E. Bates, *The Modern Short Story* (London 1972) 27.

[143]Segal, "A Psycho-Analytical Approach," 392.

[144]H. Gold, "The International Symposium on the Short Story,"
The Kenyon Review 30/4 (1968) 451.

[145]Cf. Even-Zohar, "Israeli Hebrew Literature," 433.

[146]Zussman, "Yizhar's *On the Edge of the Negev*," in *Selection*, 45.

[147]Miron, "Beyond the Boundary of the Story," loc. cit.

NOTES

CHAPTER II

[1]For a complete bibliography of his other short stories written and published between 1948-1967, see Barzel, "Nissim Aloni as a Storyteller," *Moznaim* 49/2-4 (1979) 148f. (H).

[2]Tel Aviv 1975 (H). This edition, published by Sifriat Tarmil, will be referred to as *Tarmil*.

[3]The list of his plays and the first production of each includes also: *Ha-Nesikhah ha-Amerika'it (The American Princess)*, 1963; *Ha-Mahpekhah ve-ha-Tarnegolet (The Revolution and the Chicken)*, 1964; *Ha-Kalah ve-Tzayad ha-Parparim (The Bride and the Butterfly Catcher)*, 1967; *Dodah Liza (Aunt Liza)*, 1969; *Napoleon Hai O Met (Napoleon - Alive or Dead)*, 1970; *Ha-Tzoanim Shel Yafo (The Gypsies of Jaffa)*, 1971; *Sai'r Ehad la-Azazel (The Scapegoat)*, 1973; *Eddie King (Eddie King)*, 1975.

[4]On his theatrical writing, see Abramson, *Modern Hebrew Drama*, 147-61.

[5]Cf. M. Nathan, "Conversations with Nissim Aloni," *Keshet* 8/4 (1966) 25ff. This is the first part of the "Conversations." The second appears in *Keshet* 9/1 (1966) (H) (hereafter: "Conversations").

[6]Ibid., 25.

[7]Echoes of such accusations can be found even in generally favorable reviews of his plays such as H. Boshes, "Who Likes Nissim Aloni?", *Haaretz*, 12 Nov 1971 (H); Y. Kaniuk, "On Aloni's *Aunt Liza*," *Davar*, 14 Feb 1969 (H); U. Keysari, "Aunt Liza, Say Yes to Us," *Maariv*, 21 Feb 1969 (H); Ch. Gamzu, "Nissim Aloni's *Aunt Liza*," *Haaretz*, 7 Feb 1969 (H).

[8]"Conversations," *Keshet* 9/1, p. 31.

[9]Cf. Ch. Shoham, "Childhood in the Shadow of Fear," *Maariv*, 26 Dec 1975 (H).

[10]See "To Be a Baker, *Tarmil*, 128.

[11]*Massa*, 5 Oct 1956 (H).

[12]*Keshet* 1/1 (1958-1959). This story as well as the previous one did not appear in Eng. translation. When quoted hereafter the trans. is by this author, and the references are to the *Tarmil* ed.

[13]*Keshet* 1/3 (1959). This story appears in English translation by T. Sandbank in S. Y. Penueli and A. Ukhmani's anthology *Hebrew Short Stories*, Vol. 2 (Tel Aviv 1965). Unless otherwise stated, all subsequent references to this story are to this translation and ed.

[14]*Keshet* 2/4 (1960). This story appears in an English translation by M. Oren and D. Krauskopff in *Modern Hebrew Stories* (New York 1971). Unless otherwise stated, all subsequent

163

references to this story are to this translation and edition. Although most of these stories appeared at the end of the fifties, they belong in a study of childhood stories of the sixties, not only because of being published in *Keshet*, the quarterly that from its very beginning became the forerunner of the sixties, but because their impact on the genre of childhood stories written in Israel in the sixties was considerable.

[15]This point is made by several critics; see G. Ramras-Rauch, "The Two Faces of Fantasy," *Massa*, 12 Dec 1975 (H); Ch. Pesah, "Into the Great Darkness," *Haaretz*, 14 Nov 1975 (H) and Barzel, "Aloni as a Storyteller," loc. cit.

[16]Cf. H. Yaffé, "The Stories of Nissim Aloni," *Al Hamishmar*, 2 Jan 1976 (H).

[17]Cf. Ramras-Rauch, "Two Faces of Fantasy," loc. cit.

[18]Hereafter: "Soldier." Edirne (formerly Adrianople) is a Turkish town situated near the Greek frontier on both banks of the Tunca River, at its confluence with the Maritsa. From ancient times it has known many wars. It was occupied by the Russians in 1829 and 1878. During the first Balkan War it was taken from the Turks by the Bulgars in 1913, after 155 days of siege. The Turks reoccupied it during the second Balkan War. The Greek army took it in 1920. It was restored to Turkey in 1922.

[19]Cf. Barzel, "Aloni as a Storyteller," 154ff. An alternative view is discussed above, p. 61.

[20]See S. N. Eisenstadt, *Israeli Society* (London 1967) 380f.

[21]See "Conversations," *Keshet* 8/4, p. 23.

[22]Ibid., 24.

[23]A Polish Jewish writer (1892-1942), he was murdered by the Nazis in his native Drohobycz. His books include *Sanatorium Under the Sign of the Hourglass*, trans. Celina Winiewska (London 1978).

[24]J. Picowski, "On the Cross-Roads of Three Cultures," *The Jewish Quarterly* 27/1 (1979).

[25]"Conversations," *Keshet* 8/4, p. 24.

[26]Coveney, 160. Coveney's description of Dickens, in the same place, could be applied as well to Aloni's subsequent artistic creativity: "In one sense, he continued, throughout his life, to see the world with children's eyes. This may have been the source of his love for the fantastic, and the basis of his comedy in the grotesque, of his seeing his characters as just that little larger than life."

[27]Note the common root in Hebrew of man (*gever*, גבר), and heroism (*gevurah*, גבורה).

[28]The Hebrew spelling of his nickname reads like Adirne, which connotes the word *adir* (אדיר), mighty and powerful.

[29]In his discussion of Joyce's *A Portrait of the Artist as a Young Man*; Coveney, 311.

[30] G. Steiner, "Eros and Idiom," in *On Difficulty and Other Essays* (Oxford 1978) 100.

[31] "I am a first-rate sentimentalist. I cry in all the wild west movies"; "Conversations," *Keshet* 8/4, p. 12.

[32] Steiner, "Eros and Idiom," 105.

[33] The first connection between prostitutes and this monastery is made in "Soldier," p. 8: "Near the monastery there were stalls of red dates and the prostitutes sat in the sun with legs spread apart." The red dates are an erotic symbol in Aloni's stories. The Hebrew word for date, or palm-tree, *Tamar*, has biblical sexual connotations as a palm-tree (Song 7:7, 8) and as a name of a woman associated with sex (Genesis 38; 2 Samuel 13). In the Genesis story, Tamar is thought to be a prostitute.

[34] Cf. S. Freud, *The Interpretation of Dreams*, The Standard edition of the complete psychological works, Vol. 5 (London 1964). Snakes are identified as a genital symbol of the male organ (p. 357), and "every water-pipe is a reminder of the urinary apparatus" (p. 346).

[35] Ibid., 354.

[36] Cf. L. J. Stone and J. Church, *Childhood and Adolescence* (New York 1968) 484.

[37] Filled with sexual symbols (cistern, mountain, river of warm milk), this dream also conveys an inherent apprehension (the defecation and the fall) and appears to belong to the literature of childhood sexual complexities marked by post-Freudian influences; this literature stresses childhood and early adolescence as "periods of acute sexual torment and potential trauma," and translates the painful initiation of the child into "the more intimate terms of emotional and sexual spoliation"; Coveney, 337.

[38] Freud, *Interpretation of Dreams*, 354, 684.

[39] C. Lévi-Strauss, *The Raw and the Cooked* (London 1970) 335f.

[40] Ibid., 334.

[41] The correct literal translation "tongues of fire" (*leshonot esh*, לשונות אש) is more erotically suggestive.

[42] The boy's attraction to fire can be related to a possible influence on his imagination of the verbal resemblance in Hebrew between *esh* (אש) "fire" and *isha* (אשה) "woman." The grammatical gender of fire in Hebrew is feminine.

[43] For some reason this sentence was omitted from the English translation.

[44] The correct literal translation of the last part should read: "My finger was trembling to make a hole in it" (in Hebrew, *le-nakev*, לנקב); note the resemblance in Hebrew between *nekev* (נקב) "hole," and *nekevah* (נקבה) "female."

[45] Taking the girl to see the owl may suggest a wish to have intercourse with her, if one considers the superstition that the sound of an owl hooting among houses is a sign that an unmarried girl has just lost her virginity; see P. Haining, *Superstitions* (London 1979) 95.

[46]See Shoham, "Childhood in the Shadow of Fear," loc. cit.

[47]The paradox of the blind seeing stems from the saying "the angel of death is all eyes" (*Avodah Zarah* 20). Cf. Yizhar's "A Story" (182) where he calls Death "A Thousand Eyes"; on the opposite tradition--of the angel of death as blind--see below, n. 146.

[48]See "Conversations," *Keshet* 9/1, pp. 38, 43.

[49]N. Frye, "The Road of Excess," in *Myth and Symbol*, ed. B. Slote (Lincoln 1963) 14 (hereafter: Slote).

[50]Coveney, 231.

[51]Cf. D. Hertz, "Beneficial Conservatism," *Yediot Ahronot*, 21 Nov 1975 (H).

[52]See Booth, *Rhetoric of Fiction*, 136.

[53]Cf. *Child Development Through Literature*, ed. E. D. Landau, S. L. Epstein and A. P. Stone (Englewood Cliffs 1972) 87 (hereafter: Landau).

[54]See Coveney, 230.

[55]See above, p. 71.

[56]In the *Keshet* interview Aloni admits that he is constantly writing about a man whose desires are irrepressible and who constantly acts foolishly; see "Conversations," *Keshet* 9/1, p. 43.

[57]Landau, 247.

[58]Since the socio-economic status of the father is not defined in these stories, it is difficult to tell how much of a counterpart, socio-economically speaking, Shoeblack is to the narrator's father.

[59]From a Freudian standpoint, this suggests Oedipal traits. Cf. Bettelheim, *Uses of Enchantment*, 113: "The Oedipal boy, who feels threatened by his father because of the wish to replace him in Mother's attention, casts Father in the role of the threatening monster. This also seems to prove to the boy how dangerous a rival to the father he is, because otherwise why would this father figure be so threatening?"

[60]Cf. Bettelheim: "Red is the color symbolizing violent emotions, very much including sexual ones." Ibid., 173.

[61]The balcony is associated with sin (while the roof is associated with punishment--from the roof Shmeel, the avenger, intends to blow up the world, subconsciously punishing his mother); on the balcony Shmeel's mother is high on a pedestal, and at the same time on display like a prostitute waiting for customers. That the narrator has such a feeling is reflected in his dream, in which he sees Goldberg shoving his hand under the dressing gown of Shmeel's mother while she stands on the balcony ("Shmeel," 186).

[62]Coveney, 221.

[63]Such a fantasy also crosses Holden's mind when he asks his roommate at school: "What's the routine of joining a monastery?"; Salinger, 61.

[64]See R. Patai, *Israel Between East and West*, 2nd ed. (Westport 1970) 129ff.

[65]"Conversations," *Keshet* 8/4, p. 12.

[66]Ibid., 8.

[67]Twice in this page.

[68]For a suggested connection between Sultana in the role of Lilit and the *shedim*, see above, p. 78.

[69]On the belief in the magical powers of a mirror, see S. Thompson, *Motif-Index of Folk-Literature* (Copenhagen 1955) 2.217. He mentions an African belief in a magic mirror that kills enemy soldiers.

[70]In contrast to Yizhar, Arabs are not mentioned in Aloni's childhood stories, and he does not comment on Jewish-Arab relationship. In Yizhar's stories, the Arab is introduced mainly for nostalgic and pastoral purposes, which Aloni's stories clearly lack. Also, although the background of Aloni's stories is the period of the Mandate, there is no mention of the British in a local context, nor of the tension between the *Yishuv* and the British. Furthermore, there is no way of telling whether the soldiers in the stories are Jews or British.

[71]*Massa*, 5 Sept 1956 (H).

[72]E. Fromm, *Man for Himself* (New York 1947) 237.

[73]Landau, 291.

[74]See B. Evron, "A New View of Nissim Aloni," *Yediot Ahronot*, 8 Aug 1975 (H).

[75]J.-P. Sartre, *The Psychology of Imagination* (London 1972) 141.

[76]Cf. Frye, *Anatomy of Criticism*, 195; Bettelheim, *Uses of Enchantment*, 213.

[77]"Conversations," *Keshet* 8/4, p. 20.

[78]Ibid., 17.

[79]Ibid., 35.

[80]F. Fergusson, "'Myth' and the Literary Scruple," in *Myth and Literature*, ed. J. B. Vickery (Lincoln 1966) 139 (hereafter: Vickery).

[81]Y. Ben Porat, "Perhaps Tomorrow," *Yediot Ahronot*, 8 March 1963 (H).

[82]"Conversations," *Keshet* 8/4, p. 13.

[83]Ibid., 6. This play has never been produced or published.

[84]Ibid., 15.

[85]C. G. Jung, *Memories, Dreams, Reflections*, ed. A. Jaffé
(New York 1965) 311.

[86]Fergusson, "'Myth' and the Literary Scruple," loc. cit.

[87]H. M. Block, "Cultural Anthropology and Contemporary Literary Criticism," p. 134 in Vickery.

[88]Ibid.

[89]G. S. Kirk, *Myth: Its Meaning and Functions* (Cambridge
1970) 7.

[90]Lévi-Strauss, *The Raw and the Cooked*, 3.

[91]Ibid., 6.

[92]R. Wellek, *Concepts of Criticism* (New Haven 1963) 361.

[93]D. Bidney, "Myth, Symbolism, and Truth," p. 13 in Vickery.

[94]C. S. Lewis, *An Experiment in Criticism* (Cambridge 1965) 45.

[95]J. L. Blotner, "Mythic Patterns in *To the Lighthouse*,"
p. 243 in Vickery.

[96]"Conversations," *Keshet* 8/4, p. 36.

[97]Lévi-Strauss, *The Raw and the Cooked*, 5.

[98]Ibid.

[99]Frye, *Anatomy of Criticism*, 215.

[100]For a discussion of the *Akedah* in Aloni's plays, see
G. Ofrat, "The Sacrifice of Isaac," 350f.

[101]J. Goldin in his introduction to Spiegel, *The Last Trial*,
xvii.

[102]"Conversations," *Keshet* 8/4, p. 26.

[103]Later, in his plays, this challenge found a clear parrici-
dal expression, culminating in *Eddie King*, in which Eddie says:
"A son, Joe said to me, what he has in this life is to finish off
daddy...sometimes daddy finishes him off first...in wars"; see
Abramson, *Modern Hebrew Drama*, 158; and cf. Ch. Shoham, "Nissim
Aloni's *Eddie King* as a Mythical Drama," *Moznaim* 44/5-6 (1977) (H).

[104]See, for instance, L. Ginzberg, *The Legends of the Jews*
(Philadelphia 1946) 1.283.

[105]See E. Fleischer, *Shirat ha-Kodesh ha-Ivrit bi-Yemei
ha-Beynaim (Hebrew Liturgical Poetry in the Middle Ages)* (Jerusalem 1975) 470 (H). The *Akedah* is also connected with the
prayers of Rosh Ha-Shanah; it is mentioned in the *Zikhronot*
prayers of this high holiday. The story of the *Akedah* is the
pentateuchal reading on the second day of Rosh Ha-Shanah.

[106]See above, p. 52.

[107]This sentence was omitted in the English translation.

[108]See Ben Porat, "Perhaps Tomorrow," loc. cit.

[109]Cf. Ginzberg, *Legends of the Jews*, 198-201.

[110]Lévi-Strauss, *The Raw and the Cooked*, 142.

[111]See Gen 12:11-15; and see Ginzberg, *Legends of the Jews*, 221f.

[112]Spiegel, *The Last Trial*, xvii.

[113]*Midrash ha-Gadol* on Gen 22:19 (H); see Spiegel, *The Last Trial*, 5.

[114]*Hadar Zekenim* 10b. *Bet ha-Midrash*, ed. Jellinek, 5.157 (H), and *Minḥat Yehudah*, *Toledot*, Gen 25:27 (H); see Spiegel, *The Last Trial*, 6-8.

[115]*Midrash ha-Gadol*; see Spiegel, *The Last Trial*, 3f.

[116]*Minḥat Yehudah* and *Paaneaḥ Raza* (H); see Spiegel, *The Last Trial*, 6.

[117]*Lekaḥ Tob*, ed. Buber, 161 (H); see Spiegel, *The Last Trial*, 32.

[118]*Shibbolei ha-Leket*, 9a-b (H); see Spiegel, *The Last Trial*, 33.

[119]See Spiegel, *The Last Trial*, 17-27.

[120]Ibid.

[121]Aloni's preoccupation with this theme is evident in his play *The Scapegoat*.

[122]In a passage omitted from the English translation.

[123]See P. R. Davies, "Passover and the Dating of the Aqedah," *Journal of Jewish Studies* 30/1 (1979).

[124]Frye, *Anatomy of Criticism*, 193-97.

[125]Ibid., 193.

[126]Ibid., and cf. p. 61 above with regard to the narrator's perception of his own father as a wizard.

[127]Medusa is also the metaphor Aloni uses to describe the darkness that fell upon the *shekhunah* ("Soldier," 22).

[128]Frye, *Anatomy of Criticism*, 196.

[129]Ibid., 238.

[130]G. Róheim, "Myth and Folktale," p. 29 in Vickery.

[131]Ibid., 31.

[132]Cf. Haining, *Superstitions*, 95.

[133]Note the intentional paradox of its identification with the blind Sultana.

[134]For Aloni's preoccupation with the myth of Persephone, in his play *The American Princess*, see "Conversations," *Keshet* 8/4, pp. 11, 13; see also Ben Porat, "Perhaps Tomorrow," loc. cit.

[135]The action of *The American Princess* takes place in May. Aloni reveals that he intended it to correspond with Persephone's return to earth in the spring. See "Conversations," *Keshet* 8/4, p. 13.

[136]Tennyson, *The Life and Works of Alfred Lord Tennyson* (London 1899) 12.118.

[137]G. R. Stange, "Tennyson's Mythology: A Study of *Demeter and Persephone*," p. 362 in Vickery.

[138]Ibid.

[139]A. C. Swinburne, *Poems and Ballads* (London 1906) 195.

[140]Ibid.

[141]R. Harrison, "Symbolism of the Cyclical Myth in Endymion," p. 239 in Vickery.

[142]Another species of owl mentioned alongside *Lilit* is *sa'ir*, the smallest of the owls, the *Otus Scopus*. The word *sa'ir* refers also to a demon (cf. Lev 17:7; 2 Chr 11:15). But it is also part of the phrase *sa'ir la-azazel*, in Hebrew: "a scapegoat." Aloni's preoccupation with it was noted above.

[143]Haining, *Superstitions*, loc. cit.

[144]Ibid.

[145]A. S. Rappoport, *Myth and Legend of Ancient Israel* (New York 1966) 1.79.

[146]Samael is synonymous, in Jewish tradition, with Satan, angel of death and "head of the devils"; see G. Scholem, *Kabbalah* (Jerusalem 1974) 385-88. These associations and descriptions of him as a "blind angel" (387) arising from the etymology of the name, may reinforce the interpretation of Sultana as embodying demonic elements of Lilit. While Samael is not mentioned in the stories, Satan's presence is an intrinsic element in the lore of the *shekhunah*.

[147]Rappoport, *Myth and Legend*, 77.

[148]Cf. Scholem, *Kabbalah*, 357.

[149]Cf. A. S. Rappoport, *The Folklore of the Jews* (London 1937) 97.

[150]Compare with a Hebrew or Canaanite inscription found at Arslan-Tash, in northern Syria. This inscription that dates back to the 7th or 8th century B.C. is of a winged female demon strangling children. Scholem, *Kabbalah*, 356.

[151]*Alpha Beth de-Ben Sira*, ed. M. Steinschneider (Berlin 1858) 23.

[152] See Scholem, *Kabbalah*, 356.

[153] These nocturnal "screams" again bring to mind the owl. The connection between the oven and the owl can be seen also in the tale "The Owl was a Baker's Daughter," in K. Briggs, *A Dictionary of British Folk Tales in the English Language* (London 1970) Part A, 1.123, 443.

[154] Cf. Scholem, *Kabbalah*, 357f.

[155] Ibid., 325. In view of Aloni's flair for symbolic names, the identification of the owl with the Queen of Sheba provides an etymological clue to the name of the leader of the *shekhunah* "gang," Salomon, in whose attic the owl dwells. As another exercise in exegesis, and bearing in mind Aloni's weakness for a play on words, one could consider the following metathesis as a clue to the meaning of the owl's age: the owl is a thousand years (*shanim*, שנים) old, and King Solomon had a thousand wives (*nashim*, נשים).

[156] Scholem, *Kabbalah*, 358.

[157] C. W. Eckert, "Initiatory Motifs in the Story of Telemachus," p. 162 in Vickery.

[158] Ginzberg, *Legends of the Jews*, 274f.

[159] According to the midrash, Abraham's act broke her heart and caused her death.

[160] Not in the English translation.

[161] Frye, *Anatomy of Criticism*, 159.

[162] H. Frankfort, *Kingship and the Gods* (Chicago 1958) 157.

[163] See Kirk, *Myth: Its Meaning and Functions*, 255.

[164] R. Chase, "Notes on the Study of Myth," p. 70 in Vickery.

[165] A. Lytle, "The Working Novelist and the Mythmaking Process," p. 105 in Vickery.

[166] See J. G. Frazer, *The Golden Bough*, Part III: *The Dying God*, 3rd ed. (London 1923) 183f.

[167] Ibid., 31.

[168] E. O. James, *The Ancient Gods* (London 1960) 300f.

[169] Goldberg in this context is analogous to the narrator's father, especially in his role as the presumed lover of the woman whom the narrator desires. Destroying him is destroying the dragon. Cf. Bettelheim, *Uses of Enchantment*, 114: "The Oedipal boy projects his frustrations and anxieties onto a giant, monster or dragon."

[170] The allusion is mostly in his name, with gold representing the sun, as it was, for instance, in the case of the Incas.

[171] Cf. Rappoport, *Folklore of the Jews*, 14: "To the Persians the sun was the eye of Ormuzd, to the Egyptians the eye of Demiurgos, to the Greeks the eye of Zeus."

[172]Vickery, 162.

[173]Cf. Psa 19:5.

[174]Rappoport, *Folklore of the Jews*, 15.

[175]Ginzberg, *Legends of the Jews*, 221.

[176]Frye, *Anatomy of Criticism*, 150.

[177]In the poem mentioned above, "The Garden of Proserpine," and especially in "Hymn to Proserpine" (Swinburne, *Poems and Ballads*, 75-82).

[178]Cf. R. P. Adams, "The Archetypal Pattern of Death and Rebirth in Milton's *Lycidas*," p. 189 in Vickery.

[179]Bettelheim, *Uses of Enchantment*, 166.

CHAPTER III

[1]Before it was Hebraized the family's name was Shakherles. See I. Remba's interview with Shahar, "David Shahar Will Not Waste His Year Off," *Maariv*, 1 Aug 1969 (H).

[2]Rabbi Moses Sofer (1762-1839), an halakhic authority and leader of Orthodox Jewry in Pressburg, the center of Hungarian Jewish Orthodoxy.

[3]Constructed in 1883.

[4]The stronghold of the ultra-Orthodox Jews, a community which has a medieval character in dress and customs and which fanatically preserves the mores of the Middle-European Jewish ghetto.

[5]Orthodox elementary and advanced Jewish schools.

[6]Vladimir (Ze'ev) Jabotinsky (1880-1940), Zionist activist, soldier, orator, writer and poet; founder of the Jewish Legion, a military formation of Jewish volunteers in World War I, who fought for the liberation of Palestine from Turkish rule.

[7]*News from Jerusalem* (An Anthology of Shahar's stories in English translation) (Boston 1974) 223 (hereafter: *News*).

[8]See N. Gutkind's interview with him, "David Shahar's *The Palace of Broken Vessels*," *Hatzofeh*, 9 June 1972 (H).

[9]*Al ha-Ḥalomot (Of Dreams)* (Tel Aviv 1955) (H) - (hereafter: *Dreams*).

[10]Cf., S. Zemach, *Sheti va-Erev* (*Warp and Woof*) (Tel Aviv 1959) 86 (H); Y. Bahur, "David Shahar's *The Fortune Teller*," *Haaretz*, 26 Aug 1966 (H); G. Shaked, "Great Yearning for a Little God," *Haaretz*, 20 May 1960 (H).

[11]Tel Aviv 1959 (H) - (hereafter: *Honeymoon*).

[12]Tel Aviv 1960 (H) - (hereafter: *Caesar*).

[13]Jerusalem 1961 (H) - (hereafter: *Riki Maoz*).

[14]Tel Aviv 1966 (H) - (hereafter: *Teller* for the book, and "Teller" for the story).

[15]Jerusalem/Tel Aviv 1970 (H).

[16]Jerusalem/Tel Aviv 1971 (H) - (hereafter: *Mustache* for the book, and "Mustache" for the story).

[17]Merḥavia 1969 (H).

[18]Merḥavia 1971 (H).

[19]Merḥavia 1976 (H).

[20]Tel Aviv 1979 (H).

[21]All these stories are included in *News*, and all references to them, if not otherwise stated, are to the translations in this edition.

[22]All references to the former are to its Hebrew text in *Dreams*; all references to the latter are to its Hebrew text in *Mustache*. The quotations from them are given in the English translation of the author of this study, as are the quotations from Israeli critics and reviewers in Hebrew publications.

[23]*Meassef* 2 (1961) (H).

[24]*Moznaim* 15/1 (1962) (H).

[25]*Meassef* 3 (1962) (H).

[26]*Meassef* 5-6 (1966) (H).

[27]In *Teller*.

[28]Cf. S. Katz, *Yerushalayim ke-Mabba Ommanuti bi-Yetzirot Hazaz ve-Shahar (Jerusalem as an Artistic Expression in the Works of Hazaz and Shahar)*, a Bar-Ilan University Ph.D. dissertation (1978) 327 (hereafter: Katz, *Expression*) (H).

[29]A. Oz, in his novel *Touch the Water, Touch the Wind* (trans. N. de Lange [London 1976] 91), comically describes an immigrant Hebrew poet who could not free himself of such a myth. See D. Patterson, "Modern Hebrew Literature Goes on Aliyah," *Journal of Jewish Studies* 29/1 (1978).

[30]In his interview with Ch. Be'er, "To Collect the Broken Vessels, To Make a Reconstruction," *Haaretz*, 27 Aug 1971 (H).

[31]See his interview with Gutkind, *Hatzofeh*, 9 June 1972.

[32]Cf. R. Fürstenberg, "History Through a Cracked Mirror: On David Shahar's *His Majesty's Agent*," *Modern Hebrew Literature* 5/4 (1980) 30.

[33]Cf. Katz, *Expression*, 133; M. Baumgarten, "A Mythical City," *Jerusalem Post*, 30 July 1976.

[34]Cf. Shaked, *A New Wave in Hebrew Fiction*, 62; Luz, *Existence and Man*, 141; Katz, *Expression*, 237; Barzel, "Introduction to the Stories of David Shahar," in *Shishah Mesapprim (Six Authors)* (Tel Aviv 1972) 297 (H); A. Blatt, "People on the Border," *Hatzofeh*, 28 Aug 1970 (H).

[35]Derogatory term which expressed the *Sabra*'s negation of the Jewish pattern of life in the diaspora.

[36]*Caesar*, 113.

[37]In its English translation by W. Lever, which appears in *Israeli Stories*, ed. J. Blocker (New York 1962), and in *First-fruits*, ed. J. Michener (Philadelphia 1973), her name is spelled Tehilah. In the English translation by I. M. Lask which appears

in *Hebrew Short Stories*, ed. S. Y. Penueli and A. Ukhmani (Tel Aviv 1965), and in *Tehilla and Other Israeli Tales*, selected under a committee headed by I. Shenhar (London/New York 1956), it is spelled Tehilla.

[38] See "Moses and the Negress," a segment from *Palace*, in *News*, p. 144.

[39] Not available in English translation (hereafter: "Evening").

[40] *Dreams*, 92f.

[41] In *Mustache* (hereafter: "Old Man").

[42] Schweid and Luz differ in their interpretation of Ephraim's motive. The former maintains that it is principally a political act--Ephraim meant to revenge the humiliation of the *Yishuv* by the British (see Schweid, *Three Night Watches*, 216); whereas Luz believes it is a personal vendetta (see Luz, *Existence and Man*, 129). The latter seems to be more appropriate.

[43] Cf. J. J. Rivlin, "The Hegemony of the Ashkenazim in the Old *Yishuv*," *Moznaim* 15/4-5 (1962) (H).

[44] See M. Michaelson, "An Interview with David Shahar," *Yediot Aḥronot*, 14 Jan 1977 (H).

[45] See Remba's interview, *Maariv*, 1 Aug 1969; and I. Bezalel's interview with Shahar, "Literature and its Gods," *Massa*, 2 Sept 1966 (H).

[46] "National Military Organization." A Jewish underground armed organization founded in Jerusalem in 1931, also known as *Irgun*.

[47] Cf. Luz, *Existence and Man*, 123.

[48] Cf. Katz, *Expression*, 157.

[49] Cf. Barzel, "Introduction to the Stories of David Shahar," 297.

[50] Cf. S. Katz, *Ha-Ani ve-Gibborav be-Sippurei Shahar (The I and its Protagonists in Shahar's Stories)* (Tel Aviv 1975) 18 (H) (hereafter: Katz, *Protagonists*).

[51] Cf. Y. Zwick, "A New Meeting with Shahar's Writings," *Davar*, 10 Sept 1971 (H).

[52] Cf. Luz, *Existence and Man*, 128.

[53] It is noteworthy that in the children's book *Riki Maoz*, and in "The Little Doctor," the personality of the grandmother, especially in the former, is more pleasant and good-natured and she is portrayed as radiating warmth and affection.

[54] In his interview with Bezalel, *Massa*, 2 Sept 1966.

[55] Cf. Luz, *Existence and Man*, 127.

[56] In *News* (hereafter: "Proposal").

[57] In *Dreams*.

[58]Cf. M. Avishai, "Reality and Dream in Yesterday's Jerusalem," *Al Hamishmar*, 8 Jan 1971 (H).

[59]Cf. N. Gal-Margalit, "The Meaning Beyond the Tangible," *Haaretz*, 27 Aug 1976 (H).

[60]G. Yardeni, "An Interview with Shahar," *Moznaim* 15/2-3 (1962) (H).

[61]In his interview with Gutkind, *Hatzofeh*, 9 June 1972.

[62]Ch. Nagid's interview with Shahar, "Truth Beyond Truth," *Yediot Aḥronot*, 12 Feb 1971 (H).

[63]Cf. M. L. von Franz, "The Process of Individuation," 208f.: "The Self is symbolized with special frequency in the form of a stone, precious or otherwise."

[64]In his interview with Bezalel, *Massa*, 2 Sept 1966.

[65]Barzel, "Introduction to the Stories of David Shahar," 298.

[66]In 1963, about the period this story was written, Shahar published a book called *Ḥokhmat ha-Zen* (*Zen-Buddhist Wisdom*), a Hebrew translation of Zen-Buddhist aphorisms and parables. It is likely that this had an influence on him when writing this story.

[67]Cf. Barzel, "Introduction to the Stories of David Shahar," 299.

[68]See Scholem, *Kabbalah*, 344.

[69]On OOBE (out-of-body-experience), see R. A. Monroe, *Journeys Out of the Body* (London 1972).

[70]On the "Ari" and the Lurianic Kabbalah, see Scholem, *Kabbalah*, 420-27.

[71]In his interview with Be'er, *Haaretz*, 27 Aug 1971.

[72]On the kabbalistic concept of the "breaking of the vessels," see Scholem, *Kabbalah*, 119.

[73]Cf. Y. Zwick, "Shahar's Narrative Work," *Al Hamishmar*, 1 Oct 1976 (H); and Katz, *Expression*, 209.

[74]Scholem, *Kabbalah*, 176.

[75]Ibid., 177.

[76]Ibid., 187f.

[77]Ibid., 158.

[78]Ibid.

[79]Ibid., 181.

[80]Ibid., 158.

[81]Ibid., 181.

[82]Ibid., 4.

[83]Cf. Y. Oren, "Mysticism and Humour in Shahar's Stories,"
Yediot Aḥronot, 6 Aug 1971 (H).

[84]Cf. Katz, *Expression*, 209.

[85]Cf. Gal-Margalit, "The Meaning Beyond the Tangible,"
Haaretz, 27 Aug 1976.

[86]See Z.G., "The Fortune Teller," *Keshet* 9/2 (1967) (H).

[87]Scholem, *Kabbalah*, 3.

[88]See his interviews with Yardeni, Nagid and Bezalel.

[89]Luz, *Existence and Man*, 138.

[90]Dickstein, *Gates of Eden*, 97.

[91]Ibid. See also Ruth R. Wisse, *The Schlemiel as Modern
Hero* (Chicago 1971) 3-24.

[92]Ironically, though, in *Sefer Razi'el* (Amsterdam 1701) 34b,
and elsewhere, Samael (Satan) appears as the angel in charge of
Tuesday--something of which Shahar may or may not have been aware;
see Scholem, *Kabbalah*, 387.

[93]Scholem, *Kabbalah*, 157.

[94]For the concept of the *Sefirot* (divine emanations), see
Scholem, *Kabbalah*, 96-107; for the common order of the *Sefirot*
and the names used for them, see p. 106; for a chart showing the
interrelation of the ten *Sefirot*, see p. 146.

[95]*Hakham* is a title given to a member of the rabbinic elite.
Nicknaming this café-owner a *ḥakham* is an instance of Shahar's
ridiculing institutional religion.

[96]By contrast, the café in "Spirit," which is in another part
of Jerusalem, is associated with this element.

[97]E. M. Forster, *Aspects of the Novel* (London 1927) 74ff.

[98]When she opens the door for the narrator she is, like
Shmeel's erotic mother in Aloni's stories, "wearing a red dressing
gown and her hair was disordered" (*News*, 91).

[99]Cf. Luz, *Existence and Man*, 124; and Katz, *Expression*, 234.

[100]Cf. Shaked, "Great Yearning for a Little God," *Haaretz*,
20 May 1960.

[101]Booth, *Rhetoric of Fiction*, 158f.

[102]Cf. Katz, *Protagonists*, 13.

[103]Cf. Zwick, "A New Meeting with Shahar's Writing," *Davar*,
10 Sept 1971; Shaked, "Great Yearning for a Little God," loc. cit.

[104]W. Benjamin, *Illuminations* (London 1970) 89.

[105]This testimony is given in "The Dove and the Moon," a
segment from *Palace*, in *News*, 181.

[106]Cf. Luz, *Existence and Man*, 123.

[107]See his interview with Yardeni, *Moznaim* 15/2-3 (1962).

[108]In his interview with Be'er, *Haaretz*, 27 Aug 1971.

[109]Scholem, *Kabbalah*, 154.

[110]In his interview with Yardeni.

NOTES

CHAPTER IV

[1]Her father Chaim Kahana (d. 1976), a veteran of the second
Aliyah, was one of its founders. On the first years of this kib-
butz, which was founded in 1921, see A. Yaari, *Zikhronot Eretz
Israel* (*Memories of Eretz Israel*) (Jerusalem 1947) 2.1185-90 (H).

[2]This is the name given to it later in her collection *Under
One Roof*. Its original name was *Ba-Derekh ha-Baytah* (*On the Way
Home*). It was published in *Massa*, 9 Nov 1956 (H). Cf. her
article "My First Story," *Massa*, 1 Jan 1965 (H).

[3]Cf. Shaked, *A New Wave in Hebrew Fiction*, 168; L. Yudkin,
"Kahana-Karmon and the Plot of the Unspoken," *Modern Hebrew
Literature* 2/4 (1976) 30.

[4]Merhavia 1966 (H).

[5]Tel Aviv 1971 (H).

[6]Tel Aviv 1977 (H).

[7]Cf. G. Avinur, "Mrs. Talmon and her Girlfriends,"
Al Hamishmar, 13 Aug 1971 (H).

[8]First published in *Ammot* 10 (1964); included in *Under One
Roof*. All subsequent references to it are to its English transla-
tion by A. Jacobs as published in the anthology *Meetings with the
Angel*, ed. B. Tammuz and L. Yudkin (London 1973) (hereafter:
"N'ima").

[9]First published in *Molad* 22 (1965-1966); included in *Under
One Roof*. All subsequent references to it are to the *Molad* text.
The English translations of quotations from it are by the author
of this study (hereafter: "Heart").

[10]First published in *Shdemot* 34 (1969); included in *Magnetic
Fields*. All subsequent references to it are to the *Magnetic
Fields* text. The English translations of quotations from it are
by the author of this study.

[11]See Jung, *Man and His Symbols*, 211.

[12]See N. Gretz, "A Dramatic Event and Other Times," *Siman
K'ria* 6 (1976) 38 (H). For an approach which seeks to regard the
pattern of the encounter in Kahana-Carmon's stories through a
mystical interpretation, an exercise in reading into the text
elements which are not necessarily there, see Shaked, *A New Wave
in Hebrew Fiction*, 171f.; and especially A. Balaban, *Ha-Kadosh
ve-ha-Drakon* (*The Saint and the Dragon*) (Tel Aviv 1979) 8 (H).
The latter even goes out of his way to explain the encounter between man and woman in Kahana-Carmon's stories in terms borrowed
from Buber's philosophy. This aspect is reviewed also in S. Katz,
"Jerusalem - Heart of Light," *Bikkoret u-Parshanut* 9-10 (1976)
110 (H).

[13]Y. Baḥur sees this as typical of the narrator in all of Kahana-Carmon's stories; cf. "A Poet and an Author Under One Roof," *Yediot Aḥronot*, 4 Nov 1966 (H).

[14]Cf. Ḥulda's confession in the context of her love for Baruchin: "I am incurably sick" ("Heart," 609).

[15]Cf. R. Litvin, "Amalia Kahana-Carmon - a Fresh Introduction," *Massa*, 10 Oct 1969 (H).

[16]Compare the description of Shmeel's mother on the balcony in Aloni's "Shmeel," see above, p. 62. Each description brings out the essence of the woman on the balcony. Ronen's mother is inhibited, introversive, uncomfortable--the opposite of Shmeel's mother who is at ease, forthcoming, unafraid of erotic encounters and not pent-up, as her loose hair symbolizes.

[17]Bettelheim, *Uses of Enchantment*, 53.

[18]Ibid., 225.

[19]Ibid., 234.

[20]Ibid.

[21]Ibid.

[22]Sometimes called also King Frog; see Briggs, *Dictionary of British Folk Tales*, 258-60, 563f.

[23]Bettelheim classifies these two fairy tales in a category called "animal-groom cycle'." See *Uses of Enchantment*, 282f.

[24]According to Bettelheim, one of the typical features of the fairy tales of the "animal-groom cycle" is that although it is known that a sorceress changed the groom into an animal, it remains unknown how and why it happened (*Uses of Enchantment*, 283).

[25]A. Koestler, *The Act of Creation* (London 1964) 355.

[26]Bettelheim, *Uses of Enchantment*, 170.

[27]Ibid., 183.

[28]Ibid., 172.

[29]Ibid., 175.

[30]Ḥulda is in the same category as the young girls with regard to the problems of initiation. One can regard Ronen's childhood as a mirror of his mother's "long childhood." See Erik Erikson, *Childhood in Society* (London 1977) 13f.: "It is human to have a long childhood; it is civilized to have an even longer childhood. Long childhood makes a technical and mental virtuoso out of man, but it also leaves a lifelong residue of emotional immaturity in him."

[31]The end of the 19th century and the beginning of the 20th.

[32]By contrast, in the male writer Shahar the image "mummy" is employed to characterize an old woman at the head of the family; see above, p. 101.

[33]Cf. Bettelheim, *Uses of Enchantment*, 289.

[34]J. L. Henderson, "Ancient Myths and Modern Man," in *Man and His Symbols*, 138.

[35]Ibid.

[36]Bettelheim, *Uses of Enchantment*, 303.

[37]J. Jacobi, "Symbols in an Individual Analysis," in *Man and His Symbols*, 299.

[38]Koestler, *Act of Creation*, 358.

[39]Ibid.

[40]Ibid.

[41]Bettelheim, *Uses of Enchantment*, 234.

[42]While she does not possess the demonic character of Aloni's Sultana, the sardonic treatment of her is similar to that of the grandmother in Shahar's stories.

[43]After a character in a Franz Léhar operetta.

[44]In contrast to Aloni's and Shahar's boy-narrators who, when spying on adults, are less interested in their own parents than they are in other adults, Ronen is not as interested in other adults as he is in his mother, whose shadow he becomes as the story progresses.

[45]Henderson, "Ancient Myths and Modern Man," 132.

[46]Cf. H. Barzel, "Introduction to the Stories of Amalia Kahana-Carmon," *Six Authors*, 141.

[47]This English version is given in A. Jacobs' translation of the story.

[48]Of the Spanish school of Hebrew poets. See H. Schirmann, *Ha-Shirah ha-Ivrit bi-Sfarad u-be-Provans* (*Hebrew Poetry in Spain and Provence*) (Jerusalem/Tel Aviv 1954) 1.425ff. (H); and A. M. Habermann, *Toldot ha-Piyyut ve-ha-Shirah* (*A History of Hebrew Liturgical and Secular Poetry*) (Tel Aviv 1970) 1.182ff. (H).

[49]For further discussion of this passage as a figurative description of death, see S. Luria, "Poetry Born of Love and Its Anguish," *Moznaim* 50/4 (1980) 276 (H).

[50]For Yizhar's use of this biblical association, see above, pp. 15, 21.

[51]*Siman K'ria* 5 (1976) 266 (H).

[52]Ibid.

[53]C. G. Jung, "Approaching the Unconscious," in *Man and His Symbols*, 55.

[54]W. K. Wimsatt, *The Verbal Icon* (London 1970) 79.

[55]In Knights and Cottle, *Metaphor and Symbol*, 10-23.

[56]Ibid., 11.

[57]Ibid., 12.

[58]The contrast between the animals which symbolize the husband and the lover is not accidental. According to a common feature which Bettelheim detects in fairy tales of the "animal-groom cycle," the sexual partner is first experienced as an animal; Bettelheim, *Uses of Enchantment*, 282.

[59]Cf. Jacobi, "Symbols in an Individual Analysis," 279.

[60]See ibid., 293.

[61]Cf. Henderson, "Ancient Myths and Modern Man," 151f.

[62]Ibid.

[63]See above, p. 23.

[64]According to Bettelheim, "Psychoanalytic investigation has revealed that over-involvement in and with horses can stand for many different emotional needs which the girl is trying to satisfy. For example, by controlling this powerful animal she can come to feel that she is controlling the male, or the sexually animal-istic, within herself" (*Uses of Enchantment*, 56). In N'ima's case the erotic aspect commingles with a mystic expression, as her stallions call to mind horses in visions of the prophet Zechariah (1:8-10; 6:1-4), as well as connoting visions of the prophet Ezekiel. See Barzel, *Six Authors*, 144; and see Luria, "Poetry Born of Love and Its Anguish," *Moznaim* 50/4 (1980) 276.

[65]I. A. Richards, *Principles of Literary Criticism* (London 1959) 240.

[66]Koestler, *Act of Creation*, 327f.

[67]Silberschlag, *From Renaissance to Renaissance*, 175.

[68]Lewis Carroll, *Alice's Adventures in Wonderland* (London 1925) 84ff.

[69]Cf. Bates, *Modern Short Story*, 10, 80.

[70]Cf. B. Romberg, *Studies in the Narrative Technique of the First-Person Novel* (Stockholm 1962) 4-11.

[71]Cf. C. Brooks and R. P. Warren, *Understanding Fiction* (New York 1959) 148.

[72]Booth in his discussion of Lubbock's view of Henry James (*Rhetoric of Fiction*, 174f.).

[73]Cf. Katz ("Jerusalem - Heart of Light," 113f.) in her discussion of the Jerusalem motif in Kahana-Carmon's story "If Now I Found Grace," in *Under One Roof*.

[74]Kahana-Carmon's predilection for displaying knowledge-ability and worldliness in her writing arouses criticism among her reviewers. She is accused of pretension and affectation by

Y. Orian Ben-Herzl, *Yediot Aḥronot*, 20 Aug 1971, and 10 Sept 1971
(H). Similar reservations are voiced by Y. Friedlander, "Chapters
of a Story and Parts of a Diary," *Davar*, 30 July 1971 (H); N.
Toker, "On the Creative Writing of Amalia Kahana-Carmon," *Moznaim*
50/1 (1979) (H); and D. Miron, *Pinkas Patuaḥ* (*An Open Notebook*)
(Merḥavia 1979) 95, 100 (H).

[75]*Dictionary of National Biography* (Oxford 1971) 775.

[76]Brooks and Warren, *Understanding Fiction*, 145.

[77]See, for example, S. Grodzenski, "On Amalia Kahana-Carmon's
Stories," *Ammot* 11 (1964) (H); and see also Ch. Nagid in his reply
to Y. Orian Ben-Herzl, *Yediot Aḥronot*, 3 Sept 1971 (H).

BIBLIOGRAPHY

This selected bibliography is arranged as follows:

I. Primary

Works by each Author (grouped separately). The arrangement is alphabetical according to transliterated Hebrew titles (followed by translation).

II. Secondary

Critical works, articles or books containing such articles, about each Author (grouped separately). The arrangement is alphabetical according to the name of the critic. Hebrew titles translated (followed by transliteration).

III. General

Miscellaneous works which have contributed to the formation of the ideas discussed throughout this study. Arranged as in II, above.

* indicates that the volume includes the story of the same title (see the preceding entry).

I. PRIMARY: WORKS BY EACH AUTHOR

S. YIZHAR

Al Ḥinukh ve-Al Ḥinukh le-Arakhim
  (*On Education and Education for Values*)   Book of essays

"Aremat ha-Deshen"
  ("The Dunghill")   Short story

"Be-Fa'atei Negev"
  ("On the Edge of the Negev")   Short story

"Bubkah Shel Ḥanoch"
  ("Ḥanoch's Bubkah")   Short story

"Ephraim Ḥozer la-Aspeset"
  ("Ephraim Goes Back to Alfalfa")   Short story

"Gam Pirḥei Bar Rotzim Liḥyot"
  ("Wild Flowers Also Want to Live")   Speech

"Ḥabakuk"
  ("Ḥabakuk")   Short story

"Ha-Ḥorshah ba-Givah"
  ("The Grove on the Hill")   Short story

"Ha-Nimlat"
  ("The Runaway")   Short story

"Ha-Shavui"
  ("The Prisoner")   Short story

"Laylah Beli Yeriot"
  ("A Night Without Shooting")   Short story

"Massa El Gedot ha-Erev"
  ("A Journey to the Banks of Evening")   Short story

Midnight Convoy   A collection of stories in English translation

"Mish'olim ba-Sadot"
  ("Paths in the Fields")   Short story

"Raḥatzah ba-Brekhah"
  ("A Dip in the Pool")   Short story

"Shayyarah Shel Ḥatzot"
  ("Midnight Convoy")   Short story

Shishah Sippurei Kayitz
  (*Six Summer Stories*)   A collection of children's stories

"Sippur Ḥirbet Ḥizah"
  ("The Story of Ḥirbet Ḥizah")   Short story

Sippur Ḥirbet Ḥizah   Two stories*

"Sippur she-Lo Hithil"
  ("A Story That Did Not Begin")   Short story

Sippurei Mishor
 (*Tales of the Plain*)   A collection of stories

Yemei Ziklag
 (*Days of Ziklag*)   Novel

"Zikkaron la-Rishonim"
 ("In Commemoration of the *Rishonim*)   Speech

NISSIM ALONI

Akhzar mi-Kol ha-Melekh
 (*The King is the Cruellest*)   Play

Bigdei ha-Melekh ha-Ḥadashim
 (*The King's New Clothes*)   Play

Dodah Liza
 (*Aunt Liza*)   Play

Eddie King
 (*Eddie King*)   Play

Ha-Kalah ve-Tzayad ha-Parparim
 (*The Bride and the Butterfly Catcher*)   Play

Ha-Mahpekhah ve-ha-Tarnegolet
 (*The Revolution and the Chicken*)   Play

Ha-Nesikhah ha-Amerika'it
 (*The American Princess*)   Play

Ha-Tzoanim Shel Yafo
 (*The Gypsies of Jaffa*)   Play

"Ḥayal Turki me-Edirne"
 ("A Turkish Soldier from Edirne")   Short story

"Ha-Yanshuf"
 ("The Owl")   Short story

Ha-Yanshuf A collection of stories*

"Kayitz Aḥaron"
 ("The Last Summer")   Short story

"Liheyot Ofeh"
 ("To Be a Baker")   Short story

Napoleon Ḥai O Met
 (*Napoleon - Alive or Dead*)   Play

Sa'ir Ehad la-Azazel
 (*The Scapegoat*)   Play

"Shmeel"
 ("Shmeel")   Short story

DAVID SHAHAR

"Al ha-Ḥalomot"
    ("Óf Dreams"; English translation entitled "Uncle Zemach")
    Short story

Al ha-Ḥalomot
    (*Of Dreams*)   A collection of stories*

"Al ha-Ḥataim ha-Ketannim"
    ("Óf Little Sins")   Short story

"Al ha-Tzlalim ve-ha-Tzelem"
    ("Of Shadows and the Image")   Short story

"Be-Erev ha-Kayitz"
    ("On a Summer Evening")   Short story

"Devarim she-be-Teva ha-Adam"
    ("Things in the Nature of Man")   Short story

"Eshet Ba'alat ha-Ov"
    ("The Woman with the Familiar Spirit")   Short story

Ha-Massa le-Ur Kasdim
    (*Journey to Ur of the Chaldees*)   Second volume of *The Palace
    of Broken Vessels*

"Ha-Metziah"
    ("The Find")   Short story

"Ha-Rofe ha-Katan mi-Reḥov ha-Ḥabashim"
    ("The Little Doctor")   Short story

Harpatkotav Shel Riki Maoz
    (*The Adventures of Riki Maoz*)   Children's book

"Ha-Zaken u-Bitto"
    ("The Old Man and His Daughter")   Short story

Heikhal ha-Kelim ha-Shevurim
    (*The Palace of Broken Vessels*)   A five-volume novel in
    progress

Ḥokhmat ha-Zen
    (*Zen-Buddhist Wisdom*)   A Hebrew translation of Zen-Buddhist
    aphorisms and parables

Kayitz be-Derekh ha-Neviim
    (*Summer on Prophets Street*)   First volume of *The Palace of
    Broken Vessels*

"Keisar"
    ("Caesar")   Novella

Keisar   A collection of stories*

"Ma'aseh be-Roke'ah u-bi-Geulat ha-Olam"
    ("The Pharmacist and the Salvation of the World")   Short story

"Maggid ha-Atidot"
    ("The Fortune Teller")   Short story

Maggid ha-Atidot   A collection of stories*

"Moto Shel ha-Elohim ha-Katan"
("The Death of the Little God")   Short story

Moto Shel ha-Elohim ha-Katan   A collection of stories*

News from Jerusalem   A collection of stories in English translation

"Pinik Mevakkesh Et Yadah Shel ha-Almah Simon"
("The Proposal")   Short story

"Sefamo Shel ha-Apifior"
("The Pope's Mustache")   Short story

Sefamo Shel ha-Apifior   A collection of stories*

"Shi'ur Rishon"
("First Lesson")   Short story

Sokhen Hod Malkhuto
(*His Majesty's Agent*)   Novel

Yerah ha-Devash ve-ha-Zahav
(*Honeymoon and Gold*)   Novel

Yom ha-Rozenet
(*The Day of the Countess*)   Third volume of *The Palace of Broken Vessels*

AMALIA KAHANA-CARMON

"Be'er Sheva Birat ha-Negev"
("Beer Sheba the Capital of the Negev")   Short story

Bi-Kfifah Ahat
(*Under One Roof*)   A collection of stories

"Hinumah"
("Bridal Veil")   Short story

"Im Na Matzati Hen"
("If Now I Found Grace")   Short story

"Keta la-Bamah be-Taam ha-Signon ha-Gadol"
("A Passage for the Stage in the Grand Manner")   Essay

"Lev ha-Kayitz, Lev ha-Or"
("Heart of Summer, Heart of Light")   Short story

"N'ima Sassoon Kotevet Shirim"
("N'ima Sassoon Writes Poems")   Short story

Sadot Magnetim
(*Magnetic Fields*)   Two short stories and a short novel

"Sippuri ha-Rishon"
("My First Story")   Newspaper article

Ve-Yareah be-Emek Ayyalon
(*And Moon in the Valley of Ajalon*)   Novel

II. SECONDARY: CRITICAL WORKS ABOUT EACH AUTHOR

S. YIZHAR

Averbuch, Y.   "Days of Ziklag" ("Yemei Ziklag") in Nagid, *S. Yizhar -
A Selection of Critical Essays on His Writings*; see below.

Barzel, H.   "Yizhar's New Stories" ("Sippurav ha-Ḥadashim Shel S.
Yizhar"), *Yediot Aḥronot*, 18 October 1963.

_____.   "Yearning and Rebuke" ("S. Yizhar: Kemihah ve-Tokhaḥah"),
Yediot Aḥronot, 16 May 1973.

Barzilay, I.   "The Reflection of Youth in Yizhar's Mirror" ("Demuto
Shel ha-Noar ba-Aspaklariah Shel Yizhar"), *Bitzaron*, October
1959.

Blatt, A.   "S. Yizhar - Whither?" ("S. Yizhar - le-An?"), *Hatzofeh*,
7 February 1964.

Breslawsky, M.   "Musings on the Book of Perplexity" ("Bi-Tehiyah
Al Sefer ha-Tehiyah"), *Mibbifnim* 21/2-3 (1959).

Cohen, A.   "Yizhar's *Tales of the Plain*" ("*Sippurei Mishor* le-S.
Yizhar"), *Davar*, 9 October 1963.

Elad-Lander, P.   "Of One Beginning" ("Al Hathalah Aḥat") in Nagid,
S. Yizhar - A Selection of Critical Essays on His Writings;
see below.

Green, A.   "On Yizhar's New Stories" ("Sippurav ha-Ḥadashim Shel
S. Yizhar"), *Hapoel Hatzair*, 8 October 1963.

Gur, I.   "More on Yizhar's Style" ("Od Al Signono Shel Yizhar"),
Al Hamishmar, 8 June 1951.

Ha-Ephrati, Y.   "A Study in 'A Dip in the Pool'" ("Iyyun be-
Raḥatzah ba-Brekhah") in Nagid, *S. Yizhar - A Selection of
Critical Essays on His Writings*; see below.

Halpern, I.   "A Brave and Perplexed Generation" ("Dor Gibbor
ve-Navokh"), *Davar*, 20 March 1959.

_____.   "In Search of the Path to Faith" ("Ḥippusei Derekh
la-Emunah"), *Davar*, 28 April 1959.

Kariv, A.   "S. Yizhar" in Nagid, *S. Yizhar - A Selection of
Critical Essays on His Writings*; see below.

Kena'ani, D.   "In the Convoy and Outside It" ("Ba-Shayyarah
u-Betzidah"), *Orlogin* 5 (1952); also in Nagid.

Keshet, Y.   *Lockets* (*Maskiyyot*), Tel Aviv 1953.

Kidan, A.   "The Final Analysis" ("Ha-Maazan ha-Sofi"), *Keshet* 1/1
(1958).

Kramer, S.   *The Changing of the Guard in Our Literature* (*Ḥillufei
Mishmarot be-Sifrutenu*), Tel Aviv 1959.

_____.   "A Song of Ḥasidim" ("Zemer Shel Ḥasidim"), *Moznaim*
25/3 (1967).

Kramer, S. *Realism and Its Decline* (*Realizm u-Shevirato*), Ramat Gan 1968.

Kressel, G. *Cyclopaedia of Modern Hebrew Literature* (*Leksikon ha-Sifrut ha-Ivrit ba-Dorot ha-Aḥronim*), Vol. 2, Merḥavia 1967.

Kurzweil, B. "Comments on a Chapter from a New Novel by Yizhar" ("He'arot le-Perek me-Roman Ḥadash le-S. Yizhar"), *Haaretz*, 30 August 1957.

_____. "The Great Disappointment" ("Ha-Akhzavah ha-Gedolah"), *Davar*, 22 August 1958.

_____. "Comments on the State of Our Literature Today" ("He'arot le-Matzav Sifrutenu be-Shaah Zo"), *Haaretz*, 18 September 1963.

_____. *Our Modern Literature - Continuation or Revolution?* (*Sifrutenu ha-Hadashah - Hemshekh O Mahpekhah*), Jerusalem/ Tel Aviv 1965.

_____. *Between Vision and the Absurd* (*Bein Hazon le-Vein ha-Absurdi*), Jerusalem/Tel Aviv 1966.

_____. "The Art of Storytelling, or the Conversion of Life into Literature" ("Ommanut ha-Sippur O Literarizatzia Shel ha-Ḥayyim), in Nagid, S. *Yizhar - A Selection of Critical Essays on His Writings*; see below.

Lichtenbom, I. "On Three Authors" ("Al Shloshah Mesapprim"), *Moznaim* 4/1 (1956).

Luz, Z. *Existence and Man in Israeli Literature* (*Metziut ve-Adam ba-Sifrut ha-Eretzyisraelit*), Tel Aviv 1970.

Megged, M. "With Yizhar's *Days of Ziklag*" ("Im Yemei Ziklag le-S. Yizhar"), *Massa*, 26 and 28 September 1958.

Michaly, B. Y. *Fruit of the Land* (*Pri ha-Aretz*), Tel Aviv 1966.

_____. "The Ethos That Failed" ("Ha-Etos she-Hikhziv"), *Moznaim* 35/3-4 (1972).

Miron, D. "The Hero in Yizhar's Stories" ("Ha-Gibbor Etzel Yizhar"), *Haaretz*, 16 September 1960.

_____. "The Landscape in Yizhar's Stories" ("Ha-Nof Etzel Yizhar"), *Haaretz*, 28 October 1960.

_____. "On Yizhar's Last Two Stories" ("Al Shnei Sippurav ha-Aḥronim Shel Yizhar"), *Haaretz*, 1 December 1961.

_____. *Four Faces in Contemporary Hebrew Literature* (*Arba Panim ba-Sifrut ha-Ivrit Bat Yamenu*), Jerusalem/Tel Aviv 1962.

_____. "Beyond the Boundary of the Story" ("Me-Ever li-Gvul ha-Sippur"), *Haaretz*, 13 December 1963.

_____. "S. Yizhar: Some General Observations," *Midnight Convoy and Other Stories*, Jerusalem 1969.

Moked, G. "Between Author and Leaders" ("Bein Sofer le-Manhigav"),
     Yediot Aḥronot, 30 July 1965.

Nagid, Ch. (ed.). S. Yizhar - A Selection of Critical Essays on
     His Writings (S. Yizhar Mivḥar Maamrei Bikkoret Al Yetzirato).
     Tel Aviv 1972.

Pachter, M. "Tales of the Plain" ("Sippurei Mishor"), in Nagid,
     S. Yizhar - A Selection of Critical Essays on His Writings;
     see above.

Ratosh, Y. "Escape to Reality, 'A Night Without Shooting'"
     ("Ha-Beriḥah El ha-Metziut, 'Laylah Beli Yeriot'"), in Nagid,
     S. Yizhar - A Selection of Critical Essays on His Writings;
     see above.

Sadan, D. "Smilansky Yizhar," in Kressel, Cyclopaedia of
     Modern Hebrew Literature; see above.

Sandbank, S. "Longing for the Open" ("Ha-Gaaguim El ha-Patuaḥ"),
     Ammot 2/2 (1963).

Schweid, E. "Four Stories in a Different Light" ("Arba'ah
     Sippurim be-Or Aḥer"), Massa, 27 March 1959.

_____. "Turning to God in the Young Hebrew Literature"
     ("Ha-Peniyah le-Elohim ba-Sifrut ha-Ivrit ha-Tzeirah"),
     Molad 17/129-30 (1959).

_____. "Perplexity on Perplexity" ("Mevukhah Al Mevukhah"),
     Massa, 1 November 1963.

_____. Three Night Watches (Shalosh Ashmorot), Tel Aviv 1964.

_____. "Protest for the Sake of Conformity" ("Meḥa'ah Tzorekh
     Hashlamah"), Massa, 26 September 1965.

_____. "Before Locked Gates" ("Lifnei She'arim Neulim"), in
     Nagid, S. Yizhar - A Selection of Critical Essays on His
     Writings; see above.

Shaked, G. "Reflections on the Literature of the War of Libera-
     tion" ("Hirhurim Al Sifrut Milḥemet ha-Shiḥrur"), Massa,
     4 and 13 October 1967.

_____. A New Wave in Hebrew Fiction (Gal Ḥadash ba-Sipporet
     ha-Ivrit), Merḥavia 1971.

_____. "The Outsider and the Convoy" ("Ha-Peli ve-ha-Shayyarah,
     Al Shayyarah Shel Hatzot"), in Nagid, S. Yizhar - A Selection
     of Critical Essays on His Writings; see above.

Shalev, M. "Confusion and Sadism" ("Mevukhah ve-Sadizm, Ḥirbet
     Ḥizah"), in Nagid, S. Yizhar - A Selection of Critical Essays
     on His Writings; see above.

Shoham, U. "The Open Plain, the Closed Orange Grove, and the Arab
     Village" ("Ha-Aravah ha-Petuḥah, ha-Pardess ha-Sagur, ve-ha-
     Kefar ha-Arvi), Siman K'ria 3-4 (1974).

Stavi, M. "S. Yizhar and the Reading of His Books" ("S. Yizhar
     ve-ha-Keriah be-Sefarav"), Haaretz, 5 November 1951.

Ukhmani, A. "The Strength and Weakness of Yizhar's Writings"
    ("Gedulatah ve-Hulshatah Shel Yetzirat Yizhar"), *Massa*,
    19 February 1953.

————————. *Towards Man* (*Le-Ever ha-Adam*), Merhavia 1953.

————————. *Human Voices* (*Kolot Adam*), Ramat Gan 1967.

Yaffe, A. B. "Yizhar's War Stories" ("Sippurei ha-Milhamah
    Shel Yizhar"), *Al Hamishmar*, 3 October 1949.

Yudkin, L. *Escape into Siege, A Survey of Israeli Literature
    Today*, London/Boston 1974.

Ze'ev, W. "Eventful Days" ("Yamim she-Neshimatam Gevohah"),
    Mibbifnim 21/2-3 (1959).

Zemach, S. "Midnight Convoy" ("Shayyarah Shel Hatzot"), in Nagid,
    S. *Yizhar - A Selection of Critical Essays on His Writings*;
    see above.

Zussman, E. "Yizhar's *On the Edge of the Negev*" ("Be-Fa'atei
    Negev le-S. Yizhar), in Nagid, S. *Yizhar - A Selection of
    Critical Essays on His Writings*; see above.

NISSIM ALONI

Aran, D. "Three *Shekhunah* Stories by Nissim Aloni" ("Shloshah
    Sippurei Shekhunah Shel Nissim Aloni"), *Al Hamishmar*,
    13 January 1961.

Ben Ammi, N. "All the Magic of the Stage" ("Kol Kismei ha-Bamah"),
    Maariv, 13 October 1971.

Ben Porat, Y. "Perhaps Tomorrow" ("Ulai Mahar"), an interview
    with Aloni, *Yediot Ahronot*, 8 March 1963.

Bezalel, I. "The Theatre, the Mask..." ("Ha-Teatron, ha-
    Massekhah, u-Bikhlal..."), an interview with Aloni, *All is
    Written in the Book* (*Ha-Kol Katuv ba-Sefer*), Tel Aviv 1969.

Barzel, H. "Nissim Aloni as a Storyteller" ("Nissim Aloni ki-
    Mesapper"), *Moznaim* 49/2-4 (1979).

Boshes, H. "Who Likes Nissim Aloni?" ("Mi Ohev Et Nissim Aloni"),
    Haaretz, 12 November 1971.

Dovev, L. "Monologue, Conversation, Hide-and-Seek" ("Monolog,
    Sihah, Mahboim"), an interview with Aloni, *Bamahane*, 9 Novem-
    ber 1971.

Evron, B. "A New View of Nissim Aloni" ("De'ah Aheret Al Nissim
    Aloni"), *Yediot Ahronot*, 8 August 1975.

Gamzu, Ch. "Nissim Aloni's *Aunt Liza*" ("Dodah Liza le-Nissim
    Aloni"), *Haaretz*, 7 February 1969.

Hagar, E. "A Chat with Nissim Aloni" ("Sihah Kalah Im Nissim
    Aloni"), *Al Hamishmar*, 22 February 1963.

Hertz, D. "Beneficial Conservatism" ("Shamranut ha-Poelet le-
    Tovah"), *Yediot Ahronot*, 21 November 1975.

Kaniuk, Y.   "On Aloni's *Aunt Liza*" ("Al Dodah Liza Shel Aloni"),
     Davar, 14 February 1969.

Keysari, U.   "Aunt Liza, Say Yes to Us" ("Dodah Liza Haggidi Lanu
     Ken"), *Maariv*, 21 February 1969.

Nathan, M.   "Conversations with Nissim Aloni" ("Sihot Im Nissim
     Aloni"), *Keshet* 8/4 and 9/1 (1966).

_____.   "Code, Love and the Creative Spark" ("Ha-Tzofen,
     ha-Ahavah, ve-ha-Zik Shel ha-Bore"), *Maariv*, 27 July and
     10 August 1973.

_____.   "Inside the Sphinx" ("Bi-Kravav Shel ha-Sfinks"),
     Maariv, 13 June 1975.

_____.   "Nissim Aloni" ("Nissim Aloni"), *Maariv*, 24 September
     1976.

Pesah, Ch.   "Into the Great Darkness" ("El Tokh ha-Hoshekh
     ha-Gadol"), *Haaretz*, 14 November 1975.

Ramras-Rauch, G.   "The Two Faces of Fantasy" ("Shtei Panim
     la-Fantasiah"), *Massa*, 12 December 1975.

Shoham, Ch.   "Childhood in the Shadow of Fear" ("Yaldut be-Tzel
     Eimah"), *Maariv*, 26 December 1975.

_____.   "Nissim Aloni's *Eddie King* as a Mythical Drama"
     ("Eddie King le-Nissim Aloni ke-Mahaze Mitos"), *Moznaim*
     44/5-6 (1977).

Yaffe, H.   "The Stories of Nissim Aloni" ("Sippurei Nissim
     Aloni"), *Al Hamishmar*, 2 January 1976.

DAVID SHAHAR

Avinur, G.   "The Hebrew Story after the Six-Day War" ("Ha-Sippur
     ha-Ivri le-Ahar Milhemet Sheshet ha-Yamim), *Moznaim* 34/5-6
     (1972).

Avishai, M.   "Reality and Dream in Yesterday's Jerusalem" ("Metziut
     ve-Halom bi-Yerushalayim Shel Etmol"), *Al Hamishmar*, 8 January
     1971.

Bahur, Y.   "David Shahar's *The Fortune Teller*" ("Maggid ha-Atidot
     le-David Shahar"), *Haaretz*, 26 August 1966.

Barzel, H.   "Trends in Israeli Prose" ("Megammot ba-Proza ha-
     Israelit"), *Moznaim* 10/5-6 (1960), and 12/5-6 (1961).

_____.   "Introduction to the Stories of David Shahar" ("Mavo
     le-Sippurei David Shahar"), in *Six Authors* (*Shishah Mesapprim*),
     A Collection of Contemporary Hebrew Short Stories, ed. and
     introduced by H. Barzel, Tel Aviv 1972.

Baumgarten, M.   "A Mythical City," *Jerusalem Post*, 30 July 1976.

Be'er, Ch.   "The Death of the Little God" ("Moto Shel ha-Elohim
     ha-Katan"), *Haaretz*, 25 September 1970.

Be'er, Ch. "To Collect the Broken Vessels, to Make a Reconstruc-
    tion" ("Le-Esof Et Shivrei ha-Kelim, la-Asot Rekonstruktzia"),
    an interview with Shahar, *Haaretz*, 27 August 1971.

Ben-Naḥum, D. "The Breaking of the Vessels in Shahar's Stories"
    ("Shevirat ha-Kelim be-Sippurei Shahar"), *Alei Siaḥ* 2 (1975).

Bezalel, I. "Literature and its Gods" ("Sifrut ve-Eloheha"), an
    interview with Shahar, *Massa*, 2 September 1966.

Blatt, A. "People on the Border" ("Anashim Al ha-Gevul"),
    Hatzofeh, 28 August 1970.

Fayans, E. "In the Shadow of Jerusalem" ("Be-Tzilah Shel Yeru-
    shalayim"), *Maariv*, 6 August 1971.

Fürstenberg, R. "History Through a Cracked Mirror: On David
    Shahar's *His Majesty's Agent*," *Modern Hebrew Literature* 5/4
    (1980).

Gal-Margalit, N. "The Meaning Beyond the Tangible" ("Ha-Mashmaut
    she-me-Ever la-Muḥash"), *Haaretz*, 27 August 1976.

Gutkind, N. "David Shahar's *The Palace of Broken Vessels*"
    ("David Shahar, Heikhal ha-Kelim ha-Shevurim"), *Hatzofeh*,
    9 June 1972.

Hagorni, A. "Place - Jerusalem; Time - Past" ("Ha-Makom
    Yerushalayim, ha-Zeman Avar"), *Mabbat Ḥadash*, 2 November 1966.

Harel, I. "Shahar's Jerusalem" ("Yerushalayim Shel Shahar"),
    Maariv, 9 October 1970.

Kadari, S. "The Dreams About the Palace of Broken Vessels"
    ("Ha-Halomot Al Heikhal ha-Kelim ha-Shevurim"), *Hayom*,
    17 October 1969.

Katz, S. "The Uncle Protagonist and the Old Mother in Shahar's
    Stories" ("Ha-Dod ha-Gibbor, ve-ha-Em ha-Zekenah be-Sippurei
    Shahar"), *Davar*, 27 August 1971.

_____. "On the Narrator in Shahar's *The Fortune Teller*" ("Al
    Demut ha-Mesapper be-Maggid ha-Atidot le-Shahar"), *Bikkoret
    u-Parshanut* 4-5 (1974).

_____. "The Protagonist and the Narrator in the Stories of
    David Shahar" ("Demut ha-Gibbor ve-ha-Mesapper be-Sippurei
    David Shahar"), *Yerushalayim* 9-10 (1975).

_____. *The I and Its Protagonists in Shahar's Stories (Ha-Ani
    ve-Gibborav be-Sippurei Shahar)*, Tel Aviv 1975.

_____. "The Soul of Things and Time" ("Nishmat ha-Devarim
    ve-ha-Zeman"), *Yediot Aḥronot*, 19 March 1976.

_____. *Jerusalem as an Artistic Expression in the Works of
    Hazaz and Shahar (Yerushalayim ke-Mabba Ommanuti bi-Yetzirot
    Hazaz ve-Shahar)*, a Bar-Ilan University Ph.D. dissertation,
    1978.

Luz, Z. "The Chasms of the Soul in Jerusalem's Alleys" ("Tehomot
    ha-Nefesh be-Simtaot Yerushalayim"), *Bikkoret u-Parshanut* 1
    (1970); also in his *Existence and Man in Israeli Literature*,
    Tel Aviv 1970.

Michaelson, M. "An Interview with David Shahar" ("Reayon Im David
    Shahar"), *Yediot Aḥronot*, 14 January 1977.

Moked, G. "The Journey to Ur of the Chaldees" ("Ha-Massa le-Ur
    Kasdim"), *Akhshav* 2 (1973.

Nagid, Ch. "Truth Beyond Truth" ("Emet she-me-Ever la-Emet"),
    an interview with Shahar, *Yediot Aḥronot*, 12 February 1971.

Neumann, E. "Simplistic and Symbolic Realism in David Shahar's
    Stories" ("Realizm Pashtani ve-Simli be-Sippurei David
    Shahar"), *Haboker*, 29 April 1960.

Oren, M. "Nonconformist 'Caesar'" ("'Keisar' Nonconformisti"),
    Maariv, 27 May 1960.

Oren, Y. "David Shahar: Yearning for the Hidden Life" ("David
    Shahar: Kissufim El ha-Ḥayyim ha-Genuzim"), *Haaretz*,
    25 July 1969.

_____. *"Day of the Countess* - in the Middle of the Road"
    ("Yom ha-Rozenet be-Mahatzit ha-Derekh"), *Yediot Aḥronot*,
    3 September 1976.

_____. "Mysticism and Humor in Shahar's Stories" ("Mistikah
    ve-Humor be-Sippurei David Shahar"), *Yediot Aḥronot*,
    6 August 1971.

Orian Ben-Herzl, Y. "Jerusalem's Version" ("Nusaḥ Yerushalayim"),
    Massa, 11 February 1972.

Raviv, Y. "On the Palace and on the Vessels" ("Al ha-Heikhal
    ve-Al ha-Kelim"), *Davar*, 12 September 1969.

Remba, I. "David Shahar Will Not Waste His Year Off" ("David
    Shahar Lo Yevazbez Et Shnat Hufshato"), an interview with
    Shahar, *Maariv*, 1 August 1969.

Schweid, E. "Between Past and Future" ("Bein Avar le-Atid"),
    Beterem, 4 November 1955.

Shaked, G. "Great Yearning for a Little God" ("Kissufim Gedolim
    le-Elohim Katan"), *Haaretz*, 20 May 1960.

_____. "Jerusalem in Literature" ("Yerushalayim ba-Sifrut"),
    Bamaḥane, 17 September 1971.

Shapira, S. "The Death of the Little God" ("Moto Shel ha-Elohim
    ha-Katan"), *Massa*, 25 September 1970.

Yardeni, G. "On the Dreamer and his Dreams" ("Al ha-Ḥolem
    ve-Ḥalomotav"), *Massa*, 12 April 1955.

_____. "An Interview with Shahar" ("Reayon Im Shahar"),
    Moznaim 15/2-3 (1962).

Z. G. "The Fortune Teller" ("Maggid ha-Atidot"), *Keshet* 9/2 (1967).

Zarḥi, N. "Arrow Aimed into the Night" ("Ḥetz Mekhuvvan le-Tokh
    ha-Laylah"), an interview with Shahar, *At* 118 (1977).

Zartal, A. "The World of Lonely People" ("Olaman Shel Demuyot
    Bodedot"), *Davar*, 18 October 1970.

Zehavi, A. "The Texture of Shahar's Stories" ("Rikmat Sippurav
    Shel Shahar"), *Hayom*, 2 September 1966.

_____ . "A Daring, Original Literary Experiment" ("Nissui
    Sifruti Mekori ve-Noaz"), *Massa*, 5 November 1976.

Zemach, A. "Excessive Proximity" ("Kirvah Yeterah"), *Molad* 13
    (1970).

Zemach, S. *Warp and Woof* (*Sheti va-Erev*), Tel Aviv 1959.

Zwick, Y. "A New Meeting with Shahar's Writing" ("Pegishah
    Mehuddeshet Im Yetzirato Shel David Shahar"), *Davar*,
    10 September 1971.

_____ . "Shahar's Narrative Work" ("Yetzirato ha-Sippurit Shel
    David Shahar"), *Al Hamishmar*, 1 October 1976.

AMALIA KAHANA-CARMON

Avinoam, M. "The Stories of Amalia Kahana-Carmon" ("Sippurei
    Amalia Kahana-Carmon"), *Al Hamishmar*, 25 September 1966.

Avinur, G. "Mrs. Talmon and Her Girlfriends" ("Marat Talmon
    ve-Havroteha"), *Al Hamishmar*, 13 August 1971.

Bahur, Y. "A Poet and an Author Under One Roof" ("Meshoreret
    u-Mesapperet bi-Kfifah Ahat"), *Yediot Ahronot*, 4 November
    1966.

Balaban, A. "When Two Plus Two Makes More Than Four - or Less"
    ("Ke-she-Shtaim ve-Od Shtaim Yoter me-Arba u-ke-she-Pahot"),
    Siman K'ria 6 (1976).

_____ . *The Saint and the Dragon* (*Ha-Kadosh ve-ha-Drakon*),
    Tel Aviv 1979.

Baram, I. "Eighteen Worlds" ("Yud-Het Olamot"), *Kol Haam*,
    18 November 1966.

Barzel, H. "Introduction to the Stories of Amalia Kahana-Carmon"
    ("Mavo le-Sippurei Amalia Kahana-Carmon"), *Six Authors*
    (*Shishah Mesapprim*), Tel Aviv 1972.

Bezalel, I. "A Personal Version" ("Nusah Ishi"), an interview
    with Kahana-Carmon, *Massa*, 18 November 1966.

Blatt, A. "Of Landscapes and People" ("Al Nofim va-Anashim"),
    Hatzofeh, 23 December 1966.

Brunovski, Y. "Amalia Kahana-Carmon's *And Moon in the Valley of
    Ajalon*" ("Ve-Yareah be-Emek Ayyalon le-Amalia Kahana-Carmon"),
    Haaretz, 2 July 1971.

David, Y. "A Young and Tender Branch" ("Anaf Tzair ve-Rakh"),
    Gazith 22/1-4 (1964).

Friedlander, Y. "Chapters of a Story and Parts of a Diary"
    ("Pirkei Sippur ve-Kitei Yoman"), *Davar*, 30 July 1971.

Gretz, N. "A Dramatic Event and Other Times" ("Meora Dramati
    u-Zemanim Aherim"), *Siman K'ria* 6 (1976).

Grodzenski, S. "On Amalia Kahana-Carmon's Stories" ("Al Sippureha
    Shel Amalia Kahana-Carmon"), *Ammot* 11 (1964).

_____. "The Glowing Halo" ("Ha-Hilah ha-Nogahat"), *Davar*,
    30 July 1971.

Hagani, A. "Under One Roof" ("Bi-Kfifah Aḥat"), *Ḥotam* 118 (1966).

Ḥof, A. "The Will to be at the Top" ("Ha-Ratzon li-Heyot be-Si"),
    Davar, 9 July 1971.

Kahana, A. "An Interview with Amalia Kahana-Carmon" ("Reayon Im
    Amalia Kahana-Carmon"), *Siman K'ria* 7 (1977).

Katz, S. "Jerusalem - Heart of Light" ("Yerushalayim Lev ha-Or"),
    Bikkoret u-Parshanut 9-10 (1976).

Litvin, R. "Amalia Kahana-Carmon - a Fresh Introduction"
    ("Amalia Kahana-Carmon - Hitvadeut Ḥadashah"), *Massa*,
    3 October and 10 October 1969.

Luria, S. "Poetry Born of Love and Its Anguish" ("Shirah ha-Ba'ah
    be-Ahavah ve-Yissureha"), *Moznaim* 50/4 (1980).

Miron, D. *An Open Notebook* (*Pinkas Patuaḥ*), Merḥavia 1979.

Nagid, Ch. "Is It Really Neo-Bombast?" ("Ha-Omnam Neo-Melitzah?"),
    Yediot Aḥronot, 3 September 1971.

Orian Ben-Herzl, Y. "The Triumph of Bombast" ("Nitzḥon ha-
    Melitzah"), *Yediot Aḥronot*, 20 August 1971.

_____. "Nonetheless - Gibberish" ("U-ve-Khol Zot Leshon Atz
    Kotzetz"), *Yediot Aḥronot*, 10 September 1971.

Shaked, G. "Your Essence Versus Mine" ("Tamtziot Ata le-Umat
    Tamtziot Ani"), *Moznaim* 24/2 (1967).

_____. "The Beaten Drum" ("Ha-Tof ha-Mukke"), *Moznaim* 33/2
    (1971).

Telpaz, G. "The Woman in the Back Seat" ("Ha-Isha ba-Moshav
    ha-Aḥori"), *Maariv*, 25 June 1971.

Toker, N. "On the Creative Writing of Amalia Kahana-Carmon"
    ("Al Yetzirat Amalia Kahana-Carmon"), *Moznaim* 50/1 (1979).

Yudkin, L. "Kahana-Karmon and the Plot of the Unspoken," *Modern
    Hebrew Literature* 2/4 (1976).

III. GENERAL: MISCELLANEOUS WORKS

Abrams, M. H. *The Mirror and the Lamp*, New York 1953.

Abramson, G. *Modern Hebrew Drama*, London 1979.

Adams, R. P. "The Archetypal Pattern of Death and Rebirth in
    Milton's Lycidas," in Vickery, *Myth and Literature*; see
    below.

Akavyahu, Y. "The Father Image in New Poetry" ("Demuto Shel
     ha-Av ba-Shirah ha-Tzeirah"), *Meassef* 8-9 (1968).

Alterman, N. *Column Seven* (*Ha-Tur ha-Shevii*), Tel Aviv 1948.

Amir, A. (ed.). *The Best of Keshet* (*Keshet Makor*), Ramat Gan 1979.

Arian, A. (ed.). *Israel - A Developing Society* (*Israel - Dor
     ha-Hithavut*), Tel Aviv 1979.

Ariés, P. *Centuries of Childhood*, trans. R. Baldick, London 1962.

Auerbach, E. *Mimesis*, trans. W. Trask, Princeton 1953.

Barzel, H. *Poetry and Heritage* (*Shirah u-Morashah*), Tel Aviv 1971.

_____. *Metarealistic Hebrew Fiction* (*Sipporet Ivrit Metareal-
     istit*), Ramat Gan 1974.

Bates, H. E. *The Modern Short Story*, London 1972.

Benjamin, W. *Illuminations*, ed. with an introduction by H.
     Arendt, trans. H. Zohn, London 1970.

Bettelheim, B. *The Uses of Enchantment*, London 1976.

Bezalel, I. *All is Written in the Book* (*Ha-Kol Katuv ba-Sefer*),
     Tel Aviv 1969.

Bidney, D. "Myth, Symbolism and Truth," in Vickery, *Myth and
     Literature*; see below.

Block, H. M. "Cultural Anthropology and Contemporary Literary
     Criticism," in Vickery, *Myth and Literature*; see below.

Blocker, J. (ed.). *Israeli Stories*, New York 1962.

Blotner, J. L. "Mythic Patterns in *To the Lighthouse*," in
     Vickery, *Myth and Literature*; see below.

Boas, G. *The Cult of Childhood*, London 1966.

Booth, W. C. *The Rhetoric of Fiction*, Chicago/London 1973.

Bowra, C. M. *The Romantic Imagination*, London 1950.

Bradbrook, M. C. "The Image of the Delinquent in Literature
     1955-1960," in Knights and Cottle, *Metaphor and Symbol*;
     see below.

Briggs, K. *A Dictionary of British Folk Tales in the English
     Language*, Part A, Vol. 1, London 1970.

Brooks, C., and Warren, R. P. *Understanding Fiction*, 2nd ed.,
     New York 1959.

Brooks, V. W. *The Ordeal of Mark Twain*, rev. ed., London 1934.

Bucknall, B. J. *The Religion of Art in Proust*, Urbana/Chicago/
     London 1969.

Carroll, L. *Alice's Adventures in Wonderland*, London 1925.

Cassirer, E. *An Essay on Man*, New Haven 1945.

Chase, R. "Notes on the Study of Myth," in Vickery, *Myth and
    Literature*; see below.

Coveney, P. *The Image of Childhood*, rev. ed., London 1967.

Daiches, D. *A Study of Literature for Readers and Critics*,
    London 1948.

Davies, P. R. "Passover and the Dating of the Aquedah," *Journal
    of Jewish Studies* 30/1 (1979).

De Waele, J.-P., and Harré, R. "Autobiography as a Psychological
    Method," in Ginsburg, *Emerging Strategies in Social Psycho-
    logical Research*; see below.

Dickstein, M. *Gates of Eden*, New York 1977.

Eckert, C. W. "Initiatory Motifs in the Story of Telemachus,"
    in Vickery, *Myth and Literature*; see below.

Eisenstadt, S. N. *Israeli Society*, London 1967.

_____, Adler, Ch.; Bar-Yosef, R.; and Kahana, R. (eds.).
    Israel - A Society in the Making (Israel Ḥevrah Mithavvah),
    Jerusalem 1972.

Eliade, M. *The Sacred and the Profane*, trans. W. Trask, New York/
    Evanston 1961.

Eliav, A. *Land of the Hart (Eretz ha-Tzvi)*, Tel Aviv 1972.

Eliraz, I. "The *Akedah* as a Theme in Israeli Drama" ("Ha-Akedah
    ke-Motiv ba-Drama ha-Israelit"), *Massa*, 9 November 1971.

Elon, A. *The Israelis: Founders and Sons*, London 1971.

Empson, W. *Seven Types of Ambiguity*, 3rd ed., London 1953.

_____. *Some Versions of Pastoral*, London 1950.

Erikson, E. *Childhood and Society*, rev. ed., London 1965.

Even-Zohar, I. "Israeli Hebrew Literature: A Historical Model"
    ("Ha-Sifrut ha-Ivrit ha-Israelit: Model Histori"), *Ha-Sifrut*
    4 (1973).

Fergusson, F. "'Myth' and the Literary Scruple," in Vickery, *Myth
    and Literature*; see below.

Fleischer, E. *Hebrew Liturgical Poetry in the Middle Ages
    (Shirat ha-Kodesh ha-Ivrit bi-Yemei ha-Beynaim)*, Jerusalem
    1975.

Forster, E. M. *Aspects of the Novel*, London 1927.

Foss, M. *Symbol and Metaphor in Human Experience*, Princeton 1949.

Frankfort, H. *Kingship and the Gods*, Chicago 1958.

Frazer, J. G. *The Golden Bough*, Part III: *The Dying God*, 3rd ed.,
    London 1923.

Freud, S. *Totem and Taboo*, trans. A. A. Brill, New York 1918.

_____. *The Interpretation of Dreams*, The Standard Edition of the Complete Works, Vol. V, London 1964.

Fromm, E. *Man for Himself*, New York 1947.

_____. *The Forgotten Language*, London 1952.

Frye, N. *Anatomy of Criticism*, Princeton 1957.

_____. "The Road of Excess," in Slote, *Myth and Symbol*; see below.

Ginsburg, G. P. (ed.). *Emerging Strategies in Social Psychological Research*, Chichester/New York/Brisbane/Toronto 1979.

Ginzberg, L. *The Legends of the Jews*, Vol. 1, Philadelphia 1946.

Gold, H. In "The International Symposium on the Short Story," *The Kenyon Review* 30/4 (1968).

Gouri, H. *Wind Rose* (*Shoshanat Ruḥot*), Tel Aviv 1960.

Gretz, N. "Changes in Hebrew Literature: the Transition from the Palmach Generation to the Generation of the Sixties" ("Temmurot ba-Sifrut ha-Ivrit: ha-Maavar mi-Dor ha-Palmach le-Dor Shnot ha-Shishim Al Pi Emdot u-Mabbaim ba-Yetzirah"), *Ha-Sifrut* 29 (1979).

Gusdorf, G. "Conditions and Limits of Autobiography," in Olney, *Autobiography: Essays Theoretical and Critical*; see below.

Habermann, A. M. *A History of Hebrew Liturgical and Secular Poetry* (*Toldot he-Piyyut ve-ha-Shirah*), Vol. 1, Tel Aviv 1970.

Haining, P. *Superstitions*, London 1979.

Hamenachem, E. (ed.). *The Israeli as Jew* (*Ha-Israeli ki-Yehudi*), Givataim 1974.

Harding, D. W. "The Hinterland of Thought," in Knights and Cottle, *Metaphor and Symbol*; see below.

Harrison, R. "Symbolism of the Cyclical Myth in *Endymion*," in Vickery, *Myth and Literature*; see below.

Henderson, J. L. "Ancient Myths and Modern Man," in Jung, *Man and His Symbols*; see below.

Hindus, M. *The Proustian Vision*, London/Amsterdam 1954.

Hooke, S. H. (ed.). *Myth and Ritual*, London 1933.

Jacobi, J. "Symbols in an Individual Analysis," in Jung, *Man and His Symbols*; see below.

Jaffé, A. "Symbolism in the Visual Arts," in Jung, *Man and His Symbols*; see below.

James, E. O. *The Ancient Gods*, London 1960.

James, H. *The Art of Fiction*, New York 1948.

202   Israeli Childhood Stories

Jung, C. G. *Symbols for the Transformation*, trans. R.F.C. Hull,
      New York 1956.

_____. *The Archetypes and the Collective Unconscious*, trans.
      R.F.C. Hull, New York 1959.

_____. "Approaching the Unconscious," in *Man and His Symbols*;
      see below.

_____. *Memories, Dreams, Reflections*, recorded and ed. A.
      Jaffé, New York 1965.

_____, and von Franz, M.-L. (eds.). *Man and His Symbols*,
      London 1964.

Kena'ani, D. *Between Them and Their Time* (*Beinam le-Vein
      Zemanam*), Merḥavia 1955.

Keshet. "To the Heart of the Matter" ("El Shorshei ha-Devarim"),
      a post-Yom Kippur War Symposium, *Keshet* 16/2 (1974).

Kierkegaard, S. *Fear and Trembling*, London/New York/Toronto 1939.

Kirk, G. S. *Myth: Its Meaning and Functions*, Cambridge 1970.

Klein, M. (ed.). *New Directions in Psycho-analysis*, London 1955.

Knights, L. C., and Cottle, B. (eds.). *Metaphor and Symbol*,
      London 1960.

Koestler, A. *Promise and Fulfilment*, London 1949.

_____. *The Act of Creation*, London 1964.

Landau, E. D., Epstein, S. L., and Stone, A. P. *Child Development
      through Literature*, Englewood Cliffs 1972.

Langer, S. K. *Philosophy in a New Key*, Cambridge 1942.

Laqueur, W. *A History of Zionism*, New York/Chicago/San Francisco
      1972.

Laskov, S. *The Biluim* (*Ha-Biluim*), Jerusalem 1979.

Lerner, L. *The Uses of Nostalgia*, London 1972.

Lévi-Strauss, C. *The Raw and the Cooked*, trans. J. and D. Weight-
      man, London 1970.

_____. *The Savage Mind*, London 1966.

Lewis, C. S. *An Experiment in Criticism*, Cambridge 1965.

Lubbock, P. *The Craft of Fiction*, London 1954.

Lytle, A. "The Working Novelist and the Mythmaking Process," in
      Vickery, *Myth and Literature*; see below.

Malinowski, B. *Myth in Primitive Psychology*, London 1926.

Massa. "The *Massa* Symposium on Poetry and Criticism in the Last
      Twenty Years" ("Simpozion Massa Al ha-Shirah ve-ha-Bikkoret
      be-Esrim ha-Shanim ha-Aḥronot"), *Massa*, 30 April 1968.

Michener, J. A. (ed.). *Firstfruits*, Philadelphia 1973.

Monroe, R. A. *Journeys Out of the Body*, London 1972.

Müller, M. F. (ed.). *The Sacred Books of the East: The Brihadāranyaka Upanishad*, Oxford 1884.

O'Connor, F. *The Lonely Voice*, New York 1963.

O'Faolain, S. *The Short Story*, New York 1951.

Ofrat, G. "The Sacrifice of Isaac in Israeli Drama" ("Akedat Itzhak ba-Drama ha-Israelit"), *Moznaim* 49/6 (1979).

Olney, J. *Metaphors of Self: The Meaning of Autobiography*, Princeton 1972.

_____ (ed.). *Autobiography: Essays Theoretical and Critical*, Princeton 1980.

Oren, Y. "Reflections on 'Dor ba-Aretz'" ("Le-Ḥeshbono Shel Dor ba-Aretz"), *Moznaim* 27/6 (1968).

_____. "The Crystallization of a Generation" ("Hitgabshuto Shel Dor"), *Maariv*, 18 and 25 April 1980.

Oz, A. *Touch the Water, Touch the Wind* (*La-Gaat ba-Mayim, la-Gaat ba-Ruaḥ*), trans. N. de Lange, London 1976.

Patai, R. *Israel Between East and West*, 2nd ed., Westport 1970.

Patterson, D. "Modern Hebrew Literature Goes on Aliyah," *Journal of Jewish Studies* 29/1 (1978).

_____. "Some Aspects of the Transference of Hebrew Literature from Eastern Europe to Eretz Yisrael," in *Sefer Meir Wallenstein, Studies in the Bible and Hebrew Language Offered to Meir Wallenstein*, Jerusalem 1979.

Penueli, S. Y. "The Rest of the Story" ("Yeter ha-Sippur"), *Al Hamishmar*, 30 January 1959.

_____. "On Need, Will and Form in Literature" ("Al Tzorekh, Ratzon ve-Tzurah ba-Sifrut"), *Massa*, 18 April 1962.

_____, and Ukhmani, A. (eds.). *Hebrew Short Stories*, Vol. 2, Tel Aviv 1965.

Picowski, J. "On the Cross-Roads of Three Cultures," *The Jewish Quarterly* 27/1 (1979).

Postman, N. *The Disappearance of Childhood*, New York 1982.

Poulet, G. "Proust and Human Time," in *Proust A Collection of Critical Essays*, ed. R. Girard, Englewood Cliffs 1962.

Propp, V. *Morphology of the Folktale*, trans. L. Scott, Austin 1968.

Rabikovitz, D. (ed.). *The New Israeli Writers*, New York 1969.

Rabinovitch, I. *Major Trends in Modern Hebrew Fiction*, trans. M. Roston, London 1968.

204   Israeli Childhood Stories

Ransom, J. C. "Criticism as Pure Speculation," in Stauffer, *The Intent of the Critic*; see below.

Rappoport, A. S. *The Folklore of the Jews*, London 1937.

_____. *Myth and Legend of Ancient Israel*, Vol. 1, New York 1966.

Reid, I. *The Short Story*, London 1977.

Richards, I. A. *Practical Criticism*, London 1935.

_____. *The Philosophy of Rhetoric*, New York 1936.

_____. *Principles of Literary Criticism*, London 1959.

Ricoeur, P. *The Rule of Metaphor*, trans. R. Czerny with K. McLaughlin and J. Costello, London/Henley 1978.

Rivlin, J. J. "The Hegemony of the Ashkenazim in the Old *Yishuv*" ("Ha-Hegemoniah Shel ha-Ashkenazim ba-Yishuv ha-Yashan"), *Moznaim* 15/4-5 (1962).

Róheim, G. *Animism, Magic and the Divine King*, London 1930.

_____. "Myth and Folktale," in Vickery, *Myth and Literature*; see below.

Romberg, B. *Studies in the Narrative Technique of the First-Person Novel*, trans. M. Taylor and H. B. Borland, Stockholm 1962.

Sachar, H. M. *A History of Israel*, Oxford 1977.

Salinger, J. D. *The Catcher in the Rye*, London 1951.

Sartre, J. P. *The Psychology of Imagination*, London 1972.

Schirmann, H. *Hebrew Poetry in Spain and Provence (Ha-Shirah ha-Ivrit bi-Sfarad u-be-Provans)*, Jerusalem/Tel Aviv 1954.

Scholem, G. *Kabbalah*, Jerusalem 1974.

Schultz, B. *Sanatorium Under the Sign of the Hourglass*, trans. C. Winiewska, London 1978.

Segal, H. "A Psycho-Analytical Approach to Aesthetics," in Klein, *New Directions in Psycho-analysis*; see above.

Seventh Day. Siaḥ Loḥamim, a post-Six-Day War Symposium, Tel Aviv 1967.

Shenhar, I. (ed.). *Tehilla and Other Israeli Tales*, London/New York 1956.

Shumaker, W. *Literature and the Irrational*, New York 1960.

Silberschlag, E. *From Renaissance to Renaissance*, Vol. 2, New York 1977.

Slote, B. (ed.). *Myth and Symbol*, Lincoln 1963.

Smith, J. S. *A Critical Approach to Children in Literature*, New York 1967.

Spengemann, W. C. *The Forms of Autobiography*, New Haven 1980.

Spicehandler, E. (ed.). *Modern Hebrew Stories*, New York 1971.

Spiegel, S. *The Last Trial*, trans. J. Goldin, New York 1967.

Stamboliani, G. *Marcel Proust and the Creative Encounter*, Chicago/London 1972.

Stange, G. R. "Tennyson's Mythology: A Study of *Demeter and Persephone*," in Vickery, *Myth and Literature*; see below.

Stauffer, D. A. (ed.). *The Intent of the Critic*, Princeton 1941.

Steiner, G. *The Death of Tragedy*, London 1963.

_____. *After Babel: Aspects of Language and Translation*, London 1975.

_____. *On Difficulty and Other Essays*, Oxford 1978.

Steinschneider, M. (ed.). *Alpha Beth de-Ben Sira*, Berlin 1858.

Stone, L. J., and Church, J. *Childhood and Adolescence*, 2nd ed., New York 1968.

Swinburne, A. C. *Poems and Ballads*, London 1906.

Tal, U. "The Land and the State of Israel in Israeli Religious Life," *Proceedings of the Rabbinical Assembly*, Vol. 38 (1976).

Tammuz, B., and Yudkin, L. (eds.). *Meetings with the Angel*, London 1973.

Tennyson. *The Life and Works of Alfred Lord Tennyson*, Vol. 12, London 1899.

Thompson, S. *The Folktale*, New York 1946.

_____. *Motif-Index of Folk-Literature*, Vol. 2, rev. and enlarged ed., Copenhagen 1955.

Twain, M. *Huckleberry Finn*, London 1955.

Ukhmani, A., Tanii, S., and Shamir, M. (eds.). *A Generation in the Land* (*Dor ba-Aretz*), Merḥavia 1958.

Vickery, J. B. (ed.). *Myth and Literature*, Lincoln 1966.

_____. "Myth and Ritual in the Shorter Fiction of D. H. Lawrence," in *Myth and Literature*.

Virgil. *Eclogues, Georgics, Aeneid I-VI*, trans. H. R. Fairclough, rev. ed., London 1935.

von Franz, M. L. "The Process of Individuation," in Jung, *Man and His Symbols*; see above.

Wallenrod, R. *The Literature of Modern Israel*, New York 1956.

Weisinger, H.   "The Myth and Ritual Approach to Shakespearean
    Tragedy," in Vickery, *Myth and Literature*; see above.

Wellek, R.   *A History of Modern Criticism*, London 1955.

_____. *Concepts of Criticism*, New Haven/London 1963.

_____, and Warren, A.   *Theory of Literature*, 3rd ed., London
    1956.

Wimsatt, W. K.   *The Verbal Icon*, London 1970.

_____, and Brooks, C.   *Literary Criticism*, New York 1957.

Wisse, R. R.   *The Schlemiel as Modern Hero*, Chicago 1971.

Wohl, R.   *The Generation of 1914*, London 1980.

Yaari, A.   *Memories of Eretz Israel* (*Zikhronot Eretz Israel*),
    Vol. 2, Jerusalem 1947.

Year.   *A Year After the War* (*Shanah le-Aḥar ha-Milḥamah*), a post-
    Six-Day War Symposium, Ein Shemer 1968.

Zemach, S.   *Essay and Criticism* (*Massah u-Bikkoret*), Tel Aviv
    1954.

INDEX

DATE DUE

GAYLORD

PRINTED IN U.S.A.